i12467

JEWISH GUIDED IMAGERY

JEWISH GUIDED IMAGERY
A How-To Book
For Rabbis, Educators and Group Leaders

DOV PERETZ ELKINS

GROWTH ASSOCIATES
Princeton, NJ

Copyright © 1996 Dov Peretz Elkins

Second printing 1999.

ISBN 0-918834-16-3

Library of Congress Catalog Card Number: 96-94061
Printed by Princeton Acadmic Press, Princeton, NJ
Printed in the United States of America

This book has been composed in Adobe Caslon with titling in Friz Quadrata. Designer and typesetter: Maia C. Reim.

For a complete catalog of books contact:

Growth Associates Publishers
212 Stuart Road East
Princeton, NJ 08540-1946

(609) 497-7375

e-mail: elkins@tigger.jvnc.net
www.DPElkins.com

This book is dedicated in loving memory of my friend

MAX RATNER

Citizen of Bialystok, Jerusalem, and Cleveland

Guided Imagery Exercise in Memory of Max Ratner

❍ *Gradually close your eyes, relax, and see on the movie screen*
of your mind, a kind, gentle and generous man.
See a man who is a devoted husband, father, grandfather, brother and uncle,
See a man who is a loyal son of Israel,
A committed supporter of the synagogue and Jewish education,
A man who values learning and books,
Who is astute in the ways of business as well as the ways of the heart,
A leader in philanthropy and generosity,
A man of vision and purpose,
A man with values and ideals,
A man who is wise yet gentle,
Who is at home anywhere that Jews live,
A man who did more than his share to further the cause of Israel and humanity,
And you will see someone resembling Max Ratner, zecher tzaddik livracha.
Now open your eyes, try to live your life as Max did,
and rejoice in your lot in life. ❍

All our history is no more than accepted fantasy.
—Voltaire

First in the mind, later into action.
—Shabbat hymn, *Lekha Dodi*

I the Lord will pour out My spirit on all flesh;
Your sons and daughters shall prophesy;
Your old shall dream dreams,
Your young shall see visions.
—Joel 3:1

I am certain of nothing but the holiness of the
Heart's affections and the truth of the Imagination.
—John Keats

Contents

"Jacob's Ladder" by Jeremy Stadlin

Acknowledgements

MANY distinguished educators and scholars contributed their time and effort to the improvement of this book. I am deeply grateful for the time and effort of my friends and colleagues, Audrey Friedman Marcus, Murray Wilkow, Mel Silberman, Howard Kirschenbaum, Rabbis Sam Joseph and Stuart Kelman, and Belleruth Naparstek. Naturally, any shortcomings the book may have are solely the responsibility of the author.

I am exceedingly proud that two of my children were involved in bringing this book into being. Jonathan Elkins read the entire manuscript and offered countless stylistic suggestions. Jeremy Stadlin contributed the beautiful sketch at the beginning of the book.

Maia Reim deserves special credit and appreciation for the labor of love she offered in designing the book. Her attention to detail, her artistic talent, and her technical expertise all combined to make the appearance of the book as professional and beautiful as it is.

I am ever in the debt of Jack Canfield for his friendship, guidance, and support. I am grateful to Jack for introducing me to the art of guided imagery over two decades ago. The kind words he wrote about this book and its author are appreciated more than they are deserved.

I am grateful to my friend Yitzhak Buxbaum for permission to reprint a brief passage from his excellent book, *Storytelling and Spirituality in Judaism*, and for the permission of its publisher, Jason Aronson Inc., Northvale, NJ © 1994. Thanks are due also to the American Jewish Committee for permission to reprint portions from the series "What Being Jewish Means To Me."

Most of all I am grateful to the students in my workshops and classes throughout the world with whom I honed my skills in leading guided imagery exercises.

Dov Peretz Elkins
Princeton, New Jersey
Erev Purim, 5756

Chapter 1

WHAT IS GUIDED IMAGERY?

The heaven of today is the earth of tomorrow.
—Yechiel Michel of Zlotchov

The essence of faith is in the power of imagination, because whatever the intelligence understands has no connection to faith.
—Rabbi Nachman of Bratslav

*If you wish to see the valley
climb to the mountain top.*

*If you desire to see the mountain
rise into the clouds.*

*But if you seek to understand the clouds
close your eyes and think.*
—Kahlil Gibran

ALL OF US use imagery more than we realize. Imagery simply means creating mental images, like imagining. It is a process that is genetically imbedded into our brain. Every time we close our eyes and try to remember some past event, we are using mental images. Trying to remember where we left our keys, we retrace our steps over the past few minutes or hours, to create a visual image of ourselves coming to the point where we now find ourselves.

Trying to think of a friend's name, we may first picture her home, her clothing, the last time the two of us were together.

We visualize (one form of imagery) while we sleep (it's called *dreaming*), while we rest (*imagining*), and while we stand in line at the bank to relieve the boredom (e.g., picturing in our mind how to solve a problem with which we've been struggling).

Not a day, or even an hour goes by without our creating some form of mental imagery.

Imagery forms in our brain in many forms. Some images are seen, or visualized, and others come to us through hearing, smelling, tasting or touching. Often these images come together. For example we can imagine in the "movie screen in our mind" eating an ice cream cone. Such an image will involve seeing, touching, smelling and tasting the ice cream. When we use the term "imagery" we mean calling up past memories, or creating new experiences, through our five senses. The concept of imagery will become more clear in later parts of this book.

Whenever I am in a city which has the kind of police or ambulance sirens which resemble those in Europe, I immediately call to mind my trip to Paris *thirty years ago*! It was the first time I heard this kind of alarm.

Another vivid experience I recall comes from when I was six years old. I was at a summer camp in the beautiful Pennsylvania Pocono mountains. I was standing outside on the front steps of my cabin, and staring out at the magnificent panoramic view laid out before me. I remember the exhilarating smell of the flowers and trees, the incomparable sight of God's natural world presenting itself in full bloom before my eyes. It was early in the morning, and the only sound I could hear was the rustling of the leaves and birds chirping. Even as a young child I made a promise to myself: that I would always remember this incandescent moment (a phrase I would not have used at the time). I have kept my promise to myself, and return often to that unforgettable moment. I did not realize at the time that it was my senses which created such a powerful image of sight, sound and smell, that would enable me to keep that promise.

Experts in guided imagery tell us that our ability to recreate images of seeing, hearing and touching come from the brain's cerebral cortex, the seat of higher mental functions. Other imagery, which is induced by smelling or experiencing emotions, may come from more primitive brain centers.

What is important in learning about imagery is that we can now utilize a portion of our brain that has heretofore been greatly under-utilized. Feeling, remembering, thinking, imagining, creating, drawing, singing, praying, dancing, and other important learning skills can be greatly enhanced by the use of imagery, because it taps into a deeper part of our brain.

USES OF IMAGERY

In the last thirty to forty years, imagery has been studied and developed by specialists in many different fields.

Psychologists and psychiatrists have been using it to help people remember forgotten events in their lives which have become repressed and cause unconscious problems. When these memories are surfaced, people often become free of old fears, anxieties and phobias. Thus, imaging helps people become mentally healthier and happier.

Without knowing it, people have been using visualization and imagery for personal healing in many different kinds of situations. A well-known author, Gerta Klein, has written about her experiences in a concentration camp during the Holocaust. She writes that during the evenings, after a painful day of degradation and hard labor, she would use her imagination to conjure up the vision of her life before the Second World War. In her imagination she pictured the beauty of her home, the lovely living room where there was peace, security and love. She saw her father seated in an easy chair, reading the newspaper. She viewed in her mind her beloved mother, sitting and embroidering. She visualized her brother doing his homework. She saw and heard herself playing the piano. The music and the serenity of this warm scene soothed her, and gave her great peace of mind. But Gerta did one more important thing, based on her internal imagery. She vowed that she would survive in order to recreate that bucolic scene once more in reality. Thus, her imagination provided for her a sense of strong motivation, and a goal to work for. The clear picture and the peace of mind provided by her imagination gave her a clearly experienced state of reality which her mind, body and entire organism could work together to achieve. Her imagination provided her a sense of hope and meaning which her current harsh reality could not. Using imagery she was able to survive, to write and speak about her experience, and to share it with the entire world.

More recently, people in the healing professions have been using imagery to help heal people. Using *active* imagery people have learned to enlarge their bronchial tubes and relieve their asthma. Others have created internal pictures of their white blood cells acting as sharks to attack vulnerable germs or diseases like lupus or cancer. One practitioner assigned his students the task of practicing such an image at home and then measured their white blood cells, finding that they measurably increased, thus enhancing their immune system. Many people claim to have cured themselves (sometimes with a guide or teacher) using imagery and visualization.

Using *receptive* imagery, psychologists have helped people reach deep into their subconscious and find out why certain psychophysiological symptoms existed. One person, for example, discovered that every time he went out on a date he got sick, an unconscious way of not having to face his fears of getting involved in a relationship.

Dr. Bernie Siegel, a surgeon on the staff of Yale University Medical School, has popularized the use of imagery and other psychological approaches to healing in his several best-selling books. Through its effects on the nervous system, it is thought that imagery helps marshal the resources of the body's immune system to fight disease, thus bringing healing and strength.

Still others have used imagery to experience themselves winning a game of tennis, sinking a ball into the basket, or getting a hole in one on the links. Studies have shown that people who practice a sport in their mind's eye have had as much as, or sometimes even more effect than those who actually practice on the field. Clearly, imagery has had an important impact on athletic performance. The book, *The Inner Game of Tennis*, gave people many ideas for practicing their game even when far from the court. Other similar books followed on basketball, volleyball, golf, and a variety of other sports.

Millions of viewers watched, during the 1984 Los Angeles Olympic Games, as the athletes, hailing from countries across the globe, mentally rehearsed their specific athletic activity as a way of enhancing their performance. Many will surely remember the high jumper, standing at the starting line, moving his head and eyes, rehearsing every move his muscles and limbs were about to make in accomplishing his feat.

Writers, artists, sculptors, composers, and other creative artists have used their imaginations to create, practice and improve their performance in their field of specialty. It is said that Mozart created many of his magnificent compositions by hearing them performed completely in his head, and then set them down on paper in musical notes. University courses have developed over the past decades to assist budding artists to awaken their creative muse through a variety of methods, including guided imagery.

Countless scientists have reported that their most important discoveries were made through their imagination. Albert Einstein stated that he discovered the theory of relativity by seeing himself riding on a beam of light, and that words played no role in his vision. Henri Poincaré, a 19th century French mathematician, who discovered Fuchsian functions, tells us: "Ideas rose like clouds; I felt them collide until pairs interlocked . . . ." He describes receiving ideas in bed while in a semi-hypnogogic state.

In today's business world human resource experts often incorporate guided imagery into their training in management development of high level corporate executives. It is employed in exercises for planning, evaluating, improving interpersonal relationships, personal growth, corporate development, new product development, and many other creative functions.

In recent years many talented and creative educators have begun to utilize guided imagery to enhance their students' capacity to learn better and more quickly, with more fun and imagination, by employing techniques of active and receptive imagery. We shall explore some of these techniques in this book, and give examples of how they may be applied to practical learning experiences in the classroom, the home, the synagogue and almost anywhere one finds oneself.

Imagery has the potential for becoming one of the most potent techniques for learning developed in this century. Yet only in the last few years have teachers begun to employ its magical benefits.

IMAGERY IN JEWISH TRADITION

Imagery has been utilized in Jewish tradition from the earliest biblical age. In Jacob's famous dream at Bethel, he imagined a ladder stretching from heaven to earth, with angels ascending and descending. Later, in order to outsmart his crafty uncle, Laban, he placed striped rods in front of the eyes of the sheep in order to have them change their color. (In this case, visualization even has effect on animals.) In his next important dream he saw an angel of the Lord with whom he wrestled, and extracted the blessing to be called Yisrael instead of Yaakov.

The most famous biblical character whom the Jewish People has imagined throughout history is the prophet Elijah. In the biblical narrative, Elijah goes to Heaven in a fiery chariot. Since the Bible does not explicitly state that Elijah died when he went to Heaven, the talmudic rabbis have always assumed that he never died, but roamed the world doing good deeds for eternity.

We envisage Elijah at our Pesach Seder, as well as at the Brit Milah of every male child on the eighth day of birth. This invisible protective angel-like creature appears at crucial moments in our festival and life-cycle to offer God's divine blessings on Israel. We also invoke Elijah's presence in the late afternoon on Shabbat at Havdalah time, when Shabbat is about to depart, the time most resembling the messianic age. Elijah, we are told, will announce the coming of the Messiah in an age of universal justice and peace. In talmudic legend Elijah continually appears to speak to people at appropriate moments.

When we see, or create a visual image of Elijah at all these special moments, he personifies certain values, such as God's protective care, and God's ushering in the universal Age of Peace.

A later prophet, Joel, also foresees a time when God's spirit will be poured out on all living flesh, when people will prophesy and dream dreams, "and your young will see visions" (Joel 3:1).

The eighth century prophet Isaiah, in his famous Inaugural Vision (chapter 6), has a moving spiritual vision in which he sees a gigantic form of God, flowing with long robes which filled the entire Temple. Seraphim with six wings attend God, and as they fly around the Holy Temple they sing to one another: Holy, holy, holy is the Lord of Hosts, God's presence fills the entire earth! The building was filled with smoke, and the doorposts trembled in God's awesome presence. The vision (image) concludes with Isaiah responding to God's call to service with the famous, oft-repeated biblical response, *Hineni!*—"Here I am, send me!" This vision is the basis of the central prayer of the *Kedushah* (holiness), which is the cornerstone of the Amidah, the primary prayer of the Siddur (Jewish Book of Prayers).

In the first chapter of the Book of the Prophet Ezekiel we find one of the most unusual (some would say bizarre) set of images appearing anywhere in Jewish literature. Ezekiel sees an image of a flaming, radiant chariot, able to travel in all four directions, containing the figure of humans with four faces and four wings, and a calf's foot. Behind the human faces was the face of an eagle, and they contained burning coals of fire, suggestive of torches, with a radiance issuing from the fire. In later literature this strange image is called *Maaseh Merkavah*, "The Vision of the Chariot", which became the basis of many mystical studies and deep religious experiences.

Among the many talmudic legends which employ imagery as an important component of the story is the following tale. Moshe dies and goes to Heaven. He sees the Blessed Holy One busy affixing coronets on the letters of the Torah. Upon inquiry Moshe is told by God that these little flourishes on the letters of the Torah will form the basis of legal interpretations which will expand and adapt the Law for future ages, especially by one leading sage, Rabbi Akiva ben Yosef.

Moshe then asks permission to *see* this remarkable Rabbi Akiva (though Akiva lived over a millennium later than Moshe). God instructs Moshe to turn around, whereupon he finds himself in Rabbi Akiva's classroom, sitting on the eighth row, listening to Akiva's lectures. Hearing about laws dealing with issues 1300 years after his death, the biblical teacher finds himself totally lost and confounded. At that point a pupil asks Akiva the source of certain new laws, and the master answers: "It is a law given unto Moshe at Sinai." Moshe now understood that the tiny toggles on the Torah letters enabled Akiva to interpret the Torah for his generation, all based on the Torah which Moshe received from God at Sinai. Thus, Moshe was relieved (Talmud, Tractate Menahot 29b).

Instead of giving Moshe an abstract lecture on halakhic development and the history of Jewish jurisprudence, God does something much simpler. The Almighty asks Moshe to turn in the opposite direction and visualize, as if on a movie screen, an important historical moment which would occur a millennium later. The use of a visual and auditory image in this significant theological lesson made the lesson come alive in a powerful way, and shows the talmudic rabbis to be far-sighted, creative pedagogues. Through the use of creative imagery, they turned what might have been a dry, esoteric theory into a live, vital, and dynamic tale carrying a powerful message about the nature of the survival of Jewish Law, Judaism and the Jewish People.

Of all the periods in Jewish history when images were called upon to yield their richest fruits, it is the time of the mystical school of Kabbalah which produced the most consistent and structured usage of creative images. Rabbi Aryeh Kaplan, in his many books on meditation in the Bible, Kabbalah, and other Jewish literature, describes specific imagery techniques which Jewish mystics would utilize to feel a closer sense of God's presence. He describes the Kabbalists as visualizing Hebrew letters in a trance-like state, to enhance the feeling of deep spirituality. More advanced students concentrated on closing their eyes and seeing the four holy letters of God's ineffable name, YHVH. This technique, he says, is mentioned even in the Shulchan Arukh, the 16th century Code of Jewish Law, whose emphasis is on the minute details of daily ritual behavior rather than on mystical techniques.

Rabbi Kaplan reports: "By visualizing God's name, one can attain a tremendous feeling of closeness to God. One actually feels the presence of God and experiences a deep sense of awe in the presence. A number of classical Judaic sources find an allusion to such visualization in the verse, 'I have placed YHVH before me at all times' (Ps. 16:8). This type of visualization is also useful during worship and prayer."

Another imagery technique mentioned in Kabbalistic sources, described by Rabbi Kaplan, is to imagine the sky opening up and seeing oneself ascending into the spiritual realm, going up through the seven firmaments, one level at a time, until reaching the highest heaven. Once in this supernal heavenly realm one sees an infinitely large white curtain, on which is written YHVH, the Tetragrammaton. When the four letters fill one's mind totally, one is, so to speak, swallowed up in God's name. (See chapter 8, "Visualization," in Kaplan's book, *Jewish Meditation: A Practical Guide*, [NY: Schocken Books, 1985]).

In some of the liturgy, including some very popular prayers we consider to be old standards by now, we use images developed by kabbalists of sixteenth century Safed. The most popular images are those of visualizing Shabbat both as a queen and as a bride. In the popular prayer, *Lecha Dodi*, we chant about going outdoors to greet the Shabbat Bride, as Safed kabbalists would do at sunset on Friday afternoons. Toward the end of the prayer we turn around, face the door of the sanctuary and symbolically greet the Shabbat Bride, as if, personified, she were entering the room at that very moment. For many it is a highlight of the Friday night worship service.

In a famous poem/song by Chaim Nachman Bialik, poet laureate of the Jewish People in the early twentieth century, we sing about the sun setting in the trees, and going out to greet the Shabbat queen.

PEDAGOGIC USE OF GUIDED IMAGERY

The educational exercises and techniques which we will describe in this book have the capacity to produce a sense of spiritual exaltation, but that goal is not their only use. They are capable of accomplishing a very wide number of important pedagogic goals, ranging from the most simple to the most complex.

These experiential techniques can be used with children and adults of any age, from the very youngest, to the most seasoned and mature individuals. Guided imagery is used in secular classrooms in America starting with nursery school, and continuing to the most advanced management seminars in Fortune 500 corporations such as IBM, General Motors and RCA.

The use of guided imagery in the Jewish classroom can range from a short exercise to motivate a new lesson, a powerful emotional experience which solidifies an important point during the course of a discussion, to the use of the technique at the end of a lesson to summarize and integrate a wide range of information.

Using guided imagery will significantly supplement the education of the student accustomed in conventional learning to the development of the left side of the brain (generally considered to be the source of logical thought, linear processing of information, and analytical thinking). Exercises in guided imagery will promote enhancement of the right side of the brain which is the basis of artistic, imaginative, creative and spiritual development, a significant part of all knowledge, but especially religious education.

The extensive use of guided imagery in formal and informal education, for youth and adults, in Jewish settings, will finally bring into Jewish education an enormously useful set of pedagogic tools. There its use has the potential to be the most powerful and the most necessary.

The use of guided imagery techniques in Jewish groups is by no means limited to formal Jewish classrooms. Its range and power lend its usage to many other settings, including youth and adult clubs, havurot, leadership development, strategic planning, Jewish consciousness raising, and many other forms of experiential learning. It can be used effectively in such groups as Jewish Community Centers, Jewish Federations, Jewish Family Service agencies, and adult and family programming in a synagogue. The techniques and specific content suggestions offered in this book can be applied easily by a teacher/leader/facilitator to a wide variety of settings, depending on the goals, setting and interests of the leader and the group.

The power of imagination for young and old may need to be dusted off before full usage of it can be employed. Our society often denigrates the use of fantasy and creative thought. Children are frequently told, "You're just imagining it!" Or, "Stop daydreaming!" "It's only in your head." Students who stare out the window, or whose mind is focused elsewhere than the classroom are thought to be misbehaving. More often, they are creating an environment much more interesting than the one the teacher is trying to establish. Rarely is the use of creative imagination encouraged as young people grow. After a while they often cease using it, thinking that such behavior is dysfunctional, unrewarded, and sometimes even punished.

The notion of entertaining ourselves during periods of boredom, or waiting in line, or simply to activate an important element in our creative ability, needs to be taken out of mental storage, polished up and proudly displayed on the shelf in order to make it into something valuable and honored. The well-known preacher and writer, Norman Vincent Peale, tells about his daughter Margaret, who late one evening at age four, was discovered by her parents laughing and talking to herself at length. They asked for an explanation, and she replied, in innocence and pride, "Oh, I'm just laughing because I'm having such a good time with me."

Psychologists and educators are finding more and more, through the increasing research in this field, that fantasy, visualization, and other forms of guided imagery are creative and effective means to help prepare ourselves to live in an increasingly complex and confusing world, and that those who do it more seem to get along better than those who must cope without this indispensable tool.

Those who use their imagination to a greater extent in problem solving, finding new ideas, preparing for performance, relaxing and healing themselves, enhancing interpersonal relationships, learning better, and increasing their self-esteem, are people who enjoy life more, and who go farther in their personal and professional lives.

The facilitator will have to reestablish the benefits of imagination and visualization in order to make these exercises work. Constant affirmation is necessary to help people remove the rust and reburnish their extraordinary powers of creative thought. While the left brain has been trained to be used in more and more sophisticated functioning, the even more powerful and useful capacities of the right brain have been lying dormant in most individuals. It may take time to awaken this God-given gift, and the facilitator may need to be very patient. The right brain by nature needs an atmosphere of encouragement, patience, and validation, to function at fullest capacity.

In order to utilize imagery techniques to their best advantage for oneself and others, it will be helpful to review some of the reasons and goals for their use, and then to discuss important guidelines that set the stage for their most effective usage.

Chapter 2

GOALS— When and Why to Use Guided Imagery in Jewish Education

Seventy faces has the Torah. Each student envisions it differently.
—Midrash, Bemidbar Rabba 13:15

We are preceded on the road by a cluster of angels who announce: Make way for the Image of the Blessed Holy One!
—Rabbi Yehoshua ben Levi, Midrash Tehillim 55:19

Just as a tree bears year after year the same fruit and yet fruit which is each year new, so must all permanently valuable ideas be continually born again in thought.
—Albert Schweitzer

GUIDED imagery exercises can be used in a wide variety of times and places in the process of education. They can be used in formal and informal learning formats for both youth and adults. The breadth of usage they offer is much wider than one would think. It is appropriate for classrooms, youth groups, adult education, worship, personal growth, human resource development, and a host of other times and places. This flexible and powerful pedagogic technology enhances learning and helps create better human beings. Below are just some occasions in which guided imagery has been used with learners of all kinds.

1) Enhance Motivation

One of the central problems of presenting a lesson, or a workshop, is motivation—how to "hook" the learner into the subject. Very often the teacher/facilitator will present material that is of enormous personal importance to him/her, and will assume that the learner is equally interested. After a very short while it often becomes apparent that while the teacher is vitally engaged in the subject material, the student is psychologically far away. When an imagery exercise is used to open a lesson (one of its many, many uses) it can attract the learner to the subject matter, so that the material is "owned" by the learner.

Sometimes an imagery exercise that helps the student to relax, and let go of many preoccupations, can be helpful in bringing that student into the present and out of the past. The student's attention may be riveted on an insult or hurt from a teacher or colleague that occurred a few minutes ago, or on a problem at home. Picturing a pleasing scene in the woods, or on a beach, can enable the student to "let go" of the interfering thoughts and ideas, and be more ready to learn.

To motivate a language lesson, the teacher may ask the students to see themselves walking on the streets of the country in which the language is spoken, and find themselves comfortably conversing in the native tongue with passersby. To introduce a lesson on prejudice, or the Holocaust, the leader can create a mental scene in the student's imagination, of a crowd of Jews being pushed and harassed in a large square by brown-shirted Nazis. The content material presented after such an exercise may find the students much more interested and alert than before.

2) Personalize

The personalization of material by the leader comprises a sub-category of the above method of motivating a lesson. An imagery exercise helps the learner to take abstract subject material, and through screening it in her imagination, adapt it to her own specific and personal needs and interests. In a geography lesson, instead of merely hearing a lecture or reading a chapter about a foreign country, the learner may find oneself walking around in that land, smelling its agricultural products, picking its fruit, or interviewing its government officials.

A history lesson can be introduced by having the students imagine themselves having a person-to-person chat with some historical personality. A discussion about ethics might open with the learners searching the forest of their memory to come up with a situation that may be in some fashion applicable to the ethical issue about to be discussed. A lesson on myths and legends may be opened by asking the students to read a short story from the rich treasury of past tradition, and to envision an entirely different ending.

All of these brief openers are effective techniques for drawing the student into the precincts of the classroom or workshop study arena, and away from his/her own dreams and thoughts. The lesson is now ready to be "owned" and felt in the heart and soul.

3) Enhance Memory

A third reason for using guided imagery in education is to enhance memory. While some students are auditory-oriented, and learn and remember best through *listening*, others learn best by seeing or reading (visually-oriented). Some research has suggested that smell is the sense most closely linked to memory. Studies have shown that the more senses that are employed in the learning process, the better the chances are that the learner will remember and retain the material and the experience. Thus, using guided imagery before, during or after a lesson will help the learners to *remember* the material far better than they otherwise might. For example, a teacher may want the class to read and discuss a novel. If the students have heard the characters speaking (in their sensory imagination), watched them traveling and interacting, perhaps even conversed with them for a while, maybe touched their garments, or rode with them in a carriage, the chances of their remembering the story and its plot, characters and historical background, would all be greatly improved.

The old saying that a picture is equal to a thousand words is especially true when it comes to memory. In a similar vein, the Talmud tells us that hearing cannot compare to seeing.

Sometimes an effective review of a lesson can embody several modalities. Taking notes and other types of writing-related review techniques will strongly reinforce remembering. Another means of reinforcement is to ask the students to write something, then have them close their eyes and try to visualize what they just wrote. They may have to read what they wrote in their mind's eye a few times before remembering it in greater detail, but this whole process is conducive to deeper memory.

After a field trip to a kosher butcher shop or a Jewish funeral parlor, a workshop with a Torah scribe, or a visit to a Jewish museum, students can be asked to relax, close their eyes, and describe as many details as possible of what they saw. As students repeat something from their memory, in their mind's eye, other students will also picture the same scene, and strengthen their own memories of the experience.

4) Improve Understanding

Guided imagery can also be used to improve understanding. Because students have a variety of learning styles, their capacity to grasp the material increases greatly if more than the conventional methods of learning are utilized. For example, in a history lesson there may be four or five different kings and queens involved in a certain given century. For many students it is a problem to distinguish between these rulers. Using guided imagery can help. Sometimes outlandish methods, such as giving different colored faces to different individuals, or dressing them in different colored clothing, can help the student clarify which monarch is which.

If a certain dictator makes a political choice in a given narrative, it may be challenging for a student to comprehend that type of authoritarian personality. Entering into the mentality of such a ruler through a mental image, with graphic sensory detail, such as hearing the shouts of the ruler, watching the ruler's subjects shake in fear,— all will help the learner grasp the decision-making process of a dictator much more effectively than merely hearing or reading about it in a book. (Example: Have students create a mental image of Alexander III, anti-Semitic Czar of Russia from 1881-1884. Then show them a picture).

Biblical and theological stories and ideas can often present problems for students without experience in this milieu. While sophisticated theologians may consider picturing God as anthropomorphic as immature, doing so can often help as a first step to grasping an abstract concept, such as divinity, miracle, revelation, redemption, afterlife, etc. Mind pictures, followed by drawings or creation of artifacts, may concretize a lesson in a way that reading cannot. Guided imagery can be a part of such a clarifying lesson, even when it is not the whole lesson. It can lead to other means of concretizing and enhancing understanding.

Yitzhak Buxbaum, in his book on *Storytelling and Spirituality in Judaism* (Northvale, NJ: Jason Aronson, 1994, pages 114-116), points out that visualization has been an integral part of the Hasidic art of storytelling for a long time. He quotes Rabbi Nahman of Bratzlav who said that "Others *tell* a story; I *see* a story."

Buxbaum, himself an accomplished storyteller and Jewish educator, also quotes one of the Lubavitcher Rebbes, Rebbe Rashab, as saying:

> One has to know *how* to tell a story, so that it becomes alive.
> Even more important, one has to know how to *listen* to a story,
> so that the listening conjures up a complete picture, and one feels
> as if he is actually experiencing what is being described to him.

Buxbaum quotes the Rebbe Rashab's son and successor, Rabbi Joseph Isaac Schneersohn, who would sit with his eyes closed and meditate on a tale he heard. Rabbi Schneersohn said that "By my diligence in listening to stories and my love of repeating them to myself or others at every opportunity, I developed the ability to vividly imagine every story, as if I was living through what was happening, and the events were taking place before my very eyes. My powerful imagination turned every story into a living picture, a vision, as if I were actually watching the faces of the heroes of the stories."

The following advice is offered by Buxbaum for those who wish to practice the art of storytelling, a craft which has received renewed interest and attention in recent years: The storyteller should "try to visualize the people and events, imagining himself as actually present in the action. When meditating on a story in solitude, he should visualize its scenes one after another, going slowly and not leaving any scene until it has taken on a luminous form in his mind."

5) Increase the Affective Dimension of Learning

Another purpose of using guided imagery as an educational tool is to increase the affective dimension of learning. Teachers and educators of students of all ages are finding that employing the emotional, or affective, side of the learner's personality greatly enhances the learning process. Guided imagery tends to evoke much more of the learner's affective capacity than conventional learning, and hence taps into one's ability to feel more strongly—to care more deeply, to be in touch with one's joy, sadness, appropriate anxiety or fear.

In a lesson in social studies, for example, students who are examining the watershed period of the French Revolution will find that guided imagery exercises enable them to identify much more fully with the powerful forces of modernity that these events set off. Liberty, fraternity, and equality will be not just abstract ideas, but moods, feelings of personal relief, the joyfulness of anticipation, and the pride of accomplishment that accompanies a dramatically new adventure in human experience. The freedom of Jews to live in mixed neighborhoods, to study in secular universities, and to have a role in society, can be felt with much greater clarity.

The experience of a national or religious festival is "caught" as well as "taught" when guided imagery is included in a lesson. All the color, pageantry, music, poetry, ritual symbolism, and communal celebration are extraordinarily powerful when grasped by sensory learning as described in this book.

Picturing oneself as part of the signing of Israel's Declaration of Independence is much more likely to produce a feeling of joy and excitement than just reading the words, or hearing a story about it. Seeing oneself as part of the victorious Israelites, just having crossed the Reed Sea, while Pharaoh and his soldiers are covered by the returning waters, can be a most exhilarating and uplifting experience of salvation, redemption and thankfulness. Read the Song of the Sea (*Shirat Ha-Yam*) and have students imagine the ecstasy the Israelites must have felt at their rescue which caused them to break into a spontaneous chorus of song.

Unless we educate the heart and soul of the student, all the book learning and factual memorization in the world will not make the learning a permanent legacy in the fiber of the student's personality.

6) Increase Participation

Another benefit of using guided imagery in education is to increase participation. Very often the inability of a learner to become a part of a learning group in the fullest sense is due to his/her inability to have any control over the pace, goals and direction of what he/she is learning. Thus, he/she may very well become a spectator among the learners instead of a participant. Control over one's own destiny, at home, at work, or in the classroom, is an essential component of success in any endeavor. Because the process of guided imagery is so personalized to the learner, as explained above, it gives him/her the sense of having much greater control over how and what is learned, and engages the learners as more active participants in their own learning goals. Whether it is learning how to drive a car, or solving a problem in geometry, or learning cursive writing (in one's own language or a foreign one), the imagery process is much more tailored to the learning needs of the individual than is conventional group-oriented learning.

In addition to the involving nature of the guided imagery, there are benefits from the grounding phase which often produce important data that can be useful to a facilitator with a keen eye. (Details about "grounding" a guided imagery exercise can be found in chapter three of this book). Information can be generated about the learning pace of the individual, about the learner's feelings of inclusion and involvement in the learning process, about being part of the learning group, and about the alignment of the goals of the student and the teacher (child and parent, employee and supervisor, etc.).

7) Develop Priorities in Values and Ethics

Guided imagery can also assist in developing priorities in values and ethics. Because sensory learning is more apt to deal with one's personal value system, using imagery will enhance the ability to deal with questions of priorities in personal ethical and value choices, especially when combined with methodologies of Values Clarification and Values Realization, as spelled out in books by Sidney Simon, Howard Kirschenbaum, and Leland Howe (cf. *Values Clarification*, 1974, 1995). These techniques fit together very effectively.

In a lesson on the environment, a student picturing herself throwing a candy wrapper out of a car window may develop a personal feeling of revulsion, in addition to learning about the negative effects on a community. Or she may imagine herself using an aerosol can and sniffing it into her lungs. Watching the gases rise and watching their effect on the ozone layer may have such a long-lasting impact on that learner that future actions may very well be strongly and lastingly affected. In a current events lesson, the imagined encounter with the effects of hunger, destruction and wanton killing can develop a personal commitment to work for peace, and to take a more active role in government.

If a student can, through an imagery exercise, join Ruth as she agonizes about leaving her Moabite background, abandoning her family and roots as well as her idolatrous upbringing, and making the wrenching decision to cling to her mother-in-law, Naomi, the result can be very impactful. Through such an activity a student discovers important values such as loyalty, making difficult choices, religious commitment, and the constructive upheaval of positive personal change.

8) Bond with Individuals, Ethnic, Cultural and National Groups

Through guided imagery, bonds can be established with individuals, ethnic, cultural and national groups. In many educational settings, an important goal of the institution is to identify effectively with a variety of other, previously unfamiliar cultures. In today's multi-cultural societies it is becoming increasingly important to foster a sense of pluralism, mutual respect and appreciation for differences in language, values, ideals, dress, customs, religious beliefs and local mores. As stated above, conventional learning, through standard media, has limited range in reaching the total individual learner.

The development of understanding and appreciation by white male Americans of the cultural background of female Latinos, for example, would go a long way toward creating mutual respect. Through a lesson on the slavery experienced by ancestors of African Americans, or on the Holocaust during the period of Nazi Germany, using imagery techniques, one can come away with a profound and intense feeling, as well as cognitive appreciation of the painful historical experiences of each people's past history. This promotes understanding, bonding, and hope for enhanced future relationships.

In religious settings, classes may want to develop lessons that assist in having learners bond with people of their own respective religious traditions. Jews, for example, have a strong desire to insure the loyalty and commitment of their children to the entire Jewish People, horizontally and vertically. "Horizontally" implies creating ties with all Jews in all countries living today. "Vertically" means identifying with Jews of past generations over the vast 4000-year history of the Jewish People. The exercises in future chapters will give examples of how to do this through the use of guided imagery.

9) Deepen Spirituality

Guided imagery can also deepen spirituality. In today's world people who are formally religious and those who prefer to live by non-institutional faith, or who choose no faith at all, all seem to be searching for a more enriching spiritual life. Guided imagery experiences help people who want to enrich their spiritual life through ritual tradition, or through a specific belief in a Deity concept. It is also helpful to those who simply want their lives filled with the kind of higher aspirations which are defined today by the phrase "spiritual values."

A wide range of imagery exercises can be utilized to accomplish these goals. When dealing with religious literature, such as the Bible, the Talmud, the Koran, and various liturgies of differing religious traditions, guided imagery has unique power and adaptability to achieve the goals of the lesson.

Besides unleashing the power of a specific biblical, liturgical, or ethical tradition, imagery exercises can deal with a general sense of spiritual well-being, comfort, protection, guidance, a nurturing community, and ethical and moral sensitization. By imagining oneself communicating with a Supreme Being, or feeling supported in the metaphoric arms of a higher Power, the normal tensions, anxieties and fears of daily life are replaced by the sense of security that spiritual traditions afford their adherents.

Many educators experimenting with guided imagery come from a background in transpersonal education, and are finding that using symbolism, metaphors, ancient myths and archetypal images brings their students a heightened and deepened spiritual consciousness. They consider this to be one of the primary goals of all education, human growth and spiritual development.

10) Deepen Prayer and Meditation

There is an additional benefit that accrues from combining guided imagery with prayer and meditation: it can lead to an enhancement of spiritual awareness of, appreciation for, and involvement in ancient, medieval, and modern spiritual texts.

Religious educators are usually people who have an interest in finding more effective ways to enter the life of authentic prayer experiences in stronger and more mystical ways. Despite the spate of popular tracts and self-help books in the field of religious development and prayer enhancement, it seems to be a constant effort to teach individuals who have not grown up in a spiritual environment to capture the ability to take advantage of the many rich benefits of a life of regular prayer. Using guided imagery is one of the most effective ways to accomplish this.

Prayer is by nature a right-brain activity which is enhanced by entering a quiet, receptive state of consciousness, and slowly reaching into the deeper recesses of our mind. These recesses are the place within us where we are more capable of actualizing the prayer experience. Non-verbal approaches to help us find such spaces are much more effective than conventional, verbal methods.

Preparatory experiences, such as total physical relaxation, and quieting and slowing down the ever-racing mind, are important first steps in creating the mood of which we are speaking. All the ways we use guided imagery are conducive to this mode of being. After quieting our frenetic minds we may be more able to find other possibilities, including imagining ourselves having conversations with God, or with significant spiritual figures, past and present, real and imaginary.

Imaging oneself moving in prayerful body postures, utilizing hands, eyes, feet and other body parts, using special spiritually-oriented music for accompaniment, can add to the repertoire. Utilization of prayer metaphors, rituals and symbols in imagery settings can become extremely effective tools for developing the niche in our consciousness that fosters deepened prayer. Teaching prayer in educational settings has far too often been confined to skill training such as reading Hebrew, Latin, or other liturgical languages, arranging activities that encourage rote memorization, and racing through traditional litanies of ancient words as if the sole purpose of prayer were to see who can reach the finish line first. With the methods described in this book the religious educator will have a significant new tool to combine conventional technical prayer skills with the development of authentic personal spirituality in prayer.

11) Enhance Relaxation and Reduce Stress

Guided imagery can also enhance relaxation and reduce stress. All education suffers from the general plague rampant in our modern frenzied society: modern persons are simply too busy and scattered to achieve any significant task, especially one that requires the kind of attention and concentration that learning does. Any pedagogic device that brings a greater sense of calm, the capacity to focus on the task at hand, and the ability to be fully present, will add greatly to the learning process.

The relaxation methods described elsewhere in this volume, even if not followed by an imagery exercise, can alone advance a student's sense of being more fully present in the classroom, and enhance any person's capacity to focus more clearly and fully. In some cases, that is all that is needed to proceed to the next step in the lesson plan. When a group (or an individual) is a bit more distracted than usual, and learning is impeded in such a manner that going on to another task would seem fruitless, using one or two imagery exercises will go a long way toward making the balance of the day more productive and enjoyable.

For example, ask students or participants to imagine the activity from which they just came, and watch themselves walk away from it, leaving it completely behind. This will ease the transition to their new place. Another way to bring them into the present and let go of the immediate past is to have them take a personally-chosen metaphor that relates to some part of the new activity that is about to begin, and "play" with it on the screen of their minds. Or, one might simply get them into a relaxed place with some deep breathing, and then tell them to pay complete attention to the process of their body — their posture or heartbeat, for example — or the colors in the room, and people they are with. This will bring their attention away from any personal distractions and into the immediate situation.

In general, the repeated use of relaxation and tension-reducing activities will increase the capacity to learn and remember, heighten the potential for use of any mind-related activity, reduce possible interpersonal conflicts, make life more enjoyable, and reduce illness and accidents. Can one ever have enough practice finding the quiet, serene and tranquil place deep within?

Studies by one of the major researchers in the field of guided imagery in education —the late Beverly Galyean—reported that students who practice centering and focusing exercises in the classroom demonstrate a reduced amount of disruptive behavior (*Journal of Humanistic Psychology*, Vol. 21, No. 4, Fall, 1991, p. 64).

12) Learn How to Learn

Guided imagery can help students learn how to learn. Many modern educators, such as Carl Rogers, Abraham Maslow, Virginia Satir, Jack Canfield, Sid Simon, Howard Kirschenbaum, Hanoch McCarty, and many others in the school of humanistic education who combine skill in education, psychology and spirituality, have frequently pointed out that the most important skill one can impart in any educational setting is to give the learner the requisite tools to continue to learn. Far more important than any thing one learns from a teacher or a book is the personal practice of knowing how to be one's own teacher for the rest of one's life.

Research studies have shown that after people graduate college, they forget over 90% of the information they garner during their four years of sitting at the feet of their professors. The truly lasting and important things which they come away with are the profound personality changes that have taken place during the exposure to these significant mentors, and the tools they have developed to continue a process of life-long learning.

The repeated practice and development of the ability to utilize one's imagination are a very important part what is needed to grow in an ever changing and increasingly complex society. Imagery skills are indispensable for personal fulfillment in life, for increasing sensitization to living with a wider diversity of people, for our ability to fashion a human soul that can "grow itself" in rational, affective, physical, and spiritual domains, and for making the utilization of higher consciousness an ever more important part of being in this planet.

Beverly Galyean pointed out that guided imagery in the classroom is used in three distinct ways: 1) to enhance students' capacity to reach their "higher selves," and to "open avenues to more profound levels of consciousness and being"; 2) as a means for developing attentiveness, concentration and effective learning through practice in relaxation and centering; 3) to increase one's ability to absorb cognitive subject matter in the basic curriculum.

13) Foster Creativity and Innovation

Use of guided imagery is one of the most potent tools for fostering creativity and innovation. Professionals and nonprofessionals in every human endeavor are always looking for new ideas and new ways to accomplish their goals.

It is widely agreed that greater use of creativity in the field of education is always a welcome enterprise. Our world faces continuing problems in population growth, environmental pollution, nuclear dangers, medical and other scientific dilemmas, despite great progress in these and other areas. The need for innovative solutions to old and new problems will no doubt continue to beg for previously undreamed of solutions. Few of our leading innovators are using guided imagery today as one of many tools to solve our pressing problems.

To create an ever-greater number of Galileos, Edisons, Pasteurs, Einsteins, Dostoevskys, Shakespeares, Freuds, Renoirs, Mozarts, Mahlers, Schweitzers, Heschels, Bubers, Neibuhrs, Pope John XXIIIs, Mother Teresas, Martin Luther Kings, and other creative spirits who will transform our world in necessary and enriching ways, we need to foster a climate of innovation to brighten our universe with fresh and exciting approaches to every field of human endeavor.

Schools, factories, governments, eleemosynary and corporate entities have a need for a revitalized spirit of innovation and creativity among their workers, their policies, their organizational and community culture, to keep themselves aligned to an ever-changing and expanding global consciousness. Since the leaders of our new world or-der must come from our youth, and the schools and homes from which they emerge, we must continually infuse our educational institutions and learning environments with a self-renewing mood of search, change, adaptability, learning and growth, creative innovation, and acceptance of true progress in open, democratic and healthy societies.

Among the many new technologies being developed in the field of education and consciousness expansion, few have the great potential for expansion of our creative capacities than does the use of creative imagery.

14) Increase Vitality of Organizations and Institutions

Finally, the use of guided imagery has the potential to increase the vitality of orga-nizations and institutions. The many uses enumerated in the above sections refer in the main to enhancement of individual learning and growth, even though there is an obvi-ous beneficial spillover effect on organizations, institutions, and society at large. In this last section I want to focus on what guided imagery can achieve for the culture of a large body of people, such as a school, a school system, a corporation, a local or national government, a church, synagogue, mosque or other religious institution.

We have referred earlier, in passing, to the phenomenon known as a group or cor-porate culture. Every large body of people has a set of norms and standards, whether spoken, written, or simply "known" in an informal way, sometimes even on a subcon-scious level, by which its members live. When the members of a group share a sense of elan and excitement about the way the group functions, and when there is a spirit of change, growth, progress, creativity and innovativeness in the group's culture and spirit, each member is affected by it.

The use of guided imagery in a group or organization can help build a spirit of willingness and readiness to innovate and to be ever more creative.

Additionally, some of the specific types of usage of guided imagery lend them-selves easily to producing a corporate climate of change and innovation. Guided imag-ery exercises can be used to determine future goals for the organization by asking mem-bers to imagine what the organization will be like in the future. For example, have participants see themselves flying in a helicopter over the building or room of the group. They can "picture" what is going on, what is being produced, how people are behaving, and view new goals for tomorrow. A specific script for this imagery exercise will be found later in the book.

Experts in communication can imagine the new types of telecommunication that will be available to us in coming decades. Those who work in the computer field can discover in their mind's eye what new uses computers will be put to in coming years, and how such computers will look and work. Consultants in human resources can "picture" what kinds of training and development will be available for students, scientists and workers in the future. Teachers can "discover" new methods of teaching and learning that will help them achieve their goals more quickly, easily and effectively in days and months to come. In virtually every field, people can plan, strategize and more effectively organize their groups, institutions and societies by use of different types of guided imagery techniques.

A teacher-training workshop can include, for example, an exercise in which the students see themselves sitting in a classroom fifty years from now, listening to what the teacher is saying, looking around and seeing how the chairs are arranged, what is written on the chalkboard, what kinds of technological hardware and software, or other new and better technology are functioning in the classroom. At the end of such an exercise, the small groups of learners can sit together and share what they experienced in their imagination during the exercise, and creatively piggy-back on the ideas of other members.

Repeated and regular usage of advanced guided imagery can also help reduce conflict, establish a more positive esprit-de-corps, ensure cutting-edge innovativeness and cooperative functioning, that will enhance the spirit and mood of the group's culture.

By using guided imagery, through relaxation of the mind, accessing of the right-brain functions of our consciousness, and entrance into that mystery land of our altered states of mind, we can produce a sense of vitality, mutual sharing, joy in creativity, and the sense of fulfillment and optimal organizational health that builds strength, growth, and the continued expansion of a group's ability to function effectively together and individually.

Chapter 3

GUIDELINES FOR USING CREATIVE GUIDED IMAGERY

Imagination grows by exercise and contrary to common belief is more powerful in the mature than in the young.

—W. Somerset Maugham, *The Summing Up*

I N ORDER to facilitate a guided imagery exercise effectively, the following guidelines should be kept in mind.

1) Be Invitational

An attitude of casualness and calm should pervade the room when a guided imagery exercise is being used. The facilitator should introduce the activity in a spirit of fun and learning. This is one of a wide variety of pedagogic strategies that a teacher or group leader may utilize in the course of a learning day, and should be treated the same as any other one.

Having said that, it is also important to note that the very nature of asking an individual or a group to turn inward and tap the powers of imagination has the potential to be threatening to some people. For this reason there are several approaches during the use of these activities which make it easier for anyone for whom any threat might be present.

The facilitator should be invitational (cf. *Inviting School Success: A Self-Concept Approach to Teaching and Learning* by William Watson Purkey [Belmont, CA: Wadsworth Pub. Co., 1978]). This means asking, or inviting, participants to follow various directions in the course of the session. For example, the leader might say: "Now I would like you to find a comfortable place to sit (or lie)." Instead of "Sit comfortably, and relax."

Phrases like "please," "when you are ready," "If you can. . . .," "Let's try to. . . ." will go a long way toward creating a climate that is invitational.

An important ingredient in an invitational atmosphere is to explain to the group the rule of "I pass." That means that at any time, during any part of this exercise, anyone who wishes may skip a part or the whole just by saying "I pass." This gives the participant total permission to withdraw from any section of any activity in which he/she feels at all uncomfortable. The rule must be enforced in a sincere and non-judgmental fashion. Sometimes when I lead an imagery exercise I announce the "I pass" rule, and then explain that even though I sincerely mean what I say, I also assure the group that if they **do** choose to participate, I will be very sensitive in respecting their private space. I will let them set the limits of how much they do and how much they are willing to share afterward as the exercise is processed in a small group. This does not deny the "I pass" rule, but it gently and non-threateningly encourages participants not to have to fall back on it unless they really believe they need to do so.

While it does not happen often, there are occasions when doing an imagery exercise, especially one involved with personal values, religious convictions, or theological views, that a person feels that his/her privacy is being invaded, or for whatever reason, it is an area they want to keep to themselves. This must be fully respected, or any potential learning will be vitiated.

The facilitator should have a positive, encouraging and confident tone of voice and general approach in introducing and leading the group through the exercise. In my experience I find that when we expect positive results, and when we think and act positively, the group will respond in like manner.

Being invitational also implies that any results of an imagery experience are acceptable. There are no "right answers." Whatever reaction, fantasy, or image one produces in the inner recesses of the mind are what is timely, necessary and acceptable for that person at that moment. If the leader passes judgment, or tries to analyze the image, or attempts to "correct" a point of view held by someone, the message will be delivered that the imagery activity should be the way the leader wants it to come out. That is counter-productive to an effective imagery session, and will shut down the flow of creativity on the part of participants.

When necessary remind participants that imagery is a normal daily activity of a healthy mind, one in which all humans engage, consciously or not. Whatever images they produce are the ones their mind generates for constructive purposes.

Imagery is safe, easy and educationally useful. All that is required is a sense of willingness and the time to carry it out in a leisurely fashion. Infrequently guided imagery exercises may generate an awareness of something very deep, which may result in some unexpected emotions, such as spontaneous sobbing, angry thoughts or words, or other sudden feelings which well up to the surface. Such experiences are cathartic and healthy, often comforting, especially when a facilitator, teacher or guide is present to give assurance and comfort, or whatever required support is necessary. This is what any parent or teacher would do in similar emotional situations. Should the participant, or the guide, feel that further exploration of these emotions is worthwhile, they may consult a psychotherapist or other mental health professional to derive the maximum learning from the experience. It is an opportunity to learn and grow, and not anything harmful or dangerous.

The use of the guidelines in this chapter will assure students that the facilitator is exercising proper care and concern for their rights and feelings, in the same way that a well-trained teacher or group leader would in any effective learning situation.

In sum, being invitational means creating an atmosphere that is warm, relaxed, gentle, non-threatening, non-judgmental, and positive in tone.

2) Practice on Yourself

As in any discipline, a teacher who personally practices what is taught is in a far stronger position to transmit the content and process of a particular field. Who would want to learn yoga from someone who is one chapter ahead of the students?

On the other hand, one need not be a life-long practitioner in order to facilitate the imagery process for others. All good teachers know that they can learn new skills by participating in in-service workshops, and then return to their professional setting and try out their new skills. As we become more and more practiced and proficient in our skills, the better we can convey what we have learned to others.

The more we can speak from personal experience, the better. As time passes, and the leader is more familiar with the highways and byways of guided imagery practices, the teaching will become more effective and variegated. In the meantime, there is no reason why we may not gradually incorporate more and more exercises as time goes on, and as we have more personal experience in practicing with a variety of imagery techniques on ourselves.

The nice thing about imagery practice is that it can be done anywhere, any time. We need not get up an hour earlier, as, for example, we do in physical exercise such as jogging or weight-lifting. Imagery exercises can be performed simply and quickly in a variety of settings that require little if any lost time.

We can practice while standing in line at the bank, post office, or supermarket; before going to sleep; upon awakening in the morning; during prayer or study; and in the process of fostering more wholesome relationships. We can practice it at home or in school, in the car (simple exercises—nothing that would divert one from full attention to the road), in self-healing, in strategic planning, and in a wide variety of other situations.

The important thing is to believe in the process, and to be convinced of its positive potential to enhance learning, growth and effectiveness. This comes with personal experience and practice over a sustained period of time.

Let's take a few minutes to do a couple of practice exercises right now. Read through the instructions once or twice, and then put the book down and try this guided imagery experience.

> ⭘ *Put yourself into a very relaxed position, in a way that is comfortable for you. (You will be able to learn more about relaxation techniques in chapter four. For now, just simply breathe out a few breaths that carry some tension and anxiety out of your body, and sit like a piece of putty on your comfortable chair). If you like, you may close your eyes. Think of some problem you would like to solve, or about some student or employee in your charge who has a problem. Next, imagine that the problem has been solved. Now imagine a scene which follows the solution of that problem. See how relieved and happy you are or the other person is. Take a minute to enjoy the good feelings that come when a burden is lifted from your shoulders. . . . Now go back a bit, and see what happened to help you or the other person find the solution. How did the answer come? From where, from whom? Take a minute to see and feel the details in your mind's eye of the unfolding of the solution. . . . When you are ready, slowly come back to the room, and return to your previous position.* ⭘

Maybe you found a solution that you could not find before, or at least a new direction in which to look. Or, maybe not. Imagery exercises are not magic, and do not always provide quick and easy answers. It is always helpful, as one step, in aiding a person to find a way through the thicket of the mazes which confront us.

Now let's do a second trial exercise. Everyone I know would like to improve some human quality in their personality, since none of us is perfect. For example, I personally would like to become more patient. My pet peeves are standing in line at a bank or supermarket, waiting for a red light or getting caught in traffic. The trait I would like to change is to reduce my impatience. Think of a trait which you would like to improve, such as being more charitable, more caring, more open-minded, more ambitious. Or whatever. Write down the trait you would like to develop on a piece of paper, such as a 3 x 5 card. It should have one word such as: patience, compassion, openness, ambition, caring, etc.

> ⭘ *Now sit comfortably again in your chair, take a few gentle breaths to let go of some of your tension, close your eyes if you like, and see that piece of paper in your mind's eye. Let the word fade away, and replace it with a picture of yourself doing something including an abundance of that trait. For example, I would picture myself standing in a long line in the supermarket. I see myself very relaxed and carefree. I am humming, and enjoying looking around the store at all the beautiful designs on the packages and food cans. I take special notice of the variety of people who are in line, and how interesting they are. (In my head, a thought appears—Who cares! Let me out of here so I can go do something important!). Let any negative thoughts float by, and bring back your nice picture*

of how you are able to enhance your positive trait. Stay with it as long as you feel comfortable. Then come back to your previous position, gradually resume your posture and state of mind and sit for a minute. ○

Let yourself absorb the experience, and see if you can integrate that image, or vision, into your life. Return to that positive imagined experience at some later time when you would like to work again on developing this trait.

Now you have already practiced two imagery experiences! As you become more experienced and proficient in using them in many different ways, you will find how useful they are, and how helpful they can be to others (students, clients, children, committee members, etc.).

3) Practice First With Simple, Short Exercises

The scripts you will find in chapters five and following require preparation, explanation, and relaxation exercises for maximum benefit. There are other venues for shorter and simpler exercises which can help you accustom yourself to using the technique of guided imagery. For example:

a) At home

Try some exercises with members of your family without the elaborate preparation techniques suggested in chapter four. Simply invite your child or spouse to use their imagination. Using words like "Let's pretend that. . . ." or "Imagine that. . . .", or "What if. . . ." is often sufficient to lay the groundwork for an unstructured guided imagery exercise.

Discussing a political or international conflict, it may be enough to say "Imagine that you were a member of such-and-such a (national, ethnic, racial or religious) group, how would you react in this situation? In discussing an argument someone had with a friend, teacher, or neighbor, one might suggest: "Pretend that you were the other person in the argument, how would you feel? What would you have said? How would you have reacted? . . ."

Sitting down to a holiday meal, you might suggest to family members: "Before we recite the prayer before eating, let's pause a minute and imagine that some of the people who cannot be here are sitting across the table from us." (These might be people who could not attend, or people who have passed away). "See how it is to have their face in our mind's eye, hear their voice, guess what they might be saying, thinking, or doing."

b) During religious worship

If you are a rabbi, teacher, or someone conducting religious services, you might think of introducing a prayer with a brief invitation to imagine some scene, idea, or condition.

"Before the prayer for peace, suppose each of us thinks in our mind about what it would look like if there were total harmony and unity throughout the world."

"As we begin the section of the *Shema* let's focus our minds on the unity of all of God's children as expressed in the word *echad*, or *one*."

"Before we recite the *Ma-ariv Aravim*, which talks about the miracle of the sunset and the cycles of nature, see if you can see a beautiful sunset in your mind, or hear the birds chirping as the sun rises in the morning, or smell the lovely scent of flowers in the field as the springtime fades into summer. . . ." It is always useful to suggest a variety of visual, auditory and other images since people have different capacities to call up sensual images in their consciousness. Some are more visual, others are better at auditory images, and others prefer smell, touch or taste.

"Before we conclude the service today, think about some ways you might bring the mood of our prayers into your life in the hours and days ahead. . . ."

4) Overcome Resistance

There are several things which a facilitator can say to make the experience more appealing and acceptable to the participant. Especially when this is the first time someone is trying a guided imagery exercise, it is good to help him overcome whatever resistance he may have.

a) As pointed out earlier, assure the group that nothing harmful can happen to them, and that they will not lose control of themselves.

b) Tell them that you have done these exercises before, and that even though you and others were skeptical before trying it, it surprised you in turning out very successfully.

c) Inform the group that since they may not have tried this before, you will be asking for their reactions at the end of the experience. This will help participants to feel involved and motivated to experiment, knowing that their reactions may be helpful to you. In fact, group reactions will assist you in modifying the script or the experience the next time you use it.

d) Suggest that one of the common pitfalls in the experience of trained users of guided imagery is the "interfering voices" which come to the surface. While the script is being read it is not uncommon for people to think thoughts that may tend to block their ability to create images. Slowed, regularized breathing often helps to eliminate this inner "chatter." Since some are better at auditory images than visual images, include some sounds, such as a rain drop, a person talking, a cantor singing, water falls, the ocean roaring, etc. Have them shake hands with someone, or touch a ritual object (such as a silk tallit). Have them speak to people, or ask questions. This will help the auditory learner overcome blocks to pure visual images.

5) Follow Guided Imagery Exercises with a *Grounding* Exercise

As we have emphasized above, guided imagery can be a very powerful tool for learning, healing and growth. But the entire process of utilizing an imagery exercise includes *follow-up*. This enables the imagery, which by nature is ethereal and ephemeral, to be brought down to earth, or, to use the professional term, to be *grounded*.

An imagery exercise is an inner experience, using one or more of our senses: seeing, hearing, touching, smelling, and/or tasting. It enables the practitioner to restore old memories, create imaginary situations, invent new ideas, and generally to act more creatively and lively in life. An image is often vague and undefined. It is like a painting without a frame. Or a melody line without accompanying musical support. An even better analogy is that it is like taking a trip around the world without telling anyone a word about your experiences when you return. You feel like you are hanging in mid-air or waiting for the other shoe to drop.

An effective imagery exercise that is not followed by a grounding experience is an incomplete learning experience. The student will have eaten an unripened fruit. It may produce nausea instead of a deep feeling of satisfaction and satiation.

There are many ways to ground an image, and make it a more clear and permanent part of one's growth and development. Grounding will give more depth, better perception, fuller understanding, and greater appreciation to the image that has been called forth. It will enable the learner to apply, adapt and re-evoke the imagery experience at later times for further use and development.

Henry David Thoreau once wrote: "If you have built castles in the air, your work need not be lost; that is where they should be. Now put foundations under them."

Here are ways in which one can *ground* a guided imagery experience:

a) Talk about it

The facilitator can ask participants to form small groups of two, three, or four, to share what happened during their experience. Talking about it, expressing in concrete words what happened in the brain in metaphoric symbols, word or sound pictures, or abstract concepts, will help the imagery participant make the experience more real and down to earth.

Talking about an important or deep experience will help the person to express and ventilate any strong feelings, or flesh out any incomplete pictures that came up. Images by nature are vague and foggy. Talking, sharing, and discussing can assist the person to turn the experience into something more tangible and usable. He/she can apply it to many different realms of life, and draw forth more of its implications. The talking, dialog and discussion can frame the image in a way that makes something beautiful out of raw materials that otherwise might leave one wondering, confused, questioning, or perplexed. Dialog partners can ask simple questions which draw out the imagery participant and help the person recall parts of the image which were there but perhaps not fully noticed.

The facilitator can ask participants to find a partner with whom to discuss their experience. If more time is available, after finding a partner let each couple find another couple and make a foursome. Groups can be divided at random, or the facilitator can use any number of strategies for forming small groups.

Suggested strategies for forming small discussion groups:

Birthdays – The leader can decide on the best size of each group (2, 4, 6, etc.) and then divide the group up by asking for people to announce their birthdays. If it's groups of four, then the four earliest birthdays in the year are group one, the next four are group two, etc.

Name Tags – Give people different colored name tags to designate in which group they will be.

Names From History – Select famous historical personalities and give out names on index cards. For example, if the goal is to have groups of four, four cards can say "The Four Sons of the Haggadah," "The Four Matriarchs," or four of the sons of Jacob, four cities in Israel, four important dates in Jewish history. Shuffle the cards and give them out at random, asking members to find others whose cards have something in common.

Hebrew Names – Count off groups by the first Hebrew letter of each person's name. Begin with people who have a name that starts with **alef** and continue until you have four (or whatever number you desire). Continue through the entire alphabet until everyone is in a group of the desired size.

Calendar Order – Give each person an index card with the name of a Jewish holiday. Everyone must find a group with all the people who have the same holiday. If you want groups of six, for example, give out sets of six cards with the name of a holiday written on it. Alternatively, ask members to form groups whose holidays are clustered in a certain season of the year. For example, the high holidays and Sukkot will go together, Hanukkah and Tu BeShvat, Pesach and Lag B'Omer, Shavuot and Tisha B'Av. The number of cards given out in each category is determined by how many persons the leader wants in each group.

(For more suggestions for forming groups, and other ideas for group facilitation, see Mel Silberman's excellent handbook, *Active Teaching* (Boston: Allyn & Bacon, 1996).

Leading Questions

In talking or writing about an imagery experience, some of these questions may be helpful:

1) What was the experience like?

2) What was different or special about it?

3) What did you learn from it?

4) What surprised you while going through it?

5) Was it easier or harder than you thought it would be?

6) Would you like to try it again, on another occasion?

7) What stands out most about this experience?

8) How did this experience differ from other learning experiences you have had?

9) If you were to repeat the experience, how might you change it?

10) If you have used guided imagery before, was this easier or harder than last time?

b) Write about it

Any of the grounding techniques can be used alone or together with other similar activities, depending on how much time is available, and how deep and personal the subject matter. Whenever possible, it is advisable to have an individual do something private, such as write or draw the experience, and then selectively share parts of their expression with a partner or small group. With less time available, talking can be sufficient.

Writing experiences can consist of anything from a simple paragraph or two describing freely whatever the person wants to set on paper, to a more elaborate expression, such as a poem, a narrative, an essay, a diary entry, etc. The length and depth of the writing will depend on the judgment of the facilitator, the need of the experiencer, and other factors affecting the learning group.

If writing is not followed up by small group sharing, then the facilitator may want to ask a few participants at random to share parts of their writing, just to give a flavor to the larger group, and to permit everyone to get a sense that they are not alone in this enterprise.

c) Draw something

Since images by nature emerge from the right side of the brain, it is often possible to capture parts of their message in a non-verbal symbol, such as a drawing. Giving students some paper and crayons will give them free reign to ground the image that has been floating around in their heads on paper, in concrete symbols. Things may appear on paper which the person may not even have been totally conscious of, but did emerge from the guided imagery nevertheless.

If the participant is willing and interested in doing it, drawing can be one of the most effective and useful ways to ground an imagery experience. However, s/he may have to be convinced of its efficacy in order to give it a try.

As in writing, the drawings and any comments the maker of the drawing wishes to express about it can then be shared in small groups, and then selectively, in highlights, before the entire group by a few volunteers.

d) Do something artistic besides drawing

Some people may want to do something more involved and extensive than drawing, such as composing a song, making a clay figure, or making up a dance. Or they may find other means of artistic expression which embody what their creative imagination provided. People will often enjoy keeping these objects as a permanent record of this experience, giving them personal joy and satisfaction at a later time. In one group in which I was a participant, each person was asked to create some clay object which summarized the life of another group member. This followed a number of other interpersonal experiential exercises. My partner molded a small but beautiful clay megaphone, and gave it to me as a gift. It symbolized for my partner the fact, as he put it, "that I am a man with a message." I keep this beautiful clay megaphone as a permanent source of inspiration and encouragement, and often gaze upon it when feeling doubts or misgivings about my work and influence on my students.

6) Practicing Imagination Skills

It is a very useful and practical way to get into the mental and psychological mindset of using guided imagery to do a few short "mental gymnastics" exercises which utilize imagination skills. This gives learners the confidence to know that they can do it, and also gives them a brief flavor of the contribution that using their sensory imagination has for the general growth of their imagination skills.

Explain to students that in conventional education we utilize only a small part of our brain. For many years education was limited to developing skills that are known as cognitive, or rational, skills. Little or no time was devoted to developing our emotional and feeling abilities, which are no less important life skills, and vital to human growth and development. Likewise, most educational experiences of past years omitted the skills needed to think of creative new ideas, to make progress in the arts and sciences, to develop civilization through music, literature, plastic arts, business, science, and medicine, all of which need imaginative ways to make progress in pushing back the barriers of the unknown.

It is a very exciting adventure to develop imagination skills. That is what guided imagery can do for us. Let's demonstrate how to do this, and then practice a few brief exercises.

You may want to say to the learners: "Since using our imagination requires accessing deeper, unused parts of our brain, we need to become very calm and relaxed to reach this part of our mind. In some ways it is like being hypnotized, but in guided imagery we are in complete control of what we do, and we never lose our ability to stop what we are doing and return to our normal state of consciousness. No harm can come to anyone using visualization or guided imagery. When using guided imagery techniques for educational purposes we do not enter into anyone's personal psychological problems. You can rest assured these are strictly educational techniques, and are used more and more widely all over the world in education, science, health, sports and in many other areas. Today it can be considered an almost universal skill of teachers and educators, as well as therapists and human resource development consultants."

[Notice that we have been using the following symbol to indicate the content of the script of an imagery exercise: ○. This symbol will note the beginning and ending of an exercise, the words which the facilitator will read (word for word, or in modified form) to the group. Some facilitators may want to tape the imagery exercise, and then play it to the group. You may get someone with a good reading voice, or just practice doing it yourself before taping. This has the advantage of being able to participate in the exercise along with the group. There is a professionally prepared tape available for purchase with this book. Check the order blank on the last page].

○ *Are we ready? Please get into a comfortable position, and relax. Let all your tension and tightness melt away. Take a few breaths, and with each breath exhaled, let some more discomfort, tight muscles and mental preoccupation just float away. As you sit for a minute or two, you will find that you can concentrate more easily, and focus your attention more carefully on what we are doing, letting go of all outside sensory stimulation. Pay no attention to who is sitting next to you, where you are, what is going on nearby, or to any noises that might present themselves. Just relax, and focus your attention on your own breathing. When you focus on your breathing, you are not changing it by making it slower or faster. You are just paying attention to it.*

[Note to teacher or facilitator: The above instructions must be tailored in length and sophistication to the age, level, maturity, and readiness of the participants].

If you feel comfortable, let your eyes feel very tired, and begin to close. Feel like you are sinking into your seat (or floor) beneath you. . . . (Pause). . . .

In this very relaxed state of mind we are ready to begin some guided imagery exercises.

Imagine that you see a movie screen in front of your eyes. Let some things I suggest appear on this movie screen in your mind. In addition to seeing things on your private screen, you may also smell, touch, hear and taste things. You will be using all your senses. Creating internal imagery means creating a picture that you can access with all your senses, not just sight.

Imagine a lemon on the screen in front of you. Place the lemon in your mouth. Suck on the lemon for a few seconds. . . . What is happening in your mouth, to your face, to your taste buds? Answer only in your mind. You need not speak out loud. (In fact, it is better not to, since that might disturb others in the room who are trying to concentrate).

Let the lemon fade away and disappear. See yourself sitting in a classroom. The teacher writes something on the chalkboard, but he misses once, and runs his fingernail across the board. What sound does it make? How do you react? Pay attention to what is happening in your body, as you experience this scratching on the chalkboard. . . .

Let the chalkboard fade and disappear.

Remember that anything you do in your mind is in your control. You can refuse to do anything I suggest if it is in any way uncomfortable, or something you would prefer not to do.

Now see yourself entering an extremely tall building, such as the Empire State Building in Manhattan, or any similar tall building. Enter the elevator and go to the top floor. Walk out of the elevator, and enter an office suite. Go out onto the balcony, and slowly walk toward the edge. Look down and see the traffic below. Walk around the balcony, from side to side, and keep looking in all directions. . . .

Now return to the inside of the office suite, get into the elevator, and go down to the main floor, and walk outside. Let the building fade and disappear. . . .

Whenever you are ready, come back to this room, gradually stretch your limbs, open your eyes, and be right here. ○

Think about your reactions as you sucked the lemon, or heard the scratch on the chalkboard, or walked around the balcony of the skyscraper. Did you see a gate or fence on the skyscraper balcony? No one told you to, so if you did, you were using your imagination totally independently. Think about the ways in which you took control of your imagery process, and saw or did things which were not suggested to you. See how you take care of yourself, even when the suggestion is not made to do so.

The leader may now want to conduct a discussion about what imagery powers participants have, and how they affect our mind and body, and how we react to things which we know in our rational mind are "really" not there.

What can we learn about ourselves through these exercises? About our ability to imagine, and the effects this ability has on our mind, body, emotions, and spirit?

(Allow ten to twenty minutes for discussion, as necessary).

7) Review of Suggestions For Group Learning Experiences

✿ Imagery exercises can be used for people of all ages, from the youngest child to the most mature adult, assuming proper adaptation of content, length and methodology.

✿ Sometimes it helps in school environments if the supervisor, principal, co-workers, lay boards and others are informed, casually, about the use of new and innovative techniques. An explanation about using artistic imagery and creative thinking will demystify the subject.

✿ Experiences in guided imagery can be used for *any* subject matter—science, math, history, creative arts, language, literature, political science, humanities, business, human resource development, etc.

✡ The proper place for use of an imagery exercise depends on the leader's design or lesson plan. It can be used at the beginning of a session to **motivate** participants. It can be used in the middle to **concretize** or **expand** a subject. Or it can be used at the end of a session to **summarize** or **review** a number of areas.

✡ It is wise to go from simple and brief exercises to longer and more complex ones.

✡ Frequently validate and reassure participants or students that they are doing just fine, and that the way they are handling it is perfectly acceptable. There are no wrong answers!

✡ Create a quiet atmosphere by dimming lights, putting a "Do Not Interrupt" sign on the door, and leaving enough time to complete the exercise.

✡ For those who are unaccustomed to non-conventional right-brain learning, assure them that this new method is exciting and innovative. Tell them you will invite their reactions after the experience so they will feel some ownership and control over their learning process.

✡ Use several types of images, including visual, auditory, olfactory, tactile, and taste, so that persons who favor one sense over another will be able to more easily enter the imagery experience.

✡ Make sure that you employ a **grounding** experience following the guided imagery exercise.

✡ The more you practice with your self, the more confident and competent you will be.

✡ Be invitational, accepting, warm and caring.

✡ Always be non-judgmental.

✡ End the fantasy session slowly and gradually.

8) RESOURCES

A) Books

Adelaide Bry, *Visualization : Directing the Movies of Your Mind* (New York: Barnes & Noble Books, 1978).

Jennifer Day, *Creative Visualization With Children: A Practical Guide* (Element, Inc., 42 Broadway, Rockport, MA 01966, 1994).

Richard de Mille, *Put Your Mother on the Ceiling* (New York: Viking, 1973).

Beverly-Colleene Galyean, *Mind Sight: Learning Through Imaging*, Center for Integrative Learning, 767 Gladys Ave., Long Beach, CA 90804.

Patrick Fanning, *Visualization For Change* (Oakland, CA: New Harbinger, 1988).

William Fezler, *Creative Imagery: How to Visualize in All Five Senses* (New York: A Fireside Book, Simon & Schuster, 1989).

_____, *Imagery for Healing, Knowledge, and Power* (New York: A Fireside Book, Simon & Schuster, 1990).

Shahkti Gawain, *Creative Visualization* (New York: Bantam Books, 1982).

_____, *Meditations: Creative Visualization and Meditation Exercises To Enrich Your Life* (San Rafael, CA: New World Library, 1991).

Marlene Halpin, Dominican, *Imagine That!: Using Phantasy in Spiritual Direction* (Dubuque, Iowa: Religious Education Division, Wm. C. Brown Company Publishers, 1982).

Gay Hendricks and Russell Wills, *The Centering Book* (Englewood Cliffs, NJ: Prentice-Hall, 1975).

Gay Hendricks & James Fadiman, *Transpersonal Education: A Curriculum for Feeling and Being* (Englewood Cliffs, NJ: Prentice-Hall, 1976).

Maurice A. Howe, *Imaging—Self Exploration and Development Through Creative Use of Fantasy* (Australia, 1986; available through Creative Education Foundation, 1050 Union Road, Buffalo, NY 14224)

Aryeh Kaplan, *Jewish Meditation: A Practical Guide* (New York: Schocken Books, 1985).

Robert H. McKim, *Experiences in Visual Thinking* (Monterey, CA: Brooks/Cole Publishing Company, 1972).

Ursula Markham, *The Elements of Visualization* (Element, Inc., 42 Broadway, Rockport, MA 01966, 1991).

Belleruth Naparstek, *Staying Well With Guided Imagery* (New York: Warner Books, 1994).

Martin Rossman, *Healing Yourself* (New York: Pocket Books, 1987).

Mike & Nancy Samuels, *Seeing With the Mind's Eye* (New York: Random House Bookworks, 1975).

Mike Samuels, *Healing With the Mind's Eye* (New York: Summit Books, 1990).

Virginia Satir, *Meditations and Inspirations* (Celestial Arts, PO Box 7327, Berkeley, CA 94707, 1985).

Ronald Shone, *Creative Visualization: How to Use Imagery and Imagination for Self-Improvement* (Destiny Books, One Park Street, Rochester, VT 05767, 1988, paperback).

Valerie Wells, *The Joy of Visualization: 75 Creative Ways to Enhance Your Life* (Chronicle Books, 275 Fifth Street, San Francisco, CA 94103, 1990).

(Note: Check "Books in Print"—as some books may go out of print, or be reprinted by other publishers, or publishers may change addresses).

B) Music and Other Tapes

For background music promoting relaxation and encouraging effective internal imagery, consult the following catalogs:

1) Narada Productions, 1845 N. Farwell Avenue, Milwaukee, WI 53202

2) Sounds True, 1-800-333-9185; 735 Walnut St., Boulder, CO 80302

3) Harper Audio Cassettes, 1-800-328-5125

4) Harmonica Mundi, 213-559-0802

5) Strawberry Jam, (New Hope, PA) 1-215-862-9251

6) Big Sur Recordings, PO BOX 91, Big Sur, CA 93920

7) Celestial Harmonies, 605 Ridgefield Road, Wilton, CT 06897

8) Halpern Sounds Rx., PO Box 2644, San Anselmo, CA 94960

9) Rounder Records, One Camp Street, Cambridge, MA 02140

10) Warner/Elektra/Atlantic Corp., 111 N. Hollywood Way, Burbank, CA 94305

11) Windham Hill Productions, Inc., PO Box 9388, Stanford, CA 94305

12) *Meditations for Everyday Living* by Bernie Siegel, MD.

Write to ECaP, 1302 Chapel Street, New Haven, CT 06511.

(Tapes for physical healing, for overcoming stress, and for meditation for peace of mind.)

13) Whole Person Associates, 210 West Michigan, Duluth MN 55802-1908, 1-800-247-6789; FAX: 218-727-0505. Ask for Relaxation Audiotapes.

C) Other Resources

1) Academy for Guided Imagery, PO Box 2070, Mill Valley, CA 94942; Martin Rossman, M.D. and David Bresler, Ph.D., Codirectors. Offers workshops & seminars on guided imagery.

2) Belleruth Naparstek is a practicing psychotherapist who gives lectures, and offers audiotapes and a book (see above) on guided imagery for health. She may be reached at Image Paths, Inc., 2635 Payne Avenue, Cleveland, OH 44114, 1-800-800-8661.

Chapter 4

TECHNIQUES FOR PREPARATION

There are those who are bound by the chains of reason, and for such people there is no spiritual soaring.

—Ahad Ha'Am

SINCE guided imagery strategies often draw upon the deeper recesses of human consciousness, it is advisable to enter into a relaxed state prior to beginning the actual guided imagery exercise.

For those with little or no experience in guided imagery, it is necessary only to ask the participants to sit or lie in a comfortable place and try to let go of their tension and tightness, to breathe slowly and deeply. Often this is enough to get people relaxed sufficiently to draw upon the deeper layers of their subconscious mind.

With children and adults who might be unaccustomed to specific relaxation techniques, such as those which follow, a simple request to become more relaxed is the best way to begin. For those with more experience in guided imagery, the techniques on the following pages are among many which can be used.

It is important to **invite** participants to use these relaxation exercises. In some cases a brief discussion may be held to explain the need for and purpose of relaxation as a preparation for a guided imagery exercise. Otherwise participants might be cautious about "being hypnotized" (which is not really dangerous, but often has frightening associations attached to it) or have other unfounded assumptions. It is always best to be open and honest, and to give as much preparation and explanation as possible to make people feel at ease, and to allay any unnecessary fears. Otherwise, if anxiety and fear arise, not only will the guided imagery exercise be much less likely to work, but the participants may feel that they are being tricked or manipulated.

The simplicity and safety of guided imagery permits leaders to be completely candid when using it. Raising people's fears is unnecessary, unwise and unproductive.

As participants become more convinced of the power and usefulness of guided imagery exercises in the context in which they are involved (education, worship, training, personal growth, consciousness raising), they will be more willing and more easily and effectively able to enter these activities in a spirit of fun, imagination, and growth.

For those with experience and comfort in this kind of activity, the following methods of relaxation have been found to be especially helpful in inducing a creative and productive imagery experience.

SUGGESTED RELAXATION TECHNIQUES

I - Breathing

The most frequently used and often the simplest technique for centering and relaxing is through proper breathing.

Breath is our connection to the environment, the bridge from our body to the world. It brings life-giving oxygen which renews and invigorates every part of our body, from our brain, to our limbs, our lungs, heart, arteries, etc. Without oxygen, we cannot live, and the more oxygen we have, in proper measure, the healthier we are, and the more balanced, centered and relaxed is our body.

Yoga instructors and other spiritual teachers stress proper breathing as the key to good physical and mental health. Those who are familiar with yoga can begin with some simple yoga breathing exercises. One need not, however, be a yoga practitioner to fine-tune one's breathing, and become a more healthy and effective practitioner of good breathing methods.

There are two simple steps in learning to breathe well. First, to pay attention to our breathing, without any attempt to change it. This is referred to as "awareness." Before beginning to change anything in our body state, such as becoming more relaxed, less tense and tight, it is crucial just to know where our "base-line" is—that is, to know whether and where we are tight and tense. Before we can attempt to change our breathing to a more healthy pattern, it is important just to do a "research project" and find out if we are shallow or deep breathers, if we over-ventilate or under-ventilate.

Our bodies are conditioned from birth to respond to frightening situations with a tightening reaction. This is called the "fight-or-flight response." Through the evolutionary process, our ancestors became conditioned, when in a situation of danger (such as the approach of a tiger or other dangerous animal) to react in one of two ways: to stand and defend oneself (fight) or to run away (flight). With only these two basic tools, our evolutionary development lacks other needed responses in the modern age to different kinds of stress other than physical danger.

Today we have developed fear reactions to emotional, interpersonal, financial, life-situational problems other than physical danger. It is more appropriate to use our thinking powers and critical problem solving tools than to fight or flight. Unfortunately, since these skills are highly underdeveloped in most modern people, and evolution has not provided them for us yet, we need to be trained to use them.

One of the most effective starting points in dealing with any kind of fear or anxiety-provoking problem, is to use healthy breathing. To do that, we need to study our own breathing patterns and habits. This is to look at, be aware of, or focus on, our breathing.

The second simple step is to take some deep breaths, a few in the beginning to slow down inappropriate rapid breathing. Most of us breath too irregularly and rapidly, even when rapid breathing is uncalled for and harmful. We tighten our muscles, hold our breath (which slows rapid breathing), or over-ventilate (breathe too rapidly). When our breathing gets out of a natural and healthy pattern, the life-bringing oxygen we need to function at our optimum level is interrupted, and we become tired, our muscles and joints are inflexible, and we lose our capacity to live a vibrant, vigorous, relaxed and enjoyable life.

Thus, practicing some simple breathing techniques will do two things for us. First, it will make us healthy, happier, stronger, give us more energy, and mental and emotional alertness. Second, it will teach us how to relax and find more inner peace, tranquility and spiritual joy in our relationships, our work, and our awareness of the world in which we live.

It is this second purpose which we are trying to realize in order to access the power to create a mental image. Since imagery occurs through our so-called "right-brain," from which our creativity and spirituality primarily emanate, the more we train ourselves to relax, especially through proper breathing, the better, more effortlessly, and more quickly we are able to access the hidden powers of our mind and soul.

Training for good breathing consists, then, in first taking a moment to pay attention to (focus on) our breathing. After a period of becoming more adept at focusing on and assessing our breathing patterns, we can slowly begin to change our breathing, to make it more regulated, less shallow, deeper and more conducive to good health.

After a short while of practice, natural, deep breathing will become habitual and easy.

Some helpful factors in achieving good breathing are:

✡ A bright, cheerful, well-ventilated room.

✡ Lowering the lights is also helpful in producing a relaxing state. Nevertheless, guided imagery can be done in normal light, and this step might be postponed until participants feel safe and comfortable with the facilitator, with the group, and in practicing guided imagery.

✡ A comfortable position, e.g., sitting in a chair or cushion, or lying on a carpet.

✡ Posture that allows the breath to move freely through your mouth, lungs and the rest of your body. This means uncrossed arms and legs, unbent torso, head forward.

✡ Soft music that promotes relaxation. Resources, such as cassette tapes for relaxation and tranquility, are listed at the end of chapter three.

After a few times asking participants to focus on their breathing, they can begin to practice, either in a group or alone. Suggest to them that placing a hand on the stomach will enable them to recognize if their breathing is deep enough to fill their lungs, all the way to the base, which reaches down toward the abdominal cavity.

A more advanced breathing activity is to keep the mouth closed, breathe in and out only through the nostrils, feeling the breath fill the lungs and watching the abdomen rise and fall. Following that, learners may try taking a very deep breath through the nostrils, hold to a count of three, and exhale to three more counts, emptying the stale air completely from the body. Repeat this several times, with the mouth closed.

Practicing these breathing exercises will bring greater awareness of the importance of breath in the relaxation process.

After a few practice sessions, it will only be necessary at the beginning of a guided imagery exercise, to say, in your own words, something like this:

[Remember the symbol we shall use for beginning and ending a guided imagery exercise: ○].

○ *Pay attention to your breathing. Now begin to take a few deep, refreshing breaths, and let your breathing process become deep, regular, and wholesome, giving you more energy and letting go of tension and tightness each time you breathe.* ○

Repeating a brief set of instructions about breathing, whether for its own sake, or as an introduction to one of the other relaxation exercises listed below, will reinforce the participants' ability to train their breathing, and accomplish the desired state more quickly and easily each time it is practiced.

II - Other Simple Preparation Techniques

Have students/participants find a comfortable position, take a minute to relax, and let go of whatever is on their minds. Ask them to feel their body become very peaceful. Then proceed with one of the following relaxation/centering techniques.

1) Sending Light

Imagine a strong light (perhaps from a giant Menorah or Ner Tamid) suspended high above you. Feel the rays of the light going through your entire body bringing relaxation and release.

2) Watching the Ocean

You are sitting on the beach, watching the waves. It is late afternoon, and most bathers have left the beach. It is quiet and the sun is setting. You just sit and stare at the soft waves coming in and out. With each wave you relax deeper and deeper.

3) Computer Screen

Imagine a large computer screen in front of you. It takes up so much room, that it is all you can see. A rose, or daisy, or some other beautiful flower floats across the screen, slowly. Watch it go by. Let your thoughts float by along with the flower.

4) Wind

The temperature in the room is just the way you like it. You feel very comfortable. Nothing bothers you. A soft wind begins to blow over you, quieting your entire being. It feels very soothing and quieting. It helps you relax more and more.

5) Sun

You are sitting or lying in a very comfortable place. The day is beautiful, and there are no clouds in the sky. The sun is strong, but not too hot. The warmth of the sun penetrates your skin and warms your entire insides. Your heart feels very warm and loved. You feel strong and confident, and very calm.

6) Palms

Place your hands on your eyes, gently and softly. Your hands have a magical power that brings peace and comfort to your head. The warmth and relaxation begin to move slowly through your entire body. There is a warm, healing energy that flows from your hands to all your nerves, muscles and limbs. You are making yourself feel healthy and whole.

7) Favorite Picture

In your mind's eye you see a favorite photograph from your family album, or in a frame on a wall in your home. Watch the photograph and look at it slowly and carefully. Let the memories of the photograph flood your mind.

8) Candles

The Shabbat candles have just been lit. Watch them glow. See the peace of Shabbat enter the room. Watch how everything becomes more quiet, peaceful and harmonious.

9) Echad

Say the word Hebrew word *echad* (one) to yourself over and over again. Each time you say it, you feel closer to God. You feel protected and cared for. It is a comforting and relaxing feeling; you are secure and at ease.

10) Wine Cup

Someone is pouring wine into a beautiful silver cup [a kiddush cup, if you wish].

Watch as the wine pours from the bottle into the cup. It pours and pours, as a waterfall, not stopping and not spilling. You feel joyous and calm as you watch. Keep watching, and feel more and more serene and tranquil.

11) Mountain

You are sitting in a field at the bottom of a tall mountain. You look up at the mountain and see a beautiful, peaceful sight. Just sit and keep your eyes focused on the lovely sight. As you watch, you feel more and more relaxed.

12) Music

[The facilitator plays a piece of quiet instrumental music]. Listen to the music, and let it permeate your entire body, making you feel good and relaxed. See how the music quiets your body, and makes you feel relaxed and serene.

* I am indebted to my teacher and friend, Jack Canfield, from whom I learned some of these techniques.

III - Advanced Preparation Techniques

1) Body Parts

Sit or lie in a comfortable position. Uncross your legs and arms.

Take a few deep breaths. Relax. Close your eyes.

Let the tension flow out of your body. As you breathe out, let all the anxiety and tightness flow slowly out of every part of your body.

Focus your attention on your toes. Relax your toes. Now your ankles. Relax your ankles. Next, your calves. Find them completely relaxed. Relax your knees. Your thighs. Relax your groin.

Let all the muscles and all the nerves in your stomach completely relax.

Relax your chest. Let go of any tightness in your chest. Breathe deeply and slowly.

Focus your attention on your fingers. Relax your fingers. Relax your wrists and your hands. Relax your lower arms, your elbows, your upper arms and your shoulders.

Find yourself completely relaxed, deeply relaxed. Feel good, totally comfortable.

Pay attention to your lower back. Let go of any tension that may be there. Relax your upper back. Let go of any tightness in your neck. Let your neck melt into total relaxation. Relax your scalp, and your face. Totally relax your jaw. Feel how free of tension your jaw is.

Your are completely and deeply relaxed, feeling good in every way.

2) Heavy Eyes

Sit or lie comfortably. Loosen any tight clothing. Breathe slowly and deeply.

Close your eyes. Roll your eyes gently backward, and as you do so, become very, very tired and relaxed.

Feel your body becoming very heavy. You are sinking deeply into the surface on which you are sitting or lying. With each second you are sinking deeper and deeper into relaxation.

3) Stairs

Sit or lie comfortably. Breathe deeply and slowly.

Close your eyes. In your imagination see yourself walking down a flight of stairs.

As you descend each step, count from 20, slowly, down to 1. With each step you are becoming more and more deeply relaxed. By the time you reach the bottom of the stairs, you are completely relaxed.

4) Chalkboard

Put yourself into a comfortable position. Breathe a few deep breaths. Find yourself becoming very relaxed. Close your eyes.

Picture in your imagination a chalkboard. See the number "20" written in large numbers on the chalkboard. Now imagine a large circle, written in chalk, surrounding the number "20".

Focus your eyes on the number "20". Let the number drift away into the distance, and totally dissolve, leaving only the circle.

Now you see the number "19" inside the circle. After a few seconds, let the number "19" gradually and slowly drift away, leaving only the circle.

Keep your eyes focused on the chalkboard. Continue watching lower numbers appear in the chalk circle, and fade away, gradually dissolving into the distance. Now you have reached number "1" and you are totally and completely relaxed.

5) Body Liquefaction

Sit or lie in a very comfortable position. Feel yourself becoming part of the surface on which you are sitting or lying. You are becoming one with the surface, melting into it. It totally absorbs you. Count from 20 down to 1, very slowly, finding yourself melting more and more into the surface beneath you with each lower number.

6) Verbal Count Down

Sit or lie comfortably, loosening any tight clothing, such as a belt. Become extremely relaxed and tranquil.

Count aloud from 20 down to 1. As you proceed from 20 to 19, etc., let your voice become softer and softer. When you pass the number 10, you find that it is harder and harder to say the numbers aloud, you are so totally relaxed. As you count lower and lower, the sound of your voice travels farther and farther away. Your voice becomes softer and softer. By the time you reach number "1", you are completely relaxed.

7) Favorite Place

Sit or lie in a very comfortable position. Become totally relaxed. Feel very calm, and tranquil. Breathe slowly and deeply.

Imagine a favorite spot, where you feel very relaxed, such as a beach, a waterfall, or a meadow. Look around slowly in your imagination.

See how comfortable and serene you feel. You have no worries or anxieties. All your cares are gone.

Everything is just the way you want it to be. You are totally relaxed and comfortable in every way.

Pay attention to all of the sights and sounds around you. Be mentally and physically aware of the smells, the sights, the sounds. What you feel and taste add to your good feeling.

You are in your own paradise, completely refreshed and relaxed, feeling good in every way.

✡ ✡ ✡

The facilitator should speak slowly and allow the relaxation technique to take effect before proceeding with any further parts of a guided imagery activity.

Feel free to modify, combine, or adjust, any of these relaxation techniques as you become more and more accustomed to them. The more you practice them, the more quickly and easily will participants enter into the realm of relaxation and comfort. The more the body becomes accustomed to relaxation practice the more quickly the nervous system will adjust to quickly entering into these relaxed spaces.

Chapter 5

GUIDED IMAGERY FOR THE BIBLE

Imagination is the beginning of creation.
You imagine what you desire; you will what you
imagine; and at last you create what you will.

—George Bernard Shaw

IN THIS chapter and those which follow, we will deal with sample guided imagery scripts for the Bible, and other literature, as well as for rituals, institutions and other uses.

The guided imagery scripts presented here will help participants in many ways. They are all geared toward enhancing the appreciation and understanding of the subject matter, and to personalizing the abstract data contained in the fields covered. The experience of seeing, hearing, smelling, touching and tasting the content of the story, chapter, law, celebration, or characters in the books and subjects dealt with will intensify and personalize the learning process in a way that conventional education never approached.

Below are some sample scripts. Remember that the symbol ❍ indicates the beginning and end of a script. This is the material which the leader/facilitator should read (or modify, as desired) in presenting the imagery exercise before the group. If there is no such symbol, then the leader can rephrase the contents into her/his own exercise.

THE CREATION STORY

Have the students imagine that the world has not yet been created. They are sitting in a large conference room, inhabiting the form of God's retinue of angels, sitting around a long table, deciding how the world will be shaped and formed. They must plan out what its contents will be, what will be created first, how long it will take to create each part of the universe, what the roles of each part will be. After everything else has been created, God decides to create human beings, Adam and Eve. Let them feel the drama of this pinnacle of creation. It is the first time that human beings appear on the stage of the planet.

Tell the students to imagine that one of them will sit in the center of the room and be Adam. Then the other students ask Adam how it feels to be the first human ever created. Is he lonely? What would he like? Is he hungry? What does he see, smell, hear? Have him describe the Garden of Eden. Interrupt his speaking and have someone else announce, in the voice of God, that a woman, a helpmate, will be created to be his partner. God puts him to sleep, a rib is removed and woman is created. What happens when Adam awakens?

Now place Eve in the Garden. Have Adam and Eve hold a conversation.

You may or may not want to proceed with the story of the serpent, and the Tree of Knowledge of Good and Evil.

The teacher may read the story together with the class before the exercise. Or, assuming the class knows something about the story, the teacher may do the guided imagery exercise and then read the story. It will be experienced completely differently after having done the imagery exercise. Another possibility is to study the Creation Story, and perhaps even some of the commentaries, and then do the exercise. The advantage is that the students will have more information to place inside the story in their minds. The disadvantage will be that the fantasy may appear too much like what they read instead of coming from their own imagination. How it is done depends on the goals of the teacher and the knowledge the teacher has of the class and its ability and readiness.

RECEIVING THE TEN COMMANDMENTS

The following represents a full sample creative imagery script. The teacher/leader will ask participants to get into a comfortable position, takes some deep breathes, become very relaxed, close their eyes, and follow the directions as they are spoken.

❍ *Close your eyes and imagine that you are Moshe climbing up Mt. Sinai. Look around at the Sinai desert. It is very warm, and you are a bit fatigued climbing the mountain. Pause for a moment and look down at the people waiting below.*

You climb higher up the mountain, and can barely see the people. They are tiny specks below. What is going through your mind right now? (Pause).

You go higher and higher, finally reaching the crevice where you hear God speaking to you. Listen carefully to what the Voice says. . . .

Before you receive the Commandments themselves, God has a conversation with you. Tell God what you are thinking. . . .

If you have any fears or trepidations, ask God what to do. (Pause).

What do you think will be written on the Ten Commandments? Why does God want you to receive them and take them down to the People? Ask God that, and any other questions you have now. . . .

You are the only Prophet in the Bible to speak to God face to face. How does that feel? (Pause).

It is time to receive the two tablets of the Ten Commandments. Describe them. How heavy are they? How big are they? What does the writing on them look like?

Think about all the generations of people who will read, study, and try to follow these laws. You have a big responsibility. What is it like? (Pause).

You may have some hesitations. Perhaps you don't want to accept them. Discuss with God any thoughts you have right now. . . .

It is time to go down the mountain. Say good-bye to God. . . . (Pause). Begin the slow walk down the mountain. As you get closer to the bottom, you hear some noises. Look and see, listen carefully. What is going on below? What are your reactions? ○

At this point, the teacher may bring the exercise to an end, or continue it further. If you were to terminate it, you might say:

○ *It is now time to return to this room. Slowly and gently, begin to end the fantasy, and bring yourself back to your (chair) (carpet) (place). Move your arms and legs; shake them a bit. When you are ready, open your eyes.* ○

It is time now for the leader to do a grounding exercise, and process the experience.

Reactions are unpredictable, but may possibly include some of the following components. The students may have felt a great sense of awe in the presence of God. They may be able to appreciate the importance of law in society, and the purpose and importance of the Ten Commandments. They may sympathize with the difficulties Moshe had in asking a whole society to take upon themselves an entirely new code of behavior. They may understand the people's reluctance to accept the Ten Words. They may develop a new appreciation for the prophet Moshe and his difficult task in leading the People of Israel. Many other things may emerge from their experience, which may be or may not be pleasing to the teacher. Be careful to be affirming and appreciative of whatever comes out. The idea is not to learn what the teacher wants, but to make Moshe's experience at Sinai a real and personal one for them as opposed to an ancient historical experience.

KING DAVID

The next imagery script will be an example of how this process can help the teacher work with biblical characters. Imagery works very well with biography and character study.

Any one of David's many persona would be excellent to use in a guided imagery exercise: David as warrior, as underdog against Goliath, as poet, as friend to Jonathan, as husband, as King, etc. Let's try the story of King David being told that he will not be able to build God's house. A sample exercise follows.

❍ *We are going to think about some of the feelings King David had when he wanted to build the Temple in Jerusalem.*

Sit back gently in your seat, and become very relaxed. Take a minute to breathe deeply and find the tension disappearing from your body. Just relax, and feel very comfortable. Let your eyes close. Your eyes are heavy, and you are able to take yourself back into history, — far, far, back into the time of the Bible.

It is the year 1000 B.C.E., and imagine that you are King David. You have risen to the highest power in the Kingdom of the Israelite People. No one has more power and authority than you, except for God. You have been a very faithful servant to God. You have fought many wars, and expanded the territory of Eretz Yisrael. You have been a great hero, and very successful.

Imagine yourself sitting on the throne of the King. How are you feeling? (Pause).

Ask your servants, and anyone in the room near you to leave. You want to be alone. . . . You have a deep desire in your heart. All your life you have wanted to do something extraordinary for God. You have composed many beautiful psalms, poems and songs, about your devotion and loyalty to God. You now have a question to ask God.

You would like to build a gigantic Temple in the capital city of Jerusalem, which you captured from the Jebusite People. You want it to be the Center of Eretz Yisrael. Imagine how the Temple you would like to build would look. . . .

Imagine that you have constructed the Temple. How do you feel? (Pause).

Now you are about to tell God of your plan. Feel the excitement building in your body. Your heart is pounding, and your adrenaline is flowing. This may be the pinnacle of your service to God and Israel.

You are alone, sitting on the throne, and suddenly you hear a voice. God is speaking to you. What do you think God will say? (Pause).

Tell God about your plan. (Pause).

God speaks to you now. Listen. . . .

God tells you that you will not be the one to build the holy Temple. Your hands have been bloodied in war. How do you feel? (Pause).

Argue with God. Don't take your defeat easily. . . .

What was your conversation like? (Pause). ❍

The leader may bring the imagery exercise to a close now. Or, before closing, David may hear God say that his son, Solomon, who will be King after him, will build God's Temple. This may give David some comfort, and not be as big a let-down for him. The teacher may decide how to end the exercise. There is no one way, no right way, to handle a guided imagery exercise. It is an art, like any other pedagogic technique, and should be handled in a way that fits with the teacher, the class, the circumstances, and other factors.

The leader continues:

❍ *You are about to return to the classroom now. Begin to come back to this room, slowly, gradually, at your own pace. When you are ready, open your eyes, sit up in your seat, feel yourself becoming more awake. Sit for a minute and think about your experience.* ❍

Now the teacher explains what the next step in the learning experience will be. Perhaps each person will find someone sitting nearby and share their experiences. Perhaps each person will want to write a brief dialogue outlining a part of one of the conversations they had with God. Perhaps they will want to draw how they felt when God told them that David will not be allowed to build God's house. The teacher may select the grounding experience, or may offer several options to the students.

This may be followed by an assignment, such as having King David write a letter to his son Solomon, giving him advice about what kind of Temple he would like his son to build, and what functions he envisions for the Temple in the life of the People of Israel. Or, perhaps two or more students can come to the front of the room. King David can share his sad news with his wife and children. Those listening can react and create a dramatic scene, reacting to David's surprising news. At some point, of course, the biblical text should be used, either in the original (if the children are old enough — in English or in Hebrew), or in summary; or reviewing the entire story in the words of the class textbook.

Some Shorter Imagery Exercises

For younger children, or for occasions when there is a limited amount of time, or for a part of a lesson in which the teacher wants the imagery exercise to be a smaller component of a fuller lesson, here are a few examples of brief exercises.

1) The Ten Plagues

◯ *Relax in your seats, and imagine that you are an Egyptian, during the time of the enslavement of the Israelite people. Since Pharaoh refuses to let the Israelites go, God punishes him and his people by bringing some terrible plagues on the land. One of them is having frogs everywhere.*

You are in bed, and you wake up, and see a frog on your pillow. What goes through your mind? You jump out of bed, and go into the eating room. There you see many more frogs. What are you thinking? Look around and see where else in the house the frogs have gone. . . . Go outside, and see if the frogs are anywhere besides your house. . . . Stop into your neighbors houses, and see if there are frogs there too. . . . All your neighbors are running out of their houses, and people are frantically running to and fro. . . .

What will you do? ◯

This is an example of a guided imagery exercise that is more open-ended. Lack of detail in certain biblical stories enables the student to fill in these events between the lines. This is a place where imagination can fill in the blanks and serve a very useful purpose. It helps to make the story come alive, get fleshed out, and become very personal.

(This, by the way, was often the function of the rabbinic midrash. Midrash is the personal imaging of the ancient rabbis, based on their previous knowledge of texts and traditions, imagining what happened "between the lines" to explain or elucidate an otherwise ambiguous biblical story).

The Ten Plagues is also an example of a story that can leave some young children with anxiety about past historical events when these events become too personal and frighten them. Always remember to tailor imagery exercises to the age and readiness of the student. With younger children it is important to bring the story to a positive closing. Remind the children that this happened long ago, that they are not Egyptians, that what God did helped the Israelites to escape from slavery, and that the story ended happily for Moshe and B'nai Yisrael.

2) Balak and Balaam

During the 40 years of wandering in the desert toward the Promised Land, the Israelite People encounter King Balak of Moab (where the Kingdom of Jordan is now). Balak is afraid of the Israelites, because he heard of their strength. He calls upon a Mesopotamian prophet, Balaam, to curse the Israelites. The story is found in Numbers, chapters 22 to 24.

As with any guided imagery exercise, it can begin the lesson to pave the way for the story that will be told, or read. Or it can come in the middle of the lesson to create special interest or excitement. Or it can be used to review and summarize what the students have learned. Let's suppose that the students have not yet read this story, or these chapters in the Torah. A sample imagery script follows.

❍ *Sit back, relax, and rest your eyes. Imagine that you are an Israelite travelling through the Sinai desert, and you come upon the border of the Moabite nation, an unfriendly people who are afraid of you. Look ahead and see the Moabite Kingdom. . . .*

King Balak of Moab calls upon a foreign prophet, Balaam, to come from his home in faraway Mesopotamia, and curse your people. Fortunately for you, since Balaam is a prophet of God, he cannot disobey God's wishes. Thus, he tells King Balak that he cannot say anything that God does not tell him.

Imagine now that you are Balaam. You are confused about the request given to you by Balak. You are offered great reward, but God warns you not to try to curse the people that is already blessed by God. Balaam disobeys and tries to go along with the King's plan. As you, Balaam, are riding your donkey, the angel of the Lord appears before you. You do not see the angel, but your donkey does. The angel is blocking the path, so the donkey turns aside. You get angry at your donkey and hit it. The angel again blocks the way, and the donkey brushes against the wall, and as he does so, your foot is crushed. You hit the donkey again. Finally, as the angel totally blocks the way, the donkey sits down and refuses to move. You get furious and hit the donkey again. What are you thinking about now? How can you proceed? . . . (Pause).

Suddenly, God opens the mouth of the donkey, and it asks you why you are being so cruel. The donkey tells you it has been loyal and faithful to you all these years. How do you answer the donkey? (Pause).

How do you react to a talking donkey? Are you dreaming? What is going on here? (Pause).

Finally, after several attempts of King Balak to make you curse the People of Israel, you repeatedly refuse. You look down from a hill and see the people in the valley below. It is a beautiful sight. You are happy to look upon the people. Because they are God's people, you can only bless them. You cannot curse them.

Looking down on the beautiful sight, you recite these words: How beautiful are your tents, O Jacob, your dwelling places, O Israel!

Your blessing is so beautiful, it will be recited by the descendants of the Israelites for countless generations, as they begin their morning prayers. How does this make you feel? . . .

Let's come back to this room now, and end our journey. At your own speed, open your eyes, stretch your limbs, and awaken. ○

3) Aaron Is Consecrated as Kohen Gadol

There is a very elaborate ceremony in the Torah for the consecration of Aharon as High Priest (Leviticus, chapter 8).

○ *Imagine that you are Aharon about to be consecrated as Kohen Gadol. There are special sacrifices and elaborate ceremonies. The whole people assemble for this important occasion. Look around you and see how many people have come to join you for this momentous event in the life of the People of Israel. . . .*

Moshe now approaches you and your sons, who will also be consecrated as kohanim, and washes you with special water, so that you will be ritually pure. You feel clean and holy. It is a special, unique feeling. Enjoy this feeling for a moment. . . .

Now you see Moshe approaching you with a special tunic, the tunic of the Kohen Gadol. You are getting very excited, and feeling so special. . . . Moshe then places the other holy garments on you—the robe, the ephod, and the breastplate, with the very holy 12 stones, representing the 12 tribes of Israel. Then he puts the priest's crown on your head. Pause and see how this feels. . . .

Now an even more holy and special moment arrives. Moshe takes some of the holy anointing oil, and pours a little bit on your head. You are now consecrated as the High Priest. You are the very first person in the history of your People to receive this unique and high honor. What does it feel like? . . . How will you use the authority of your high office?. . . What do you want to do to help your people become more holy? . . .

Think for a while. (Long pause).

Now let us return to our room, and come out of the imaginary experience we entered. Slowly, when you are ready, open your eyes, stretch your arms and legs, and sit quietly. ○

As you can see, there is no end to the possible uses of imagery exercises in studying the text of the Bible. Sometimes you want to feel the awe of a special event, such as Creation, or the Consecration of the Kohen Gadol. Other times, you may want to help students deal with the emotions of individual biblical characters, such as Moshe. In other lessons, you may want to enter into a biblical miracle, or fantasy, such as the ten plagues, or the talking donkey, or the crossing of the Reed Sea, or the receiving of the Ten Commandments. You may want to have two biblical characters dialog with each other in the creative imagination of your students. You may want to have them deal with theological issues like revelation, divine punishment, experiencing harsh consequences, accomplishing great deeds (like the conquest of the Land), etc. In yet other lessons, you may want to have your students create an image of a biblical story, and stop it in the middle, having the students complete it in their minds. Then read the ending the Torah gives, and compare the various endings.

In the next chapter we turn to some other kinds of guided imagery activities, such as those that might be drawn from the literature of the Talmud or the Midrash, from the rabbinic period which followed the days of the Bible.

Chapter 6

GUIDED IMAGERY FOR RABBINIC LITERATURE

The most imaginative men always study the hardest, and are the most thirsty for new knowledge.

—John Ruskin

MOST PEOPLE are not aware that the Judaism of the twentieth and twenty-first centuries is based primarily on rabbinic Judaism. Rabbinic Judaism is the foundation of the theology, Halakhah (Jewish Law), ritual practice, customs and ceremonies, Shabbat and festival observance, life cycle events, and basically all of what we believe, value, and practice as Jews today. While Judaism has its early roots in the Bible (mainly the Torah), it is an expanding and "evolving religious civilization" (Mordecai M. Kaplan's term, and widely accepted by most Jews today, including all denominations). The carefully crafted outline of Jewish belief and practice was so modified and adapted in talmudic times, that the rabbis of the talmudic period can be considered the creators of the Judaism we now practice.

To give the most obvious examples, the Torah tells us to observe and remember the Shabbat, but very few laws about how to do that are specified. The Talmud devotes an entire, lengthy tractate to this subject. Later codes and Responsa literature amplify and continue the tradition of legal and ritual evolution, which is an on-going process even now, in all branches of Judaism. Kashrut, the Jewish Dietary Laws, provides another example. The Torah specifies the types of animals, birds, etc. which are permitted to eat. But it is the Talmud which delineates all the rules about separating milk and meat, based on one short verse in the Torah about not boiling a baby goat in its mother's milk. The Talmud specifies the rules of separate dishes, vessels, cooking utensils, specific prayers before and after eating, ritual slaughtering methods, and other eating practices. All of these talmudic traditions are based on some brief verse or reference in the Torah, but it is the Talmud which truly creates the full canvass out of a brief biblical brush stroke.

The Talmud was written after the close of the biblical period, and was composed by rabbis, scribes and teachers, who lived from the from the third century B.C.E. to the sixth century C.E.—almost a thousand years of enormous creative and prolific thinking and writing.

Remember that guided imagery can be used before or after reading a rabbinic text, depending on the teacher's goals and lesson plan. Some time for relaxation is always in order. Skipping that step will prevent the full utilization of the exercise. Sharing time and/or some other grounding exercises should be planned before the imagery exercise begins.

In utilizing books of the rabbinic period, it is important for all who study this genre of literature to understand the use of biblical quotations. The rabbis of the Talmud and Midrash frequently quote verses from all sections of the Bible. They do this so that their interpretations and commentaries will have added authority. Their belief was that their opinions were merely an elaboration of the Bible, so it was always important to refer to the appropriate verse being verified, amplified, or used as evidence for a point.

We shall examine some passages from rabbinic literature, including the Talmud (made up of the Mishnah and the Gemara), the Midrash, and other rabbinic collections from this period. There is no specific chronological or thematic order to these passages.

However, the samples reflect a variety of ideas, historical settings, laws and ethical principles which make up this vast body known as rabbinic literature.

THE IMPORTANCE OF GIVING TZEDAKAH (CHARITY)

The facilitator can explain that there were many famous rabbis in the days of the Talmud and Midrash, the rabbinic period. When we read and discuss stories about them, we learn many important lessons from their experiences, their tales, and their sage advice. One tale tells of a conversation between two of the most famous sages of the early second century C.E., Rabbi Tarfon and Rabbi Akiva. Since the discussion relates to the giving of tzedakah, let's do some guided imagery to prepare ourselves to read this text (Midrash, Leviticus Rabba, 34:16).

> ❍ *Imagine that you have a friend who is not charitable. In your own case, when you pass beggars on the street, you reach into your pocket and give the person some change. When a charity can is passed around in a group, you always contribute, but your friend does not. When someone asks for volunteers to help clean up, or assist someone in need, you volunteer, but your friend does not. . . .*

You would like to say something to your friend, to express how good you feel when you share your money, your time, your love. . . . Think of what you would say. . . . How would you approach the subject? Imagine a brief conversation with your friend on this subject. (Pause). ◯

Next the facilitator may let a few people share their conversations, and compare (without judgment) the various possibilities, their similarities and differences, and perhaps the reasons for the particular approach, and the possible effects on the person.

Let us turn now to our midrashic text. The leader may retell the story, or the group may read the text. The story is about Rabbi Tarfon, a wealthy but miserly person. Rabbi Akiva, his friend, and the official charity collector, wanted to point out his error diplomatically, and thought of using a biblical text to persuade him. The class may want to discuss why Rabbi Akiva chose this approach (answer: since the Bible had such powerful moral and divine authority, especially to rabbinic scholars).

Rabbi Akiva approaches Rabbi Tarfon and suggests that he has a lucrative investment for him. Rabbi Akiva wants to purchase some choice property for Tarfon. Rabbi Tarfon agrees and gives him 4000 golden dinarii. Akiva proceeds to distribute the money to struggling students, and the next time the two friends meet Tarfon inquires about the investment. Akiva takes Tarfon by the hand, brings him to the Bet Midrash (House of Study), and shows him the room full of avid students, busily humming over the folios of the holy books. Tarfon asks: Which one of these has the deed to the property? Akiva places a copy of the biblical Book of Psalms in front of him. They study together several chapters, and then come to the following verse: "One who gives freely to the needy, that person's beneficence lasts forever; that person will be exalted with honor" (Psalm 112:9).

There is a minute of silence, and it dawns on Rabbi Tarfon that his investment is in the future of his students and of the Torah. The verse brings home the message that whoever gives money to the needy will never suffer from want, but will always be comfortable, both materially and spiritually. A light goes on inside Rabbi Tarfon, and he realizes what his friend Akiva is trying to tell him. Akiva then turns to Tarfon and says: "Here is the 'property' which I bought for you!"

At this point in the story, ask the students to return to a relaxed and receptive mode, and imagine what Tarfon's reaction would be. (Pause). Discuss the results of their imagery experiences.

Now resume the midrashic account: Tarfon arises from his seat, embraces and kisses his beloved teacher and friend, Akiva, and says to him: "My master, my guide—my master in wisdom, my teacher in proper conduct!" Rabbi Tarfon reached into his pocket and gave Rabbi Akiva yet more money to distribute as charity (Midrash Leviticus Rabba 34:16). It may be interesting to compare the results of the imagery exercise with the actual outcome of the story in the midrashic account.

The above illustration shows how an imagery exercise can be used to introduce a story, a literary entity, as well as how to go in and out of imagery during the reading or telling of such a story or textual passage.

PROTESTING AGAINST EVIL

One of the most important lessons from the Torah and post-biblical Jewish literature is the idea that citizens must be involved in their community. As Professor Abraham Joshua Heschel put it: "Some are guilty; all are responsible." You might begin a discussion/lesson by writing Rabbi Heschel's quotation on a chalkboard, and ask for reactions.

Next, explain that the talmudic passage about to be read/discussed relates to the same idea. First, ask the participants to take part in an imagery exercise. After all the necessary relaxation, preparation, and mood-setting, the leader may say something like this:

❍ *An important institution in your community [select a specific one, perhaps the United Way, the Jewish Federation, a local university] had just discovered that a large sum of money was embezzled by the treasurer, who needed it to pay medical bills in the family. It has become a community-wide scandal, filling much of the press and TV. There is one additional and important piece of information. The assistant treasurer knew about it, but felt uncomfortable saying anything, especially since she knew that the motive for the theft was for medical reasons.*

The assistant treasurer has just been brought in for questioning by the local police department. Imagine that you are that person, and you are being grilled about what information you had, and how long you had it. You try to protect your boss and yourself. Imagine yourself answering criminal charges to the detective questioning you. (Pause). ❍

A discussion may now take place among the group about the various levels of guilt and responsibility. You may use some values clarification exercises to rank the order in which persons in the organization bore responsibility, and indicate who else may have known and should also be implicated.

At this point you may wish to distribute a copy of the talmudic text, and read all or parts of it. (If you want to read more than the part quoted below, look up the entire reference in the Talmud, Tractate Shabbat, pages 54b and 55a).

> If anyone has an opportunity to protest the misdeeds of the members of the household, and neglects to do so, such a person bears a measure of the responsibility of the household. The same principle applies to one who can protest misdeeds in the wider community; so

does it apply to one who neglects the chance to protest the wrongdoing of the entire world.

For this reason the prophet Isaiah wrote (3:14): "The Lord will bring charges against the elders and officers of the Lord's people." If it is the officers who have sinned, then why does God blame the elders? We interpret this to mean that the elders were responsible because they did not complain to the officers.

At that moment two scholars, Yehudah and Shmuel, were sitting together when a woman appeared and cried out for help, but Shmuel paid no attention. Yehudah then said to Shmuel: "Does not my master agree with the verse in Proverbs (21:13): 'Whoever closes an ear to the cry of the poor shall also cry and not be heard'?" Shmuel then replied to Yehudah: You are a bright scholar to quote this apt verse, but I am not responsible. The one who is over me is responsible. Another scholar commented to his colleague on this episode: The one who bears the most responsibility is the Governor of the entire community, since there is none higher than him. His colleague replied: The Governor will not pay attention to someone like me! The scholar answered his colleague: Even if the Governor does not listen to you, you should protest anyway!

A good, healthy discussion can follow the reading of this passage, trying to deal with a multitude of questions regarding levels of guilt and responsibility, the chain of command of judgment, etc. Another important question is: Should one protest even when he knows in advance that it will do no immediate good? Why? Have the participants imagine a situation in which there are multiple levels of responsibility, and try to determine who will be punished most harshly, less harshly.

A good follow-up activity is to search for a news item that resembles the cases above—the one in the imagery exercise and the one in the talmudic passage. What is the lesson of the passage in Tractate Shabbat? How can we carry it out in our lives? Select several historical personalities who have, or who have not, accepted such responsibility. Create precise written definitions of "guilt" and "responsibility." Compare this entire discussion with the passage in Deuteronomy about the *eglah arufa*, or the calf whose neck was broken (21:1-9). Perhaps an assigned essay on this subject, or an essay contest, would be appropriate. Publishing the leading essays in some in-house or community paper or journal would heighten the motivation still further.

This is another example of how several guided imagery exercises can be combined with didactic, experiential and affective methodologies of other kinds. The integration of guided imagery into a broader program, design or lesson plan, can often be its most effective use.

THE IMPORTANCE OF SINCERITY

Have the group relax, breathe comfortably, do a relaxation exercise, and invite them to participate in a guided imagery exercise regarding their future.

○ *Imagine yourself five years from now. During the next five years you will achieve some very positive character traits that will win the respect and affection of your peers and colleagues, as well as those who may look up to you for guidance and instruction. One of the qualities for which you will be most admired is* <u>*sincerity*</u>. *Because we see and read about so many people in public and private life these days who lack sincerity, it is particularly noteworthy that you have been able to develop this treasured quality.*

In a club or association to which you belong, there is an annual award given to the person who is most sincere. This year YOU have been selected to receive this award.

Imagine a large hall filled with people who are presenting you with this award. Your name is now called out, and you walk slowly, and proudly, toward the dais, where the master of ceremonies is holding a large plaque so that all in the audience can see. When you arrive at the microphone, the M.C. reads the plaque, telling all about your wonderful qualities of sincerity, realness, and authenticity; qualities which you have displayed in all your dealings with other people in your work and social life. Take a minute to experience this special feeling. Savor every bit of it. (Pause).

Now project yourself into the future a few days after this special evening. Pay attention to all the telephone calls and mail you receive, all congratulating you on this award, and even more importantly, on your ability to achieve this kind of integrity.

Gradually, leave the fantasy, and come back to this room, at your own pace. Shake your arms and legs. If your eyes are closed, slowly open them, and return to your previous position. ○

If there are more than two or three people in your learning group, divide into groups of three and discuss the positive effects of sincerity and integrity. What results will come to a relationship, a family, a society, and a country when more and more people practice being sincere? Make lists of such results, and then have all the small groups come together and generate a large list on the chalkboard or poster paper for all to see.

When this part of the activity is completed, hand out a sheet of paper with the following talmudic quotation:

> The Torah, in discussing the holy ark in the wilderness, describes it as having gold both inside and outside (Exodus 25:11). Rava, a famous Babylonian rabbi, applied this lesson to scholars. He raised the question: Why must the Torah have gold inside when no one can actually see what is within? Why would it not be sufficient to have the ark covered with gold outside, and some less expensive metal inside? Rava stated that whoever is not the same inside as outside is not a true scholar! A contemporary of Rava, Abbaye, commented further: One who is not the same inside and outside is hateful, as the biblical book of Job says (15:16): "One is certainly called hateful and corrupt when that person pursues wickedness while drinking water." [Abbaye meant that drinking water, which is a symbol for Torah, while doing bad things, is a symbol of hypocrisy. Reading about morality while acting immorally is not being the same inside and outside.] Another rabbi, Shmuel ben Nachmani, said in the name of Rabbi Yonatan: We learn the same lesson from another biblical verse in the book of Proverbs (17:16): "What good is money in the hand of a fool to purchase wisdom, when he has no mind?" This is another example of an unauthentic person, who has an inside different from the outside. For example, paying for lessons when one cannot learn is done only to look intelligent and learned, when the person inside is actually ignorant, and either does not care about knowledge, or simply is not qualified to learn. (Talmud, Tractate Yoma 72b)

The rabbis continue to discuss other examples of people are not the same inside and outside. That is, who are not sincere, whole, authentic, and real people. Rather, they act one way and think a different way. They pretend one thing, but believe in another. The rabbis describe such people in a simple Hebrew phrase as *not* being "tokho ke-varo,"—the inside just as the outside. The highest degree of sincerity is to achieve the status of being "tokho ke-varo."

Students can now compare the difference between people who act sincerely with those who are duplicitous, phoney, insincere, and deceitful. Perhaps an art project would be useful to express in some concrete form what it means to be "golden" both inside and outside.

This is a good example of learning an important talmudic passage, engaging in an alternative learning style while doing so (the imagery exercise about winning the award for sincerity), and adding an important Hebrew expression which bears a profound ethical valence. The imagery reinforces several other important components of a lesson which may have a long-lasting effect upon the learner.

COMPASSION FOR ANIMALS

The facilitator should introduce the subject of "compassion for animals" by explaining that in talmudic days many wise people believed that pain and illness were the direct result of some moral failing. They did not consider the possibility of the random nature of microbes, bacteria and viruses, which attack their target regardless of the level of their ethical behavior. With that understood, we study a passage from which all can learn an important lesson about caring for living creatures (even though some may disagree with its theology).

Especially in this guided imagery exercise the leader must be careful not to assume that Judaism has only one point of view on every issue. For example, some people believe that eating meat from large animals, such as cows or sheep, is immoral, and for that reason they adhere to a vegetarian diet. Others disagree, and while they consume red meat, are content to know that kosher animals are killed as quickly and painlessly as possible.

○ *Sit back and become very relaxed. Let yourself enter a receptive mood. . . . Imagine that you are a cow, or a sheep, or a chicken. . . . What are your owners doing to you? . . . How does it feel to be fed by someone? . . . Notice how you are being pushed with a broom. . . . Think about other ways in which your every act is controlled by a human. . . . Let yourself imagine living inside the skin of an animal for a while. . . . What are some of the thoughts and feelings you are having? . . . Whenever you are ready, come back to this room, and open your eyes.* ○

Now an examination of the following passage in the Jerusalem Talmud (Tractate Ketubot, 12:3; 35a) is in order (or, if the passage is studied first, the imagery can follow).

"Rabbi Yehudah HaNasi (the Prince, President of the Sanhedrin—around 200 C.E.) lived in a Galilean town called Sephoris, and had terrible toothaches for thirteen years. What could such a famous, scholarly, and pious man like Rabbi Yehudah have done to bring on such agonizing toothaches? It happened once that he passed a calf being led to the slaughter. The calf bowed to the rabbi and said to him: O great master, please save me! Rabbi Yehudah replied to the calf: This is what you were created for!"

But the Talmudic passage doesn't stop there. The talmudic rabbis believed that pain was caused by sin, but cure was also possible, by performing good deeds. In the end, after his thirteen years of punishment, Rabbi Yehudah was cured of his toothaches. Why? The Talmud continues: "Rabbi Yehudah once passed some people who were about to kill a nest of mice. In a tone of righteous indignation, Rabbi Yehudah jumped up and shouted to the people, quoting from the biblical book of Psalms (145:9): 'God's mercies are over all works of creation.' Thus, the rabbi was cured!"

The facilitator may follow up with other passages by searching in Jewish reference works under the Hebrew phrase "Tsa-ar Ba-alay Chaim"—the Jewish aversion to "Pain of Living Creatures." The literature is voluminous. See, for example, *Encyclopedia Judaica* ("Animals"), Volume 3, pp.5-7.

THE IMPORTANCE OF SELF-ESTEEM

Sometimes stories are told in the Talmud which lend themselves very easily to a guided imagery exercise. An ethical dilemma is posed, a favorite theme in talmudic literature, in the form of an allegory, or a story. The tale is often brought to conclusion with a biblical verse as final proof.

One such story is about the famous Rabbi Akiva. This story can be read to learners while they are in a position of receptivity and relaxation, to make the encounter more real and personal in their minds. It is a good example of how a lesson on an important piece of literature can be augmented simply by closing the eyes and imagining the story as well as hearing it, without very elaborate imagery exercises.

The story is that of two people on a journey in the wilderness. One is carrying a canteen of water. The hypothetical case is this: If both drink from the little bit of water, there will not be enough water for either one of them and both will die. However, if only one drinks all the water, that person can reach civilization in time to survive. Two talmudic scholars debated the possibilities. Ben Petura argued that it is preferable for both to drink and die, so that neither has to feel guilty about the other's death. Rabbi Akiva disagreed. He quoted from the Torah: "Your brother must live beside you" (Leviticus 25:36). Rabbi Akiva read that verse to mean that unless you live, your brother's life has no meaning to you. Hence, your own life takes precedence (Tractate Bava Mezia 62a).

> ○ *Take some deep breaths and become very relaxed. . . . Imagine yourself walking in the desert with a friend. . . . It is getting extremely hot, and you have been walking very far. . . . You realize that there is not enough water in your canteen for both you and your friend to survive. This is an extremely difficult decision. The two of you sit down and analyze the problem. . . . Your choices are: 1) Each of you drinks half the water, or neither of you drinks it, in which case both of you will die from thirst. 2) You drink the water and are thus able to walk to the closest place of civilized existence. If you do that, your realize that your companion will die. 3) Give the water to your friend, so he can reach civilization, in which case you will die.*
>
> *Think about these choices. . . . (Pause). Discuss them with your friend. Think about what Jewish Tradition might advise you. (Pause). What did you decide?. . . . ○*

This is an example of how students can create their own midrash while learning from a Talmudic passage, and add their own wisdom to the ancient texts.

IMAGERY AND FANTASY IN THE TALMUD

The concluding guided imagery exercise in this chapter is brought to illustrate that the ancient rabbis had no lack of imagination and capacity to tell tall tales, or myths, which bore within them important kernels of truth, historical and ideological. As expert pedagogues, they were not adverse to embellishing history and theology by adding imaginary twists and flourishes to their narration of events.

One way to use this particular exercise is to let it illustrate the freedom of the use of human imagination in Jewish tradition, thus showing participants that the method of learning and passing on tradition in this book is an ancient and long-accepted one. This exercise could thus be used as one of the first in a more complete design covering the Talmud or another topic.

The facilitator can introduce the tale in this way: It deals with the end of an important era in Jewish history, the last days of what is called "The Second Commonwealth." This is the period when the Romans captured and destroyed the holy city of Jerusalem, burned the holy Temple to the ground, and exiled almost all of its inhabitants. It happened in the year 70 C.E., on the ninth day of the Hebrew month of Av, a significant date to remember. The ninth of Av is observed to this day as a day of mourning and commemoration of the end of Jewish independence. The Second Commonwealth came to an end much as the First Commonwealth did almost 700 years earlier, when the Babylonians under King Nebuchadnezzar destroyed Jerusalem and the first Temple.

The story tells about some of the young Kohanim (priests) who were exempt from battle, and were not yet mature enough to be in charge of Temple worship. Their sense of helplessness and hopelessness is felt in the tale. With the Temple destroyed, they had no professional mission to accomplish, and must have felt very helpless.

❍ *Let us all get comfortable now, and enter into the mood of this tale by relaxing, paying attention to our breath, uncross our arms and legs, and let our eyes gently close as we listen to the story in the words of the Talmud.*

Let us take ourselves back into that sad time of Jewish history. How depressing it must have been for our ancestors to lose everything: their political independence, their religious freedom, their national unity, and the Home of God's holy worship, the Bet Mikdash (the Temple).

The Talmud relates (Ta-anit 29a) that just as the Bet Mikdash was about to be destroyed, several small groups of young Kohanim assembled and went up to the roof of the Temple. In their hands were the keys to the Bet Mikdash. Can you see the Kohanim? . . . What did they look like? As Kohanim they could not fight in the War of Rebellion against Rome. Their task was to stay and be part of the worship until the very last moment. Their greatest fear must have been that if the Bet Mikdash were burned, they would be without purpose. As servants of the Blessed Holy One, they would not be able to accept the sacrifices brought by sincere worshipers, who dreamed to be able to ascend the Temple's steps and bring God their precious gifts. Soon that privilege would be no more. Put yourselves in their place. (Pause).

As the talmudic tale continues, these bands of Kohanim, in their heart-broken, trembling voices, cry out to Almighty God: "Master of the Universe! We are young Kohanim. We hardly had an opportunity to serve You. Our whole life we were trained to be among the faithful servants of the Creator, and assist Your holy people in offering the sincere sacrifices of their farms and their flocks. Just as we are growing old enough to assume our sacred task, the wicked enemy has deprived us of our privilege. Thus, we now return to You these keys to the Bet Mikdash, which, as it begins to burn, we no longer have any use for."

At this pathetic moment, the untried Kohanim stretch out their arms and with all their strength they throw the keys up to the skies. Watch the keys rise. . . .

Suddenly, with awe and trembling the Kohanim look up and see what looks like the palm of God's very hand, reaching down, and receiving the keys that had been thrown to Heaven. It is as if God is accepting the futility of this tragic moment, and refuses to intervene. This could only make the Kohanim feel even worse. Their sadness is now mixed with futility and fear. Imagine what they must be feeling. . . . (Pause).

With nothing more to do, nothing more to hope for, nothing more to save them from this last hour of unspeakable tragedy, the Kohanim take an unprecedented step. They join arms, jump into the fire, and breath their last breath together. Perhaps their fraternal unity and fellowship is their last drop of comfort. The end has come! . . . (Long pause).

When you are ready, come back to this room, and slowly open your eyes. ⭕

Now there should be an opportunity for the sharing of experiences. After an adequate amount of discussion, the facilitator may ask participants what they derived from the exercise. Besides learning about a major event in Jewish history from a short account in the Talmud, and identifying with the tragic and sad past of Jewish history, participants can experience a guided imagery exercise that was created by the ancient rabbis to convey to the people of their generation the meaning of the moment. They will, hopefully, realize that imagery is a method of affective and experiential learning that goes back thousands of years.

Chapter 7

EXPERIENCING JEWISH HISTORY

Imagination rules the world.
—Napoleon Bonaparte

A dream not interpreted is like a letter not read.
—Talmud, B'rachot 55b

In an Introductory Essay to the book *Polish Jews—A Pictorial Record*, by Roman Vishniac (NY: Schocken Books, 1947), Rabbi Abraham Joshua Heschel describes the spiritual life of the Jews of Eastern Europe. Rabbi Heschel points out that in the intense and ubiquitous pursuit of Torah study (Torah in the broadest sense—all Jewish knowledge from Abraham to the present), the pious Jew would not seek merely information. What was sought after were the implications and presuppositions of the information studied and discussed.

The nineteenth century Eastern European Jew studied with great imagination, heavily influenced by centuries of kabbala and Hasidism. With a vivid and artistic capacity to visualize and create, these Jews studied and added to the vast store of Jewish knowledge with their fertile minds.

Rabbi Heschel describes a seventeenth century book, *Revealer of the Deeply Hidden*, which interprets the story of Moshe pleading with God to enter the Promised Land in **two hundred and fifty-two** different ways! By letting their imagination run in a thousand directions at once, these spiritually-oriented Jews were not satisfied with the facts of history or literature. They took stories and snippets of history which historians passed down in a few sentences, and made entire tomes of them.

The reason German Jews settled in Poland, which became the seat of cities teeming with three million Jews, was because, in their imagination, two Hebrew words—*Po Lin*—"reside here"—were inscribed on a note which fell from heaven and was discovered by the German Jews fleeing eastward from their home in the days of the Black Death.

Given this traditional ability and love of weaving stories out of stories, let us turn now to two sample guided imagery scripts. These only scratch the surface of what possibilities lie in this method of learning more about our past—our story.

THE CHAIN OF TRADITION

○ *Find a comfortable place to sit or lie, and find yourself becoming very relaxed and at ease. . . . Loosen any tight clothing, and remove your glasses.*

Take some deep breaths, and let your tension and tightness disappear. . . . Uncross your arms and legs, let your eyes droop into drowsiness as they slowly become shut. . . . As you breathe out, let yourself become more and more deeply relaxed. . . .

Let yourself see a small group of people from four thousand years ago, leading a long line of followers. They are Abraham and Sarah, Isaac and Rebecca, Jacob, Rachel and Leah. . . .

Watch them marching on unpaved roads from town to town, with hundreds, even thousands, of individuals and families, following after them. . . .

Behind the matriarchs and patriarchs of Israel, are their children, the twelve tribes of Israel, and all their children and grandchildren. . . .

Down the line behind this group, let yourself see Moshe and Zipporah, and Moshe's brother Aaron, the Kohen Gadol (High Priest) and his family, and all the Kohanim who followed after him and served in the Mishkan, and later in the Bet Mikdash (Temple). . . .

Behind this one family of the tribe of Levi are those who came after them, Joshua, and then the Judges of Israel, Samson, Gideon, Deborah and others. . . .

After them are some famous early prophets—Samuel, Nathan, Elijah and Elisha. See them and their families following after, as the line becomes longer and longer. Now you can barely see the beginning of the line with Sarah and Abraham way in the front. . . .

Following behind are the kings of Israel, Saul and David, Solomon and Reheboam, and their many children, who later became kings and queens. . . .

Next come the later prophets, Isaiah, Amos, Micah, Hosea, Jeremiah, Ezekiel and Jonah. . . .

You watch as the line continues to become longer and longer, marching left and right, back and forth, throughout Israel, from the Galilee to Jerusalem to the Sinai. . . . (Pause).

As time moves a bit faster, we come to the days of the Romans, when Judea was destroyed, captured, and Jerusalem burned. The Jews begin to wander outside the borders of Eretz Yisrael, and the line snakes through many lands and different countries where strange languages and cruel leaders rule our people. The line continues to lengthen, and you watch it get longer and longer . . . longer and longer. . . . (Pause).

Abraham and Sarah are so far ahead of us now, that you can barely make out the tiny figures at the head of the line. . . .

Following now in the line are many famous rabbis, Hillel and Shammai, Gamliel and Shimon, and all their students. . . .

As the line continues to get longer and longer you have to stand on your toes to see the whole of it, from beginning to end. Next follow great teachers and writers, soldiers and scholars, merchants and statesmen and women. . . .

We follow the line as our eyes gaze on famous authors and poets, Maimonides the physician, Yehudah Halevi the poet, Saadya the philosopher, and Rashi the biblical and talmudic commentator. . . .

We enter the later Middle Ages, and we see the Jews still moving, being chased from country to country, finding new places to dwell . . . until they reach Eastern Europe and Russia, where they will live for centuries. Others are in Spain, and North Africa, Italy and Greece. . . . The line weaves, and moves, marching ahead, feet tired and thirsty, longing for security and safety, food and shelter, a place to settle and study the Torah, build synagogues and pray. . . . (Pause).

We now follow the long line of our people as it gets longer and longer, and we see people wearing modern dress, living in modern countries . . . entering universities, and living alongside their non-Jewish neighbors. Yet they still march, from place to place. Until Theodore Herzl is born in the middle of the nineteenth century, and the line begins to move back toward the Homeland once again. . . .

Towards the end of the line are Jews from all over the world, east and west, north and south, all following after their ancestors in a line that stretches longer and longer . . . longer and longer. . . .

In the rear of the line, we see Jews living in Israel, some from America, others from smaller countries in Asia, Africa, South and North America, small towns and large cities, walking in this same long line, following those who came before them. . . . (Pause).

And at the very back of the line you see yourself, and your family, your friends, your neighbors. . . .

Look ahead from the back of the line, as far as your eye can see, to the very head of the line. Jump up, or stand on a high building if you want, and see the whole line, from Abraham and Sarah, all the way back to you and your family. . . .

Watch the line, and let your mind roam and wander. . . .

See if there are any thoughts you have. . . . How are you feeling? (Pause).

Do you have any Jewish heroes whom you admire? Where are they in line? Find them and see who is standing near them. . . .

Is there anything you would like to say to those who are ahead of you, anywhere in the line. Pretend you have an invisible microphone, or a megaphone, and see if you want to say anything to any or all of the groups who are ahead of you in line. . . .

Do they answer you? Listen. (Pause).

What words, or songs, or messages, do you hear? Do you see any pictures? (Long pause).

Stay with any thoughts or feelings, or any images or fantasies which may be in your mind. . . . Let them blossom and change, or do as they please. . . .

We will be still now for a while, while our imagination wanders. (Long pause).

When you are ready, begin to return to this room, and let yourself come back where you started. Take your time, and whenever it feels comfortable, open your eyes. . . . ○

I STOOD WITH ABRAHAM

This guided imagery exercise is based on the writings of the late Rabbi Abba Hillel Silver, famous Zionist orator and one of America's foremost spiritual leaders of the first half of the twentieth century. Abba Hillel Silver was rabbi of The Temple, one of Cleveland's leading temples, while he also represented the Jewish People in its struggle to establish a homeland in Eretz Yisrael. He addressed the UN General Assembly in the late nineteen forties, pleading for a place in the world for the Jews to call home. He was an important influence in the creation of the State of Israel. From his writings and sermons, a responsive reading was created which is used in many synagogues during the High Holy Days. The following guided imagery exercise is adapted from this reading, itself an adaptation of Silver's writings.

○ *Begin to enter a receptive mode, and do all the things we have practiced in getting ready to let your imagination roam free. Be very relaxed and comfortable, focus on your breath, and find yourself becoming more and more completely relaxed. . . . Let your eyes be shut, and some interesting things will appear on the movie screen in your mind. . . .*

A book appears in front of you, a large, thick, volume, suspended in air. As it gets closer to you, you can see its title. The letters now get sharper and you see the words imprinted in large dark letters on the heavy leatherbound cover. It says: JEWISH HISTORY. . . .

Open the book, and begin to flip through the opening pages. At the top of the page of the first chapter you see a title: ABRAHAM AND SARAH.

See yourself standing with Abraham and Sarah, the founders of the Jewish People. The sun is setting rapidly in the western sky, and you watch Abraham and Sarah angling their necks upwards, staring intently, as it darkens and the stars begin to come out. As they look at the shining medley of stars, too many to count, they turn to each other and predict that our people some day will be as numerous and as bright as the stars in the heavens.

Watch the stars for a moment, and let them be for you a picture of the destiny of the Jewish People. . . . Notice any feelings you have inside of you, and stay with them for a bit. . . .

Turn the page of your book of JEWISH HISTORY, and see the title at the top of the next page. It says: ABRAHAM AND ISAAC. See yourself watching the awesome and frightening moment in which father and son are walking up towards Mount Moriah, readying themselves for the sacrifice, God commanded Abraham to offer up his only son, the son of his old age, Isaac, on the altar, to test his faith. Look into the eyes of Abraham and Isaac, and imagine what is going through their minds and hearts at this moment in which their devotion is put to the test. . . .

Move on to the next page, and watch Jacob, as he wrestles throughout the night with his special angel, his Conscience. Listen to the dialogue between the two of them, as the angel tells Jacob that his name will no longer be called Jacob, but Yisrael, because he wrestled with God and humans, and prevailed. Listen as the angel blesses Jacob. . . . What is he saying? . . .

Moving forward, turning the next page in your history book, you see Joseph, lying on a soft pillow, dreaming of sheaves and stars, and of how everyone pays honor to him. Read down the page and follow Joseph as he matures, and climbs the steps from the pit to the throne of a prince, second only to Pharaoh. . . .

We turn another page in our history book, and find ourselves standing next to Moshe, "an alien prince among an alien people." Watch Moshe as he stands before the burning bush, barefoot, listening to God's voice. Watch him as he stands with awe and trembling, gazing at this mysterious bush which burns and yet is not consumed. Is there smoke? Does the fire burn hot? Then, as God charges him to save our people, look closely at the face and body of Moshe, as he realizes Who is calling him to divine service. . . .

Moving forward, we see Moshe walking down from Mount Sinai with two heavy tablets in his hands, with the words that will change human civilization for all time. An eternal Covenant is entered into between Adonai and the Hebrew nation. Then they move forward, and you walk with them, for forty long, arduous years, hungry and frustrated, in their long march to the Promised Land. . . .

With each page turned, a new decade, sometimes a new century follows. You are now standing with Joshua at Jericho, and with Deborah by the waters of Megiddo, in her difficult battle with Sisera.

Turn another page and watch blind Samson in his agony, crying wildly and courageously as he pulls down the pillars over the Philistines. . . .

Moving forward in your history book, you now see the giant prophet Samuel, pleading with his people to stay a free nation, and not appoint a king who would send their sons to war. You hear him charging his followers to remember that their true Ruler is Adonai, the Ruler of the Universe. . . .

Now you are listening to the sweet harp of David, composing the songs and psalms which will sustain our people in times of grief and fear, hope and triumph. You see David also bow before the anger of Nathan, as he realizes that even kings must obey God's law. . . .

You are now watching King Solomon dedicating the great Temple in Jerusalem, proclaiming it to be a House of Prayer for all Peoples. You hear the pious words of Solomon, gifted poet, wise ruler and teacher, skilled diplomat and statesman, declaring that in the Temple he builds there resides a God whom the heaven and the hosts of heaven cannot truly contain. . . .

As you turn the next page you find yourself standing amidst the great moral teachers of all times, Amos and Micah, Isaiah and Jeremiah, Hosea and Malachi.

Bend your ear to hear the famous teachings which will resound forever through the world, in every synagogue, church and mosque, for millennia following, teaching men and women about justice, truth, compassion and love. . . . You hear them talking of what it means to hear the authentic voice of the Almighty Creator, God of law and of love, and how the voice of Adonai beams forth, raging in their soul, leaving them no choice but to hear it and proclaim it. . . .

As you turn the next page, you see the Temple burning to the ground at the hand of Nebuchadnezzar, and the people marching, depressed, into the land of Babylon. All is hushed as you hear their soft, and valiant pledge: "If I forget thee, O Jerusalem. . . ."

In Babylon you watch as they build their temporary, makeshift synagogues, realizing that prayer and study is as dear to God as the animal sacrifices brought to the Kohanim in the altar of the Temple, and the beautiful songs of the Levites on the Temple steps. . . .

On the next page you are marching with the people back from Babylon to Eretz Yisrael, returning from captivity, valiantly trying to rebuild their broken nation on the ruins of the past. . . . Listen to the great Scribe Ezra as he gathers the returned exiles and reads them the complete Torah, with gesticulating arms and a voice quivering with passion. . . .

Moving ahead, you now sit in a classroom and watch the scribes and sages, patiently and eagerly interpreting the words of the Torah, and building a new Torah which will be called the Oral Torah, Torah She-b'al Peh. Watch as the Mishnah and the Talmud grow into volumes and volumes of rich debate and beautiful legends. . . .

On the next page you see the lionhearted children of Mattathias, fighting in the hills of Judea against the Hellenizing enemy. You celebrate their victory over assimilation, as they kindle the small menorah in the Adonai's Temple, as a single cruse of oil miraculously burns for eight full days. . . .

Next you watch gentle Hillel, the creator of Pharisaic Judaism, that has lasted until our own time, as he summarizes the entire Torah while standing on one foot: What is hateful to you, do not unto your neighbor.

Turning the page, you watch the martyred Akiva, burning at the stake, refusing to cease learning and studying Torah, inspiring a revolution, defying an empire, and dying a martyr. . . .

As our book of JEWISH HISTORY follows, page after page, we watch our people's glory and its humiliation. You see them march from land to land, where cross and crescent reign, and you walk with them over all the highways and byways of the world. . . .

You stand together with them as they drink from the bitter chalices of pain, humiliation, cruelty, and hatred . . . pogrom and slaughter, exile and disgrace. . . . Yet, even in the madness of the surrounding world, you watch them remain sane and civilized, remaining a "light unto the nations." In the midst of brutality and darkness, you watch them light a candle of courage and hope. . . .

Turning pages to the modern world, you see the night lift and the dawn break. Liberty, fraternity and equality are the calls resounding in their ears, in Europe and America. Exultantly, they march forward with pride and relief. . . .

Shackles fall from their limbs, and their minds and hearts are emancipated from the dark middle ages of ignorance and bigotry. You watch as they enrich every land that grants them opportunity. . . .

You now watch their battered ships landing at Ellis Island, joining the throngs who find the blessings of liberty, and teaming into the cities and farmlands of America. . . .

You turn the next page, a sad, dark page. . . . Night descends once more. They suffer this time as no people has ever suffered in history. . . . You watch them as they are burned, tortured, gassed, decimated in numbers, bereft of hope, as the god of world Apathy reigns supreme in the halls and corridors of power. Morality seems gone forever. . . .

As always, there is another page. Turn it, and see our people rise, like a Phoenix, creating a rich, new and bustling life in their ancient Homeland, drawing on the teachings of justice, mercy and equality for all God's children. . . .

In the wilderness there are now saplings and rich growth. The desert begins to bloom, and new cities spread out on the sand dunes and on the hills of Judea and in the southern wastelands. . . .

You then stand by them as their hard-earned state, their precious Homeland, is threatened in the Six Day War, the Yom Kippur War, and other battles for survival, as missiles land in the heart of their cities, and their enemies cheer in jubilant celebration. . . .

You sing with them at the Kotel, and on the tarmac when Sadat comes to Jerusalem, when King Hussein signs the second peace treaty with a neighboring land. . . . You fear as buses explode, and hikers are targeted for death. You press forward to create equality for Arab and Jew when new horizons of peace burst forth in the corridors of Madrid, Oslo, Washington and Jerusalem. . . .

You watch as Jews from oppressed lands in Africa, Russia and Eastern Europe stream into the land, spreading its cities into the forests; and as science and medicine, music and literature blossom at the hands of Jews from all corners of the earth, making One People from one hundreds lands. . . .

As you turn the next page, you see a blank space. . . . There is room for you to write your own page, to fill in the blanks. You listen to the words of the poet who said that these people are "bone of my bone, flesh of my flesh, soul of my soul. . . ." They are your people, and their quest is yours. You have lived with them for four thousand years, and you pledge to live with them for all time. . . .

What will you write in the blank pages ahead? Pause and think, and then draw some pictures, on the movie screen in front of your closed eyes, of our people's future. . . . (Pause).

When you are ready, slowly come back and open your eyes. . . . ○

As before, leave ample time for grounding and sharing, to make maximum use of the exercise, and permit full integration of the experience.

Other Ideas for Use of Guided Imagery in Experiencing Jewish History

1) Create imaginary conversations between figures in history, such as Moshe and Akiva; between two Holocaust survivors; between a Holocaust survivor and a German citizen who lived during World War II; between Abraham and his sons, Isaac and Ishmael; between Ruth and Naomi; between the rationalist Maimonides and his more traditional opponents; between a medieval Jew and missionizing Christians; between a secularist and a Chasid; between an Israeli and a Palestinian, etc.

2) Enter time capsules and travel to important events or periods of history, such as the editing of the Mishnah; a debate in the House of Study between Hillel and Shammai; the beginnings of the Hasidic movement in the early 18th century; the beginnings of the Haskalah (Enlightenment) movement; going through a pogrom in Poland or Russia in the nineteenth century; traveling on a boat to Ellis Island; the proclamation of the creation of the State of Israel; the crisis of the Yom Kippur War; the results of the 1990 Jewish Population Survey; the opening of the gates of emigration for Soviet Jews; Operation Moses or Operation Solomon, which freed Ethiopian Jewry; the decision to pursue the peace process between Prime Minister Rabin and Arafat; etc.

3) An image of what American or Israeli Jewry will look like fifty or one hundred years from now.

4) An imaginary interview with a famous leader or scholar from the past, such as Ezra the Scribe, Rabbi Akiva, Saadya Gaon, the Vilna Gaon, Rashi, Maimonides, the Baal Shem Tov, Theodore Herzl, Chaim Weizmann, David Ben Gurion, Golda Meir,

Justice Louis D. Brandeis, Justice Arthur Goldberg, Rabbi Mordecai M. Kaplan, Rabbi Menachem Schneerson (The Lubavitcher Rebbe), authors such as Sholom Aleichem, Chaim Potok, Shmuel Yosef Agnon (Nobel Laureate), Elie Wiesel (another Nobel Laureate), Steven Spielberg, etc.

5) Creating an imaginary scenario which creates a different outcome of a past historical event—such as: all European Jews going to Eretz Yisrael before the Holocaust, and how the Jewish world would look today under those circumstances; if the State of Israel had been created by Herzl in 1903; if the second temple had not been destroyed; if there were no anti-Semitism during the past two centuries, etc.

Chapter 8

THE SYNAGOGUE–
Small Sanctuaries in Every Land

They see You in countless visions;
yet beyond all their visions You are One.

Hymn of Glory —*Shir HaKavod*

THE SYNAGOGUE has served as the Bet Mikdash in miniature since the days of the Babylonian Exile. The prophet Ezekiel and his followers decided that even though the majestic Temple in Jerusalem lay in ruins, the people could not survive without a place for them to pour out the deep feelings of their heart to God.

In Jewish literature the synagogue is thought of as a traveling Mount Sinai, the sacred place where Moshe talked with God. Here every Jew can speak to God, and God can speak to them. Even after the return to Eretz Yisrael at the end of the sixth century B.C.E., when the holy Temple was rebuilt, and people could once again worship God in the single central Sanctuary on Mount Zion, the synagogue provided a place where those who lived in small and large communities throughout the world could come to pray to God.

In the following two guided imagery exercises we hope that the participant will be able to strengthen his/her understanding of the role synagogues have played in the past, and the even greater role they may play in the future.

The first exercise is based in part on the short essay by Rabbi Abraham Joshua Heschel, "The Inner World of the Polish Jew" in Roman Vishniac's book, *Polish Jews* (NY: Schocken Books, 1975).

THE SYNAGOGUE AS SINAI

○ *In this exercise, we will think about how the synagogue has helped our people pray and worship God throughout the past twenty-five centuries since its birth in Babylonia.*

Find a comfortable place, and become very relaxed and at ease. Pay attention to your breath, and watch how you are becoming more and more completely calm in every part of your body. Let yourself wiggle around and find a very comfortable space for yourself. Let all the parts of your body become more and more deeply relaxed. Your eyes become heavy as you sink deeply into a state of another world. A world of the past. . . .

See in your mind's eye the many synagogues that dotted the landscape of all the countries where Jews have lived from biblical times until the present day. . . . Some are large and strong; some are little wooden shacks. Some have been proudly standing for centuries; some are makeshift rooms that are part of a house or other building. Let your eyes roam throughout the ages to different places, different countries, different centuries. See the different styles of architecture out of which the architects and builders constructed the houses of God. Some are colonial, some are moorish; some are sephardic and some ashkenazic; some are square and some round; some a single story, and some several stories high. . . .

Look inside one of the synagogues. . . . What are the people doing? . . .

See how in the prayer room the worshippers are closing themselves out of the world. Some of them are trying to purify their souls before God. . . . Others are trying to perfect the likeness of God that is their holy soul. . . .

In this holy place not only do they learn Torah and Talmud, but they are also studying the ways of the human heart, the Torah of the Heart. Many of them are simple people, but their souls are like the soul of an artist, filling their hours with mystic beauty. . . . Watch them, and see if you can feel their feelings, and experience God the way they did. (Pause).

Let your eyes roam to another room in the synagogue. Here people pour over the hoary books of Mishnah and Gemara, Rashi and Rambam, halacha and aggada. . . . It is the Bet Midrash, the House of Study. Here they did not learn about science, but about nobility. They yearned to learn how to better fulfill the words of the prayer, "My God, guard my tongue from evil." It was more important to them than learning physics and chemistry and mathematics. . . .

To the Jews in these synagogues it was more important to meditate on the sacred Psalms in order to achieve holiness, than to memorize the dates of Roman history. "To them, the house of study was not important because the world needed it; on the contrary, the world was important because houses of study existed in it" (Heschel, p. 17). . . .

In an unredeemed world they strove only to make more beautiful souls, not to amass great wealth or power. Even if they lived in grinding poverty, they did not mind, as long as they could speak with God. When the heart of the Jew was turned to God, no enemy could affect it. The Jew knew that in the eyes of the Ruler of all Rulers, no secular king or queen had sway over their lives. That they were princes and princesses in God's world, children of their Creator. Whenever they were wrapped in tallit and tefillin, no evil force could penetrate their soul. Their only job was to consecrate their soul to the sanctification of the Holy Name.

Whether it was in small towns or large cities, whether in places like Safed or Troyes, in Cordoba or Sura, the light of the synagogue spread into the community, the home, the family, and the heart of every Jewish soul. . . .

The keys to these great synagogues of the past still lie in our possession. To open their doors, all we need to do is open our hearts. . . . The treasure of Jewish spirituality is available to all of us today, as it was in the past.

Just as Moshe stood at Mount Sinai, so every Jew can stand at his or her own personal Sinai, and commune with God, receiving their own Tablets of the Law. . . .

See yourself walking into a synagogue, the one of your choice. Find in there the special feeling that our ancestors created when they poured out their heart and soul to their Maker. . . .

Stay with this feeling of transcendence, and bask in its holiness. (Pause).

If you have a prayer to recite, say it now. . . .

Whenever you are ready, come back to this room, and slowly open your eyes, and take some deep breaths, returning to your natural state of mind. ○

THE SYNAGOGUE OF TOMORROW

○ *Allow yourself to become very calm and relaxed, as you sit in a comfortable chair, or as you lie down on your back on a comfortable surface. Be aware of any tension in your body, and let it go. Find your muscles and nerves becoming light and easy, loose and relaxed. Take a deep breath and let its warm energy bring peace and healing to your body. . . .*

Let your imagination run free, witnessing in your mind's eye new things, which you have never imagined before. See new shapes and colors, beautiful scenes in nature. . . . As you exhale each breath, let yourself become more and more completely relaxed. Your mind is becoming clear and uncluttered, so you can fill it with new things from your creative imagination. . . .

We are going to design our own synagogue . . . a synagogue of tomorrow. Put any ideas of how synagogues have looked or functioned in the past behind you. Let yourself be the architect, the designer, the rabbi and the educator, the president and the member, as you put all your ideas together to create a new kind of synagogue. . . .

Let's begin with the Sanctuary, the Bet Tefilah. Create a Sanctuary unlike any you have seen before. What does it look like? . . .

See the people inside, where they are sitting, or standing, or moving. . . . Where is the Ark, the Aron Kodesh, and the Sifray Torah? . . . Where is the bema, and the desks for the leaders of the worship? How are the seats arranged? Is there any open space ? . . .

Look at the walls and the ceiling, how are they different? Listen to the sounds, and the words being said. What do you see? What do you hear? . . .

What is different about the worship? Who is leading it? Turn to the faces of the worshippers. What do you see? . . .

Where is the light coming from? . . . What kind of prayerbooks, Siddurim, do you see? . . .

Think of different kinds of events taking place in the synagogue. . . . Imagine Shabbat and different holidays. . . . Think of weddings, or funerals, or personal simchas. . . . Think about the reading of the Torah. How is it different? . . . How do people pray? How do they learn? How do they communicate with God? . . . Who are the different kinds of people who lead prayer and other events in the synagogue?

Look and see if the sanctuary is filled, or not. Why are people coming there? Watch them as they leave. . . . What do they say? How do they feel? What happened inside to make them react that way? . . .

What other rooms are there in the synagogue? What happens in them? . . .

What special groups come to visit the synagogue? Why are they visiting? What do they see, or do inside?

If you want, let yourself float in the air above the synagogue, looking down

*through the roof, and see the whole building. What does it look like?
How big or small is it? How is it different from the synagogues you know? . . .*

*How can you begin to make your synagogue become the way you want it to
be? . . .*

*Let your thoughts, images and pictures go where they want to. See whatever
else you want as you create your own synagogue. . . .*

*Whenever you are ready, begin to come back to this room. On the count of
three you will return to where you started, and bring back with you a model or
picture of the new synagogue you created. Be ready to show other people the new
kind of synagogue you just made. One . . . Two . . . Three. . . .* ○

Permit anyone who wants to share this experience with the larger group to do so.
Allow ample time for this important sharing.

Other Ideas for Synagogue Imagery Exercises

1) Imagine one particular synagogue in Jewish history, perhaps a famous one in
which some great scholar or saint prayed.

2) Imagine a synagogue that is combined with some other Jewish institution, such
as a day school, or Jewish Community Center, or others. Which ones are they? How
does the synagogue benefit from this?

3) Picture the synagogue during one specific event, such as its dedication, or the
consecration of a new Sefer Torah. Picture the consecration ceremonies of a new rabbi,
or of a young class of children, or of Confirmation services. Picture a wedding, or a
funeral, or a brit milah or simchat bat.

4) Imagine yourself walking around an empty sanctuary. Go from place to place,
open the Aron Kodesh, take out a Sefer Torah, and see what thoughts and feelings you
have.

5) Remember one special event from your past when you had a unique experience
or a transcendent encounter in the synagogue. Return to it, and stay with it. Change it
in some way, if you wish. See if it can help you return to that special spiritual feeling at
some future time.

Chapter 9

IMAGERY EXERCISES TO ENHANCE THE PRAYER EXPERIENCE

Imagination, I believe, is an important component of faith. . . . It is only if we are willing to imagine that we can hear, see and feel God's presence. . . . The deepest truths so far transcend our own limitedness that only the generosity of mind and spirit called imagination can allow us to go beyond the narrowness of self and embrace the reality of God, God's universe and God's Torah.

—Rabbi Eliezer Diamond, Asst. Professor, Jewish Theological Seminary

IN CHAPTER five we sampled some guided imagery exercises dealing with themes of the Eternal Book, the Bible. The book most frequently used by religious Jews, after the Bible, is the Siddur. The Siddur is a rich anthology of the longings of the Jewish heart over many centuries.

One way to use imagery and visualization in enhancing the prayer experience is to have participants find a relaxing position, listen to some soft, appropriate music, and read the words of some of the beautiful prayers of the Siddur, (the daily and Shabbat prayer book), or of the Mahzor, (the prayer book for festivals and the high holy days).

We have selected a number of parts of various prayer services to show how guided imagery exercises can introduce these prayers, and can intensify the prayer experience by allowing them to reach higher levels of spiritual elevation.

SHABBAT EVENING – LEKHA DODI

One of the most exquisite prayers of the Friday night service is Lekha Dodi, written by Rabbi Shlomo Alkabez in the sacred city of Safed, Eretz Yisrael, during the 16th century. Kabbalists would go out into the fields with the setting of the sun, and wait for the arrival of the Shabbat bride in their mind's eye. The image of Shabbat as a bride is a popular one. The Shabbat bride is considered to be married to the People of Israel. In Talmudic legend, each day of the week had a partner, except Shabbat. So God gave the Shabbat to the People of Israel as her partner.

❍ *Find a comfortable position, take some deep breaths, and let a wave of serenity wash over you, releasing all your tension and tightness. Find your body preparing for Shabbat with a sense of renewal and refreshment. Your extra soul, a gift given to every Jew on Shabbat, is bringing you invigoration and enlightenment. See how good it feels. . . .*

Picture yourself in the sixteenth century, in the holy, mystical city of Safed, along with Rabbi Yosef Karo, Rabbi Shlomo Alkabez, and other mystical scholars, washing, and purifying their heart, body and soul, for the coming of Shabbat.

Feel yourself getting ready for a special guest in your home. Shabbat, a lovely bride bedecked all in white, with flowing lace and a long train of silk, begins to appear in the distance. You can see the outlines of her body adorned with special garments, pure and white as clean snow, gently gliding toward your group of worshippers. . . . Watch her coming closer and closer. . . .

As the Shabbat bride gets closer and the red sun begins to set deeper and deeper in the brilliant orange sky behind, everyone feels the special aura which Shabbat brings into the community. All feel pure and clean, refreshed and relaxed, free of cares and worries, thinking only of the splendor of the next twenty-six hours of peacefulness and harmony. . . .

The children have gathered around the dinner table, waiting for their parents to return from the fields. The candles are glowing in the house, bringing Shabbat light and Shabbat joy. The kiddush cup is brim full, and the special Shabbat foods are warming on the stove. Everyone runs to the window to get a glimpse of the Shabbat bride in the distance, even as the day becomes darker and darker. . . .

In the fields, the parents begin to see the outline of the Shabbat queen more and more clearly, as excitement rises to a feverish pitch . . . Shabbat is coming. . . . Shabbat is coming. . . . Even God rejoices in the Highest Heavens, as the Blessed Holy One watches its creatures below rejoicing with the onset of Shabbat. All the flowers and trees in the field jump with dance and song, as the Shabbat bride glides by them, entering the town. . . .

With the coming of the Shabbat bride, Safed's residents break into song: Come in peace, crown of beauty and joy, we greet you with joy and song. Come to join God's chosen people, who remember and observe the special Shabbat day. Welcome, O Shabbat Bride, we greet the countenance of our beloved Shabbat! (Pause). ❍

SH'MA YISRAEL

The facilitator may want to utilize one of the relaxation exercises in chapter four, to bring about a complete and deep sense of calm and openness. Since the Sh'ma is the central liturgical affirmation of Judaism, it deserves more time and attention than other prayers. When the group is in a state of relaxation, we may begin.

◯ *Find a way to let yourself become totally relaxed, so that you can permit your imagination to roam freely. Take your time with your breathing. Pay attention to your body to prepare yourself for this uplifting imagery experience....*

We are about to recite the most important prayer in all of Judaism: The Sh'ma. It is such an important prayer because it speaks of God's unity, and thus, the unity and equality of all God's creatures. Let's start by seeing in our mind's eye the pictures of Mother Earth as seen from a satellite taken by astronauts in outer space—that beautiful bluish whitish globe that seems to hang out in space that gives us our very life.... Try to hear the great rumbling of that huge ball turning and spinning through the thick atmosphere.

We are all citizens of a global village. The earth is our small town. We travel together on spaceship earth. Picture yourself traveling along on a spaceship with all the other inhabitants of our planet....

The Sh'ma emphasizes our unity, our brotherhood and sisterhood. Think of all the different people on planet earth, and how we are related to them, being children of the same one God, Who created us all. Think of people whose faces are different shapes and sizes, whose eyes are narrower, whose lips are thicker, whose height is greater or lesser than ours.... Picture faces that are black or yellow, red or white, brown or bronze. Think of people from Africa or Asia, North or South America, Europe or Australia. Remind yourself that we are all sisters and brothers....

Imagine the streets of big cities like New York or Mexico, Tel Aviv or Tokyo, Berlin or New Delhi. Picture all the people in those cities acting and feeling like part of one loving family....

In your mind's eye imagine people who live near borders in the Middle East, Arabs and Israelis, Christians, Moslems and Jews, all walking back and forth from country to country, with no one guarding the borders. Everyone trusts everyone else because we are all God's children, one human family, filled with mutual respect and love.... (Pause).

See yourself entering a museum, where weapons are displayed, and the signs say: These instruments of fighting were used in the past, when people did not understand that we are all one united human race, all nationalities, religions, races and creeds. This is a museum which helps us remember past days when there were wars, before nuclear and other weapons were destroyed. Now just a few samples remain in this museum of history. . . .

Visitors stare at the exhibits and gasp in disbelief, as they whisper to one another: "Did people really use these horrible weapons against one another?"

Picture universities, and shopping malls, and music halls, and laboratories, where people of all faiths and nationalities work and cooperate, sharing ideas and discoveries, recognizing that the fate of each group is tied together with every other group. . . .

Feel the sense of oneness, of unity, of sharing and of love, that permeates the entire universe. . . .

Stay with that feeling for a while, and enjoy its comfort, support and reassurance. . . . As we prepare to recite the Sh'ma prayer, let's keep these good feelings in our heart, feelings of respect and affection for all citizens of the planet, all God's children in every city and every country. . . .

In a minute, we shall chant together the age-old prayer of God's unity, and of our acceptance of the rule of law and love, which has the power to govern the world. . . . ○

Take time to let participants slowly chant the Sh'ma, and then express their feelings about it in any way that seems appropriate.

READING THE TORAH

This guided imagery exercise reflects one approach to the dramatic ceremony of the reading of the Torah. The facilitator or teacher may remind the group that the whole ritual of Torah reading is filled with ancient practices. We read the Torah from a scroll rather than a book, written on parchment by the hand of a *sofer* (scribe) with special animal skin and specially prepared ink, wrapped on wooden rollers called spindles (Hebrew, *atzay chaim*). We dress the Torah with a velvet cover and silver breastplate and finials (*rimmonim*), and store it in a sacred ark where it is not visible to the congregation for most of the worship service. The ceremony for removing and replacing the Sefer Torah (Torah Scroll) is special, as the Torah is paraded around the congregation, and people stretch their arms toward the aisle to kiss it.

People are called from the congregation to recite blessings over the Torah before and after it is read. The ceremony continues, fraught with religious symbolism and spiritual affection for all that the Torah represents. Clearly, this is a dramatic, and unusual ceremony, unparalleled in any other religious culture. Understanding all of this background will help those participating in this imagery experience to feel the deep significance of this extraordinary ritual and period of study and learning.

❍ *Take some slow, deep breaths, and find yourself becoming very relaxed. . . . Scan your body to find any points of tension or tightness, and let them go. . . . As you breath in, bring energy and calm into your body. As you breathe out, let go of all the tightness and discomfort that you may discover in your muscles or nerves. . . . Allow yourself to let go, and concentrate in a passive, receptive way.*

In a few moments we shall begin the part of our worship service during which we remove the Sefer Torah from the Aron Kodesh (ark), and then read parts of it before the community, just as the ancient biblical Scribe, Ezra, did almost 2500 years ago. . . .

As we read the Torah, we re-enact the giving of these five sacred books of law and lore to Moshe at Mount Sinai. This tradition of receiving the Torah at Sinai has sustained the religion of Israel for thirty centuries. Whatever we believe about the origins of the Torah, remember that our historical mythology tells us that the Torah comes from Sinai, and it is this story that inspires the entire Torah reading ritual. Let us, then, picture ourselves standing at Mount Sinai with the tens of thousands of Israelites who were there when God gave us our Torah. (Pause).

Take a moment to feel the special feeling of being with Moshe at Sinai, as he received the Torah from the Holy Blessed Creator and Redeemer. (Pause).

The Torah describes the awesome scene at Mt. Sinai during the giving of the Ten Commandments, with swirling balls of fire, an awesome blanket of smoke creeping up the foot of the mountain and enough lightning to light a modern city. It was such an intense sight that the Israelite People had to turn away and shield their faces. What does the sight do to your eyes as you imagine it? . . . (Pause).

Keep that picture in your mind as you now see yourself about to be called to the Torah for an aliyah (honor), to pronounce the ancient blessings before and after the chanting of this week's Sidrah (Torah portion). As you sing your blessings, you are re-enacting the receiving of the Torah at Sinai. How do you feel? . . . (Pause).

Even though countless thousands of people before you, in every generation and in every country, have risen to be honored with an aliyah to the Torah, as you do it, imagine that you are receiving the Torah for the first time, along with Moshe. This is an ancient ritual, and it is also as new as the breath you are taking at this very moment. . . .

We honor the Torah because it is the Holy Book of our Tradition. Look at it opened before your eyes on the Shulchan (Torah Table) before you. It is your privilege to be standing before its ancient, holy words, being among those who are receiving it for the very first time. . . .

As you stand in front of the Sefer Torah, let your eyes flash to the present and the past, seeing the Sefer Torah before you, and seeing yourself standing at Sinai.

Imagine that there lies before you a Book so wise and so humane that it has the capacity to teach, to spread justice and love, to influence leaders and simple people, to change people's ideas and their actions, to be the moral compass of your existence. . . .

There is no book in all the world that is as holy, as unique, as important, as the one which lies open in front of your eyes. And for this moment, it is your turn to stand forward and receive it from God, as Moshe and others after him have done in every generation. . . .

Let yourself stand and look at the words in the Scroll, and picture Mount Sinai, as if it were behind you, while you are about to complete your last blessing.

Permit yourself to feel all the holiness, sanctity, reverence and awe, which exudes from this Book of Centuries. . . .

When you are ready, very slowly, let yourself return to this room, and gradually open your eyes, letting the feelings of awe and reverence remain inside you, to be called upon at any time. . . . ◯

ALENU

The Alenu prayer is a unique blend of the particular and the universal. In its two paragraphs it expresses the twin polarities of loyalty to one's own people, together with the deep concern for the welfare of a redeemed world in which all God's creatures will recognize one Creator and be part of one human family. Both ideas have been essential to the preservation and understanding of the Jewish heritage.

The focus of this guided imagery exercise will be on the act of kneeling. Kneeling is a rare part of Jewish worship, used sparingly so that the worshiper does not consider the one invisible God to be capable of concretization or materialization in any human or other form.

○ *Take some deep breaths, and find yourself becoming very relaxed. Sit in a comfortable place, remove any tightness from your body, and let yourself sink into the chair or surface on which you are sitting or lying. Picture some soft, white clouds overhead, floating by and washing your room with softness and sweetness. . . . The clouds are pure and clean, and bring wholeness and tranquility to your mind and heart. . . .*

Imagine that you are the Kohen Gadol, the High Priest, in the time of King Herod, in the first century B.C.E. Your king has expanded the holy Temple, the Bet Mikdash, to be even bigger than it was in the days of Solomon, who built the first Temple almost a thousand years before.

It is your job to lead the people of Israel in their worship from week to week, from day to day. But of all the days of the year, the holiest was Yom Kippur, when the Kohen Gadol would remove his golden tunic and put on the pure white gown for the Day of Atonement, so that he could ask for forgiveness for himself, his family, and the entire Household of Israel.

See yourself as the Kohen Gadol. There are thousands of people in the courtyard surrounding the central Sanctuary where the altar was located. Listen to the stir of conversation surrounding you as the dramatic ritual of Yom Kippur is about to begin. . . .

One of the special tasks that you must perform as Kohen Gadol is to enter the Holy of Holies, the Inner Sanctum of the Temple, where in earlier days the two tablets of the Ten Commandments were kept in the holy ark. [The tablets were lost by the time of King Herod]. There was no country in the world more holy to Jews than Eretz Yisrael, and no city more holy in all of Eretz Yisrael than Jerusalem. There was no place more holy in Jerusalem than the holy Temple, and no place within the holy temple more sacred than the tiny room in the center called the Holy of Holies, Kodesh Kodashim.

As Kohen Gadol, only you are permitted to enter that holy room, and only on one day of the year, on Yom Kippur. On that holy day, in that holy place, once a year, you are obligated to recited the true name of God, so holy that we no longer even know how to pronounce it.

It is Yom Kippur in the days of King Herod's Temple, and you, the Kohen Gadol, are about to pronounce the Name. All the holy places and holy times have joined together, as you are about to pronounce the holiest name in the world—the Hebrew name of God, as it was known only to the Kohen Gadol in the first century B.C.E. Imagine what that moment feels like right now, as you are about to pronounce the Ineffable Name (the unpronounceable, unutterable Name). . . . (Pause).

As the people standing in the Temple courtyard outside hear the glorious, awesome, Holy Name pronounced by the Kohen Gadol in purity and sanctity, they all bow and kneel, and prostrate themselves, touching their face to the ground, and respond in one voice: "Praised be God's glorious sovereignty forever and ever."

You, the Kohen Gadol, ask for God's forgiveness on this sacred day of Pardon, and as the people outside hear you, they bend and bow. You feel their motion, the scurry of finding a place to bow down with their face to the ground, pleading for forgiveness for their sins. . . .

Take a moment and think of all the things for which the people, and the other Kohanim, and you, are asking forgiveness. . . .

You, the Kohen Gadol, emerge from the Kodesh Kodashim, and the people slowly stand, feeling forgiven, and closer to God than ever before. . . .

As we are about to recite the Alenu prayer, we remember this ancient scene filled with awe and sanctity, purity and sincerity, and bring those special feelings and high intentions into the words of the prayer as we recite them. . . .

When you are ready, open your eyes, and return to this moment, to rise and recite the Alenu. . . . ○

Suggestions for Other Imagery Exercises on the Subject of Prayer

1) Open the Siddur or Mahzor to any page, and let that prayer be the subject for a creative imagery exercise. Let mature students suggest the subjects or focus for the exercise.

2) Let the participants enter a receptive, relaxed mode, and imagine themselves as one of the medieval poets writing a prayer which elaborates on one of the sections of the liturgy. Following the imagery, let them write out the words of the prayer.

3) Think of the prayer for healing, read it aloud, then let each person picture someone who is not well, and imagine them being healed.

4) Have participants enter a forest, and find a quiet place to sit down and have a conversation with God. This may be followed by any traditional prayer, such as a part of the Amidah. Have them bring with them some thoughts from their conversation with God.

5) Have the students picture themselves slowly and lovingly putting on all the garments of prayer: the kippah, the tallit, tefillin. Can students think of some new meanings for these garments?

6) Have participants imagine themselves standing at the Kotel, and think of what private prayers they might want to recite.

7) Have the students recite the words of the sentence "Sh'ma Yisrael. . . ." over and over as a mantra, as long as they wish, saying it slowly and lovingly, letting whatever images that may appear come into their mind.

8) Let the students become relaxed, and picture themselves awakening in the morning, as the leader reads to them the early morning berachot (*Birkot Ha-shachar*), which were originally written for recitation when arising from bed.

Chapter 10

DEVELOPING OUR SPIRITUAL NATURE

There are more things in heaven and on earth than you have imagined. . . .

—Shakespeare

I will place within you a new spirit.

—Ezekiel 11:19

SPIRITUALITY is a difficult concept to define. When we think of a spiritual person, what usually comes to mind is an individual whose lifestyle is filled with such things as community service, cultural pursuits, elements of the meditative and reflective personality, and other non-materialistic activities.

In Jewish tradition spirituality has taken many forms. Tradition considers people spiritual when they perform God's will through the performance of *mitzvot* (commandments), study holy books (Tanakh, Talmud, etc.), and when they take prayer seriously. At certain periods in Jewish history, groups and movements arose which stressed various aspects of the spiritual life, such as kabbalah (Jewish mysticism), Hasidism (founded by the Baal Shem Tov in early eighteenth century Russia), Musar (founded by Rabbi Israel Salanter in nineteenth century Lithuania), and the modern movement for Jewish renewal (made famous by people like Rabbis Shlomo Carlebach, Zalman Schachter-Shalomi, Arthur Green, and Lawrence Kushner in the 1960s).

Since spirituality involves so many different things, including but not restricted to prayer, we shall try to focus in this chapter on areas not included in other parts of the book, although almost every chapter of guided imagery scripts includes some aspect of spirituality in its widest sense. We shall use as a basic paradigm the kind of spiritual approach one finds in the biblical Book of Psalms, and in some Hasidic literature, helping humans feel closer to God and to God's world of beauty and love. When the Torah commands us to be holy, the Hasidic interpretation says: Be humanly holy, love

God, love Torah, and love both of them through and with the important people in your life.

[It is often helpful to play soft, spiritual music during the guided imagery exercises—especially with those included in this chapter. Pachelbel's Canon is very effective. The music of Steve Halpern is also quite good. Perhaps some appropriate cantorial or Hasidic music, depending on the subject, would be helpful].

PSALM 19 – GOD, HEAVEN AND TORAH

❍ *Lie or sit in a comfortable position. Stretch and wiggle a bit until you feel very relaxed and comfortable. As you breathe, watch all the tensions, worries and problems in your mind float away. Let go of all the things inside you which you don't need or want. Breathe in clean, pure air, which gives you a sense of renewal and refreshment. . . .*

We will read parts of the nineteenth Psalm in the Tanakh, and appreciate the uplifting ideas contained within it.

In your mind's eye, look up at the Heavens, and experience the calm beauty, the serene security it brings you. . . . "The Heavens declare the glory of Adonai . . . the sky declares God's handiwork. Each day calls out to the other . . . each night whispers to its neighbor". . . . Feel the bright light of day, and then the dark velvet cover of the night. . . . Feel the protection which the world gives you. . . . See the majesty of the white clouds against the blue sky, and feel the warmth and lightness they bring. . . . Enjoy this feeling for a while. (Pause).

"The teaching of Adonai is perfect, renewing life. . . ."

In God's world, we have a map to find our way through its mountains and valleys . . . the Torah. The Torah helps us understand and appreciate our universe and the people within it. . . .

The beautiful customs and traditions of Judaism help us live our lives in this beautiful world, becoming enlightened, enriched, and enthused about ourselves and others. . . . "The precepts of Adonai are just, rejoicing the heart. The instruction of Adonai is clear, lighting up our eyes". . . .

The words which Adonai gave us in the Torah are uplifting and inspiring. . . . The Torah teaches us how to be kind, caring people, how to help others, and reach out to the needy and the broken souls of society. . . . The Torah helps us find joy in our life, and excitement. . . . It helps find truth and clarity. . . .

"Cleanse my soul, Adonai . . . clear me of guilt and keep me from doing wrong". . . .

Let my life be pure and whole. Permit me to do right and love justice. . . .
Let me be ever closer to You and Your ways . . . to Your Torah and Your people. . . .

"May the words of my mouth and the thoughts of my heart be acceptable to
You, Adonai. You are my Rock and my Redeemer". . . . (Pause).

Stay with your thoughts and feelings for a moment. Enjoy them, and learn
from them. . . .

When you are ready, come back to this place, and gently and gradually open
your eyes, taking your time to return only when you want to. . . . ○

STANDING AT THE KOTEL

Holiness, *kedushah,* can be found in time (Shabbat and Festivals), in space (the Bet
HaMikdash—The Temple in Jerusalem), in objects (a Sefer Torah), and in people
(Kohanim). Among the holiest places in Jewish tradition is the Kotel, the Western
Wall of the Temple Mount, where King Solomon and others following him built the
first, and later, the second Temple. Since 1967 when Israel recaptured and reunited the
holy city of Jerusalem, the Kotel has been a popular place of prayer for Jews who come
from all over the world on pilgrimage.

○ *Find a comfortable place, and begin to relax. . . . When you are ready to*
let go of your environment, take some deep breaths, and find yourself becoming
more and more deeply relaxed. Take another slow, deep, cleansing breath, and
exhale as fully as you can. . . . Breathe deeply, into your belly, and then breathe
out as fully as you can. . . . As you continue breathing deeply and easily, you are
feeling more and more calm and serene. . . . As you exhale breathe out any
unwelcome thoughts, and watch your breath as it brings you purity and calm. . . .

You are now standing at the Kotel, the famous Western Wall of King
Solomon's great Temple, built three thousand years ago. . . . What does it feel like
to be there? . . . Think about all the centuries and generations of Jews who have
yearned to be able to stand where you are standing now. . . . Feel how fortunate
you are. . . . (Pause).

Picture in your mind the many Jews who made long, tiring pilgrimages to
this Wall, just to be able to be closer to God. . . . Do you see some of them standing
there, alongside you, from a century or two ago, in long black coats and fur hats,
shuckling and swaying as they whisper their prayers? . . .

Reach out and touch the stone. Feel its contours and roughly hewn edges.

Listen to the birds who have built their nests in its cracks. Hear them coo as you run your hand along the cold stone in silent awe. . . .

Even though there may be others around you at the Kotel, it is so quiet, it feels as though you are there completely alone, with God. . . . God is listening to you now. . . . Feel God's presence at the Kotel, as you begin to think of what you want to say. . . . (Pause).

Now say whatever you want to say to God. Take your time. . . . (Pause).

Perhaps you would like an answer from God. See if God would like to speak to you. . . . What do you hear God saying to you? . . . (Pause).

If you would like to write down any prayer, as many people who pray at the Kotel do, write it on a piece of paper and place it in one of the crevices between the large rocks of the Kotel. . . .

If you want, reach out to the Kotel, and take back with you the message of God, which is written on one of the papers between the cracks, and take it with you. . . . See what it says, and then fold it up and place it in your pocket to take along with you. . . . (Pause).

If there is anything else you want to say to God, do so now, before you leave the Kotel. . . . Remember that you can always come back here in your imagination, and speak to God any time you want, just by closing your eyes and coming to the Kotel in your mind. . . .

When you are ready to leave, take a few steps back, and find yourself back here in this place. . . . Take your time, and come back slowly and gradually. . . . When you are ready, open your eyes. . . . ◯

THE LIGHT OF THE MENORAH

Light is a very effective metaphor for spiritual themes. Light is ubiquitous in Jewish tradition. We need think only of such ritual objects as the Ner Tamid, the Menorah, Shabbat candles, the Shiva and Yahrzeit candles, etc. Light is soothing, calming, and freeing.

◯ Let yourself become completely relaxed. Imagine that you are walking in the middle of a beautiful, safe forest. You are strolling through a clear path and looking at the beautiful bushes and trees on either side of the winding path. . . . As you walk, you find yourself becoming more and more completely relaxed. . . . There is no hurry, so no need to walk quickly. Just saunter along, at a leisurely pace.

The farther you go along the path, the deeper you stroll into the forest, the closer you feel to God, and to God's world of beauty and serenity. . . . All the animals and wildlife in the forest are safe and secure. Nothing can hurt or harm you. . . . The growing things, plants, flowers, trees, bushes and exotic wild flowers, and the birds and other animals are all there to lend beautiful smells, sights and sounds to your walk through this beautiful and charming forest. . . . Take in the crisp smell of pine and feel the warm mist rising from the living forest bed.

Walk further in the forest, and feel how good and safe, and comfortable you feel. (Pause).

After you have walked for several hours, you are feeling even stronger than when you started. You are not at all tired or weary. You feel strong, healthy and confident. . . . You are not too warm or too cold, but just right. Everything is just right. . . . A gentle breeze is blowing, which makes you even more comfortable and happy. . . . Feel the breeze dancing gently on your face, as you feel yourself becoming more spiritually attuned, and joyful. . . .

Ahead of you is a small mountain with a large Menorah sitting on a high rock on top of it. All seven candles of the Menorah are burning brightly. As you get closer to the mountain, you see seven steps that lead to the top of the mountain. Walk slowly upward, step by step, ascending each of the seven steps. . . .

Approach the Menorah slowly and feel the warmth and beauty that emanates from it. . . . You sense something magic and wonderful as you get close to the Menorah. . . . The rays of light coming from the Menorah are very beautiful, and radiant. They bring you special feelings of joy and calm in your heart. You feel a sense of deep love and being loved. . . . The Menorah is your friend, and you may speak to it if you like. . . . (Pause).

As you watch the dancing light of the Menorah, you feel the magical light entering through your eyes and pour into your body. The rays of light from the Menorah begin to fill you with a sense of well-being and peace, of shalom. Every part of your body, every cell, tissue, muscle and bone is filled with this incredible light. . . . All the parts of you, your head, your face, your chest, your lungs and heart, your arms and hands, your legs and feet, are all filled with the beautiful light beaming out from the beautiful Menorah in front of you. . . . Now close your eyes and keep the light from escaping from you. (Pause).

Your whole being is filled with the spiritual light of the Menorah, and through it, the light of Adonai. . . . You feel purified and cleansed, inspired and uplifted. . . . Let the light swirl around your body, penetrating into every tiny crevice of your body, making you whole and healed. . . . Your mind is filled with new wisdom and joy, your heart is filled with love and compassion. . . . Let this wonderful feeling imprint itself into your soul, so that you can keep it with you always. . . . (Pause).

The wonderful feeling you feel now comes from God. Express your thanks to God for the light which you are now enjoying. . . . ○

[Parts of this exercise were inspired by Beverly-Colleene Galyean's *Mind Sight*].

ELIJAH THE WISE

○ *Allow yourself to become very relaxed, and enter the basket of a hot air balloon that will transport you to the Heavens. The balloon is a very safe and secure place to be, so you need not be concerned. Any time you want to come down, simply pull the level to lower yourself back to the ground. . . .*

Now toss out of the balloon more and more weights, so that you rise higher and higher. . . . Soon you see a white-bearded figure from the Bible floating around the skies. It is Elijah the prophet. Remember the biblical story about Elijah? Elijah never died. He ascended to Heaven in a fiery chariot, and all through the centuries he has roamed about the world, appearing at the naming of little babies, entering stealthily into homes during Pesach Seders, and showing up anywhere he wants at any time, constantly giving advice, doing good deeds, bringing laughter, cheer and hope to the world. . . .

As your balloon rises higher into the Heavens, you get closer to Elijah, close enough to speak with him. . . . Perhaps you have some questions about your spiritual life which you would like to ask Elijah. He is a very wise and kind person, and will keep anything you say to him very confidential. . . . Have a conversation with Elijah and see what advice he has for you to help you become a more spiritual person. . . . (Pause).

Since Elijah will return to our world to announce the coming of the Messiah, you may also want to ask Elijah what things we here on earth might do to hasten the coming of Mashiach, when there will be no more war or strife, and all nations, races and religions will live in peace with one another. See what Elijah's response to your question about Mashiach is. (Pause)

Now take a last moment to ask Elijah anything else you forgot to ask. (Pause).

Now it is time to thank Elijah for the wisdom he imparted to you. Thank him now. . . . If you wish, you may hug or kiss him goodbye. Ask him if it is alright with him if you come back and speak with him again whenever you wish. . . .

When you are finished, turn the lever to bring yourself gently back to earth. When you are ready, come out of the balloon, feeling very satisfied and pleased with the new information and enlightenment you received from Elijah. . . . When you are ready, return to this room, and open your eyes. . . . ⵔ

An appropriate discussion which may follow this guided imagery exercise can focus on the subject of the inner wisdom which each human being has inside, wisdom which can help us solve problems and point us in the proper direction. Through this imaginary meeting with Elijah, we utilize our own native (or divine?) wisdom which may not be available to us through normal rational channels. The process of imagery enables us to reach into a part of our brain and soul which stores much wisdom, insight, and hidden ideas, all waiting to be unlocked by Elijah to give us as precious gifts. Participants can offer examples of times when a "flash of insight" came to them, an experience similar to this type of encounter with Elijah's presence.

Other grounding exercises can follow, such as sharing groups, painting the scenes we saw, and discussing other ways to access our inner, mystical, divine wisdom.

SACRED MEMORIES

The concept of memory is essential to Judaism. A major portion of the High Holy Day liturgy is called *Zikhronot*, remembrances. The prayer recited for the departed four times a year is called *Yizkor*, or *Hazkarat Neshamot*, both referring to memorializing our loved ones who have died. The Torah is filled with admonitions demanding that we never forget our biblical experience of being slaves in Egypt. History and memory are so ubiquitous in Judaism that one cannot practice Judaism without utilizing memory as an important part of worship and celebration. This guided imagery exercise will focus on some special, holy memories, which will reinforce our connection to God and to our spiritual self.

ⵔ *Find the place within yourself that is at peace and tranquil. Remember a time when you everything was just right. Recapture that moment, and feel how good it is. . . . Notice how relaxed and at ease you are. . . . The peace of your life energizes every part of you. Your entire being is exactly the way you love to be— calm, confident, at peace, secure. . . .*

Go back into the forest of your memory and find in it a precious moment. A time when you felt very close to nature, or to God, or to another human being. Each of these can be described as holy moments. God wants us to be close and intimate with our environment and with the important people in our lives. God also wants us to be close to the divine part of ourselves. . . . Find one special, holy moment when you felt very spiritually attuned and connected. . . .

Perhaps you are in a house of worship, or out in a beautiful meadow, or by the seashore. Maybe you are having an intimate conversation with a loved one, and sharing affection or other feelings. . . . Maybe you are singing or dancing, praying or eating. . . . Whatever you are doing that feels holy, go back deeply into that experience. . . . Notice all the details of this experience. . . . Who is there with you? What are you doing? What is going on around you? . . . Look all around. . . . Remember all the smells, the taste, the touch of things. . . . What is it like to experience the feeling of a holy moment? (Long Pause).

If you would like, turn now to another holy moment. . . . Capture the image in your mind's eye of some special, sacred time, when you felt that God was in your life in a very deep way. . . . Pay attention to everything in that experience. (Pause).

What do the experiences have in common? What ways can you bring that sense of the holy back into your everyday life? . . .

Take your time, and when you are ready, come back to this room, and gently, gradually, open your eyes, and be still for a while. (Pause). ○

FOCUS ON A WORD

There are many special words in the Jewish literary heritage. Jews are the People of the Book, said Mohammed, something which all peoples recognized. Words have important meanings, especially words from the important languages Jews have used throughout history, such as Hebrew, Aramaic, or Yiddish. This brief exercise will focus on an important word which can be selected from anywhere in the four-thousand-year-old Jewish tradition.

○ *Sit or lie comfortably, and begin to assume a receptive mode. Be very calm and still, and let your breathing relax, along with all your body functions. Let your heart beat more slowly, and feel your entire being becoming like a piece of marshmallow, melting deep into the surface on which you are sitting or lying. . . .*

In this imagery exercise we will focus on one short word from our Tradition. Perhaps it is a Hebrew word, like **shalom**, *or* **sh'ma** *(listen),* **'or** *(light), or God's name,* **Adonai.** *You might pick a Yiddish word, such as* **mensch** *(a fine person), or* **shayn** *(beautiful). Or an English word, such as peace, hope, love, or justice.*

Let this word appear before your mind's eye, and see it hanging in the air.

Hear it pronounced slowly and softly in your imaginary ear. As with many of our prayers, words which are repeated have a cumulative effect on us. Keep repeating this special word to yourself, inside, so only you can hear and see. . . . After repeating it for a while, you will attain what our tradition calls **kavannah**, *or a feeling of special concentration.*

Find yourself becoming more and more calm as you keep repeating the word as long as you wish, attaining more and more **kavannah**. *Let yourself be infused with the sound and power of this word. (Pause).*

Keep repeating it now until you want to stop. . . .

When you are ready, sit quietly for a moment, and notice what repeating your special word with **kavannah** *has done to your concentration and state of mind. (Pause).*

Whenever you want, come back to this room, and return to your normal consciousness, opening your eyes, feeling energized and content. Notice how the experience deepened the sense of the divine within you. . . . ○

[Next time you do this exercise, try to do it for a longer time. Each time, make it longer, until you reach about twenty minutes, if you can.]

Suggestions for More Exercises on Spirituality

There are many books in which one can find spiritual visualizations and guided imagery exercises. The bibliography in Chapter Three will supply the reader with many of them. However, I would like to recommend two books, written by two very special people who are experts and experienced practitioners in this area of developing our spiritual selves.

In these books you will find treasures to contemplate, meditate and create imagery exercises, enough to fill the rest of your life.

1) Yitzhak Buxbaum, *Jewish Spiritual Practices* (Northvale, NJ: Jason Aronson, 1990)

Yitzhak is a kind, gentle teacher, with a great store of Jewish knowledge and human wisdom, much of which is drawn from the kabbalistic and hasidic traditions. He has written other books which are also wonderful.

2) Joan Borysenko, *Fire In The Soul: A New Psychology of Spiritual Optimism* (New York: Warner Books, Inc., 1993)

Joan is a bright, compassionate teacher and writer, cell biologist and psychologist, who draws on her Jewish roots and world traditions to bring together a wide selection of wonderful ideas in her many books. Her approach is more eclectic, and we can all learn from her depth and piety.

Chapter 11

SHABBAT SHALOM

Shabbat is a vision of the World To Come.
—Zohar

*It is only with the heart that one can see rightly;
what is essential is invisible to the eye.*
—Antoine de Saint-Exupéry, *The Little Prince*

ACCORDING to the famous late nineteenth century essayist, Ahad Ha-Am, "More than the Jewish People has kept Shabbat, Shabbat has kept the Jewish People." That oft-quoted and insightful observation summarizes the importance of Shabbat in Jewish Life from the beginnings of our people's history to the present time.

No institution or ritual encompasses more of what Judaism stands for than does Shabbat. It is a time when all Jewish values, practices and beliefs converge in one holy day. Shabbat is an unparalleled opportunity for the fulfillment of Torah study, prayer, self-reflection and meditation, the building of intimate relationships with family and friends, and the enjoyment of the material pleasures of life such as food, drink, sex and sleep. It is a time to dance and to sing, to rejoice and to celebrate.

Shabbat is a window into living a complete and rich Jewish experience, as its spirit infuses the other six days of the week. Whether observed according to every letter of the Halakhah, or in a way that is meaningful and inspiring to each individual in his/her own way, Shabbat is a day for expansion of the soul and the kindling of the spirit. The guided imagery exercises below are designed to help participants enter into the mood and ambiance of this unique day.

PREPARATION FOR SHABBAT

It is said that the journey is more important than the destination. For Shabbat this may be an exaggeration, because the experience of Shabbat is even greater than the preparation involved before it. However, the Shabbat day (from Friday just before sundown until Saturday just after sundown) is greatly enhanced by walking across its threshold with hours and even days of preparation.

❍ *Since all human beings require a combination of work and rest, Shabbat offers an opportunity to pause from our labors and concentrate on **being** instead of **doing**.*

*Find a comfortable place to sit or lie, and begin to enter the state of **being**, leaving **doing** behind. . . . To help this experience of Shabbat enter our entire being, take a few deep breaths, and with each breath exhale the worries and cares of the week days. Breathe in the spirit of Shabbat—the spirit of refreshment and renewal, of rest and relaxation, of joy and exaltation of the soul. . . .*

After a minute or two of winding down, let your eyes become heavy, and your eyelids close. . . . Roll your eyes back into your head a bit, and find yourself becoming drowsy and in a deep state of restful consciousness. . . .

Since Shabbat is such a vital part of our existence, its spirit hovers over us all seven days of the week. Everything we do, even on all the six non-Shabbat days, can be considered one long preparation for the peak experience of Shabbat.

Sunday, Monday, Tuesday, we are still floating high from the rest and joy of the previous Shabbat. On Wednesday we begin to think about what special preparations we want to do for the coming Shabbat. We shop in the supermarket and purchase special foods so that both our body and our soul can benefit from the Shabbat experience. Walk around the supermarket and load your cart with some special things which you want for this coming Shabbat. . . . What did you purchase? (Pause).

At home that evening, make some telephone calls and invite some dear ones to join you for this Shabbat evening meal, or for Shabbat lunch or Seudah Shlishit. . . . Whom did you invite? . . . How did they respond? . . . (Pause).

You decide that this coming Shabbat will be a bit extra special, even more than others. You go into a special store and buy something that will make this coming Shabbat even more beautiful in your home. . . . What are you buying? (Pause).

In the place at home where you keep your holy books, you go to the shelf with material on the weekly Sidrah, the Torah portion for this week. . . . Look over the books, and take one or two to begin your preparation for studying this week's Sidrah and Haftarah. . . . Perhaps you have a favorite commentary you enjoy reading along with the Sidrah. Take a look at some of the comments in that book. . . . (Pause).

Thursday evening you sit down to relax after dinner, and begin to read the daily paper and perhaps another of your favorite magazines. In some way an idea in this paper or magazine reminds you of an idea you just read about in the Sidrah of the week. Around the Shabbat dinner table you can share this idea with your dear ones. . . . What do you expect will be their reaction when you connect the Sidrah with contemporary thoughts and ideas? (Pause).

Thursday evening before you retire, you set the table in the dining room for Shabbat dinner. You use your best dishes and flatware, water goblets and shiny silver kiddush cups. You set out the Shabbat candlesticks, the challah plate and cover, a challah knife (only if you are a challah-slicer, and not a challah-tearer).

Friday around lunch time you check to make sure you have everything ready for Shabbat. You double-check to see if you have Shabbat candles, at least two challot (one for "Keep" and one for "Remember"—the two versions of Shabbat in the Ten Commandments), and a bottle of your favorite kosher wine. Get some lovely flowers, perhaps from your back yard, to make the Shabbat table beautiful and sweet-smelling. . . . Gaze at the flowers . . . sniff them. See how it makes you feel. . . . Now do anything else you want to add to Shabbat and make it a very special day. . . . What else did you add to make the day extra special? (Pause).

In case you are a challah baker, you take some time on Thursday evening (or Friday if you prefer) and bake a few challot. You take out your recipe from The Jewish Catalog or other source, and begin to mix the ingredients, the flour, granulated yeast, water, sugar, some raisins if you like, an oiled bowl. . . . Taste a bit of the dough (but not too much). How sweet and soft is it in your mouth? . . .

After the dough has risen for several hours, you begin to divide the dough for as many challot as you want to bake, and artfully braid it. Braiding the dough reminds you that some think of the challot as the golden hair of the Shabbat bride. . . .

Following ancient custom you separate a small chunk of challah dough and throw it into the oven, as a kind of sacrifice, reminding you of the sacrifices given to the Kohanim in the ancient Temple. When you do that you recite a special blessing from your siddur. . . . Next you brush the dough with egg wash and sprinkle it with some sesame seeds. You then bake it in the oven for about a half hour at 350 degrees. Then you remove your beautiful, golden, shiny challot from the oven and let them cool until you are ready to serve them at Shabbat dinner. . . . Look at the challot, and see how they shine. . . . In their shiny reflection you see a beautiful picture that has much personal meaning to you. . . . What is it? (Long pause).

When Friday afternoon comes, and the Shabbat bride is about to arrive, you empty your pockets of all the coins in them and drop them into the Tzedakah box. Next you take our your siddur and practice humming some of the beautiful songs which welcome Shabbat, like **Lekha Dodi** *("Come, O Sabbath Bride") or Bialik's lovely poem-song,* **Ha-Chama MeRosh Ha-Ilanot** *("The Sun on the Treetops"). . . . You take a nice warm shower, put on your Shabbat clothes, and then sit back in your most comfortable chair, now all completely ready for Shabbat. You take a short nap and fifteen minutes later you hear a gentle knock at the door. Your Shabbat guests, including the Shabbat bride, have arrived. . . . (Pause).* ○

SHABBAT CANDLES

○ *Let your eyes close and become very comfortable and relaxed. Allow some deep, slow breaths to bring peace and harmony into your body and soul. . . . See how good and at peace you feel. . . . Everything is just right. . . . Your heart is calm, you are at one with yourself and the world. . . .*

You are at home, getting ready to light the Shabbat candles. . . . The house is clean and in order. . . . The Shabbat table is set and ready. . . . The beautiful silver kiddush cups at each place highlight the white table cloth. An artistic ceramic challah plate graces the center of the table, and covering the challot is a large silk cover from Jerusalem, hand-painted with a picture of the Kotel, the Western Wall, in lovely pastel colors. The meal is prepared, the company invited. . . .

You are ready to usher in Queen Shabbat. The matches lie impatiently next to the candle holders. . . .

Before you pick up the match and strike it to make the last fire of the week, your mind wanders a bit, and you are thinking of many things. . . . First, you think about all the pious Jewish women who have kindled their Shabbat candles throughout the centuries. . . . An image comes to your mind, with one particular woman, from a different land and a different time, standing as you are, on the border of Friday and Shabbat, about to cross over into the mystic Land of Shabbat. . . . See if there is something you would like to say to this woman. (Pause).

Coming out of your reverie for a while, you prepare once again to kindle the four or five Shabbat candles, one for each of several special people in your life. . . .

Think of who these special people are, and picture each one of them. Maybe they are some people from your past, maybe from your present family. Take a minute and say a brief word to each of them before you strike the match. . . . (Pause).

Now light each candle, with love and devotion for each one, and watch the burning glow. . . . Take your time as you gaze at the different colors in their fire —the orange, the light blue, the green and the red. . . . Now you follow ancient custom by waving your arms three times in a circle from your shoulders outward, in a wide circle, extending your hands in front of you, and then closing the circle by bringing your hands back to your chest, and letting them drop to your sides. . . . When you have finished, you cup your arched hands gently over your closed eyes, and recite the b'racha. "Barukh ata Adonai, Elohenu Melekh ha-olam, asher kidshanu be-mitzvotav, ve-tzeevanu le-hadleek ner shel Shabbat." "Praised are You, Adonai, God of the Universe, Who has made us holy with Your mitzvot, and instructed us to kindle the Shabbat candles." Then you recite some other of your favorite prayers, such as: May God bring us Shabbat rest; may God bring us Shabbat joy; may God bring us Shabbat peace. Shabbat Shalom. . . . (Pause).

Tradition tells us that we have a **neshama yetera***, an extra Shabbat soul, which enters our body when Shabbat arrives. It heightens our spirit and uplifts our heart. Some say that the extra Shabbat soul even makes us taller. Certainly we are taller in our capacity to feel and care. . . . Imagine an extra soul inside yourself. . . . Pay attention to how you feel with the extra soul inside you. (Pause).*

Next, think about the week that has gone by. What special things occurred? . . . What problems did you have? Let them go now that Shabbat is here. . . . Imagine all the bad things as green ghouls and watch them running out of your body one by one. Name each ghoul as it exits your body and feel lighter as you watch it float away. . . .

What successes did you enjoy? Relish them. Imagine all the good things as colorful flowers. As each one slowly disappears, you can still smell their beautiful aroma remaining in your body and soul. . . . Bask in the satisfactions in your life. . . .

Now take a few minutes to look directly into the tip of the shimmering flame on one of the Shabbat candles. . . . As you stare into the reddish-orange, yellow-blue flame, think of a special prayer you would like to recite. . . . Take a minute to think of what to pray about, and then compose your prayer while you are standing in front of the candelabra. . . . Recite it now in a soft whisper. . . . (Pause). Imagine in your mind's eye that your prayer has been fulfilled. What does your world look like now that your prayer is fulfilled? What changes have occurred?

(Pause).

Now that Shabbat has come into your life, and you enter into the realm of Shabbat, think about what you have to look forward to . . . during the rest of the evening . . . tomorrow . . . until sundown, when Shabbat takes leave of your home. . . .

Find a comfortable chair close to the Shabbat candles, and look at them in a leisurely, relaxed manner. Take your time. . . . You have nothing to rush or hurry for. . . . Just slowly and peacefully stare at the Shabbat candles, and see what thoughts or feelings come to your mind. . . . Let them float across the stage in your mind, and see what comes. . . . *(Pause).*

As the peace and tranquility of Shabbat envelops your body, and your home, let yourself enjoy the experience. . . .

When you are ready, return to this room, and slowly open your eyes. . . . ◯

ZEMIROT — SHABBAT SONGS

◯ As you sit back or lie down comfortably in your place, you begin to hear soft music swimming across the room. . . . The music is pleasing to your soul, and it brings you calm and peace. As you listen to the music, your soul moves into different levels of consciousness, relaxing you and energizing you. . . . You enter into the spirit of the music with all your being. . . . The music is as magic, uplifting your mood, bringing you warmth and security. . . .

With a few deep breaths, you find yourself totally relaxed and tranquil. A sense of Shabbat peace washes over you, and you feel unusually whole and healed. . . .

The music of Shabbat is an indispensable ingredient in creating the unique mood of this day. The lovely tunes and poetic words of some of the traditional **zemirot**, Shabbat songs, bring an exalted spiritual dimension to the Shabbat experience.

We shall hear some of these **zemirot** swirling around inside our mind and heart, bringing the special Shabbat message, to reclaim our self, our life. . . .

Let your mind create images and sounds, smells and feelings, as you hear these beautiful songs from days long ago, and from more recent times. . . . Listen carefully. First you hear a song called **Yom Ze Mechubad** —"This Day is Honored."

As you listen to the song, let your mind wander and create whatever images which present themselves. . . . Don't force anything, just let it come if it wants to.

Yom ze mechubad. . . . *"This day is honored above all others, because on it the Rock of Ages did rest. . . . In six days you shall complete your work, but the seventh is for your God. Do not work on the Shabbat, for this day is honored. . . .*

"First is this day among all festive days. It is the Sabbatical Day, the Holy Shabbat. Thus everyone sanctifies God's name over wine, over two braided breads which are sliced and enjoyed. . . .

"Eat your fill and bless Adonai on this honored day, the God whom you love, since God blessed you among all nations. . . .

"On this day God finished the work of creation, and the heavens declare God's glory. The earth is filled with the lovingkindness of Adonai. See all that God's hand has done before resting on Shabbat. God is indeed our Rock whose work is perfect. . . . This day is so honored. . . ."

Let these words help you feel the unique meaning of Shabbat. . . .

Now we hear another song, **D'ror Yikra**. *"Freedom God proclaims for all sons and daughters of the world on this day of Shabbat. This day is surcease from labor and trouble . . . from anger and strife. . . . Rest and be at ease on this day of Shabbat. Be with your people, O God, and give them a sign of deliverance. When we are free, we shall open our lips and fill our tongue with Your praise. . . . Let all who obey You know wisdom in their soul . . . for it shall be a jewel in their crown. . . . Let all who keep Your holy laws also keep Your sacred Shabbat."*

Take your time with these words and melodies, and let them find a special place in your soul. . . .

Yom Shabbaton *is a song extolling the special character of Shabbat. "Shabbat is impossible to forget. Its sweet memory is like a rare fragrance. . . . As a dove are all who seek rest from care. Those who are weary find repose. . . .*

"This day is so honored by Your faithful. Young and old alike take special care to mind its laws. . . . Its demands are etched on the tablets in the Ten Words. Every one of our People was there at Sinai, joining in the Covenant. 'We shall do and we shall obey' they declared with one voice. . . . 'God is One' said they, and Blessed is the One who gives strength through Shabbat rest. . . .

"Thus spoke Adonai on the Mountain of Myrrh: 'Remember and Keep the Holy Shabbat.' Follow each and every one of its commands. Let Shabbat rest bring you new strength and gird your loins. . . .

"Though our People wanders in Exile as sheep who stray . . . nevertheless we swore to keep our oath, to observe precious Shabbat. . . . Your promise we long to know, to watch over Your People, and guard them from all harm. . . .

"As a dove are all who seek rest from care. Those who are weary find repose. . . ."

Hear the melodies dancing in your ears and the scenes floating in your mind, and see what gifts Shabbat brings to you. . . . Take your time as your imagination wanders. . . .

When you are ready, come back to this room, and slowly, gradually, open your eyes. . . . ❍

HAVDALAH

❍ *It is time to wish farewell to your visitor, the Shabbat Queen. . . . Find a place that is comfortable, and prepare to relax and let yourself part from the special guest who accompanied you for the past twenty-six hours. You have just spent a complete day in relaxation and repose. . . . You feel the blessings in every fiber of your being which Shabbat HaMalkah has brought to you. Your body and soul are renewed and refreshed, and you reluctantly say good-bye to Shabbat. . . .*

You and your family or friends go to an open space outdoors, perhaps in the back of your home, or in a wooded area, anywhere that is open to the sky. . . . The sun has set, the red ball of deep orange has sunk deep into the horizon, and it is all black now, except for a sliver of moon and some stars lighting the planet. . . .

In your heart is a mixture of joy and sadness. You have experienced a full day of wonder. A day filled with all the beautiful things in which human beings at their best can participate—prayer and study, delicious meals and ample rest, time for friends and for books, time for singing and talking, for the uplifting of the soul to the heights of heaven. . . .

As Queen Shabbat departs, gather with some special people in your life, and begin to sing of Elijah. "Eliyahu Ha-Navi . . . Eliyahu ha-Tishbi. . . ." Elijah symbolizes the coming of the Messiah. Shabbat afternoon, now ended, is the time most like the messianic era, when all is peaceful and harmonious. A time when there is sweet Shalom in every nook and cranny of the universe. . . .

Together with your dear ones make a circle. In the darkness light a long braided candle. . . . See the shadows of your friends' faces through the glimmer of the candle. . . . As you stand together, arm in arm, a figure dances into the middle of the circle. As the words "Eliyahu Ha-Navi" resound among the trees in the distance, a blithe spirit rejoices with you, as if from heaven itself. . . . The figure of Elijah has joined you, and assists you as you sing farewell to Queen Shabbat. Watch Eliyahu dance in the middle of your circle. . . .

Suddenly the figure evaporates, and the candle still burns, bringing light and joy, happiness and mirth, to you and all Jews everywhere. . . . Listen to one of your group chant the Havdalah blessing, announcing the separation between Shabbat and the mundane, Israel and the nations, light and darkness, between Shabbat and the six days of Creation. . . .

First a blessing is chanted over the wine, giving sweetness to your sorrow, lightness to your heavy spirits. . . . Next, over the beautiful aroma of spices in the castle-shaped box with a tiny door to open and inhale the fragrance inside. . . . As our Special Shabbat Soul (the **neshama yetera**) departs, the extra soul that enters the body of every Jew when Shabbat arrives, we need the whiff of spice to restore us to full vitality. . . . Finally, each person clutches his or her fingers toward their face, over the braided multi-wicked candle of Havdalah, and watches the shadow between the crevices of the fingers and the palm. In that distinction between dark and light, see the difference between Shabbat and weekdays. Let it remind you that you are now returning to the ordinary, trying to steal some precious holiness from Shabbat to bring along with you for the next several days. . . .

Think about some of the special things you did during the Shabbat which is now ending. . . . (Pause).

Remember some of the songs you sang, the prayers you chanted, the people you spoke with. . . . Let these memories stir around inside yourself. . . . Pick out one of them and stay with it for an extra moment. . . .

Was there someone in synagogue whom you had not seen in a while, and were happy to see again? . . . Did you read a book which brought you new knowledge or uplifted your soul with some charming insights? . . . Was there a special dish which you tried for the first time? . . . Try to remember all the wonderful things you did on this Shabbat. . . . Now it is time to let go of your Guest, and say good-bye. (Pause).

Did the Shabbat Queen bring you a few moments of reflection to think about the path of your life, the direction you are traveling? . . . What new understanding did you achieve about yourself, about life, about God, during this Shabbat? . . . Are you ready now for a week ahead that will be enriched by the pause which Shabbat brought into your life? . . . (Pause).

What can you do next Shabbat to bring new clarity to your work, to your relationships, to your family, to your own existence? . . . Learning from all the *wonderful things which this Shabbat brought you, can you think of ways to spread the wealth of the Shabbat experience to make yourself an even richer person next Shabbat? . . . (Pause).*

How can the symbols of Havdalah stretch the harmony and bliss which you experienced during this Shabbat into the days ahead? Think of the wine, the spices, the bright light. How can these symbols bring new sweetness, new aroma, and new light into your sometimes tired and weary life? How can you bring these life-giving gifts to the days and weeks of those who are important to you? (Pause).

It is time to softly hum the song of Eliyahu one more time, and as you do so, pour some wine into the dish which holds the tall Havdalah candle. The light of the candle is now turned downward into the droplets of the shiny purple wine, and the light is extinguished. Some puffs of smoke ascend from the dish, and the humming becomes ever softer. . . . Shabbat is a memory. The week has returned. You are now strengthened and renewed for a better week than the one before. . . . You are ready to return to another part of your life. . . .

When you are ready, come back to this room, and gently and slowly open your eyes. . . . ◯

Chapter 12

YOU SHALL REJOICE IN YOUR FESTIVALS

The High Holy Days and the Pilgrimage Festivals

In every generation each Jew is to imagine oneself going out of Egypt.
—Pesach Haggadah

THE HEBREW poet laureate of modern Palestine, Chaim Nachman Bialik (d. 1934), suggested that just as there are peaks and valleys in space, so there are peaks and valleys in time. The peaks in time are the Festivals. Rabbi Samson Raphael Hirsch (d. 1888, Frankfurt, Germany), leader of the neo-Orthodox movement of modern times, once said that the Jewish Calendar is the catechism of the Jew.

There is no doubt that the Jewish holidays are primary today in Jewish observance and Jewish consciousness. Jews whose attendance at synagogue and whose prayer life is minimal will still actively observe many, if not most, of the Jewish Festivals, whether at home or in synagogue. This is equally true of non-observant Israelis whose ties to ritual Judaism are well-known to be very tenuous. Perhaps some of the guided imagery exercises below will help clarify and strengthen these important ties which remain for many Jews among their most important connections to their Heritage. For those whose Jewish lives are fuller in other ritualistic, intellectual and spiritual ways, the exercises can raise their present commitment to an even higher level.

We shall follow the chronological order of the calendar year in presenting these exercises.

THE SHOFAR

◯ *Imagine yourself sitting in synagogue on the morning of Rosh Hashanah, and the Hazzan is repeating the Musaf Amidah. Excitement builds as you approach the blowing of the shofar. . . .*

In your mind's eye take yourself back to other times at Rosh Hashanah services when the shofar was blown. Recall many different people who have blown the shofar in years gone by. Out of the forest of your memory recall the person who blew the shofar in the synagogue you attended as a child. . . . Bring back the sight, sounds, smells and other senses of that early shofar blowing experience. What was it like? . . .

Now hear the blasts of the shofar one more time. . . . Another year has passed. The crisp air outside as you entered the synagogue reminds you that Fall has come again. Summer is over, vacation time has gone, and the new school year, the organizational program year, and the Jewish calendar year, are about to resume. . . . Notice the twinge of sadness about losing the summer that has zipped by so quickly. . . . Nevertheless you are excited about what things are in store for you in the coming year. . . .

Just before the Baal Tekiah raises the shofar to his lips, the rabbi explains some of the meanings that Jewish history has given to the blowing of the shofar. Listen carefully. . . .

Listen as the rabbi retells the famous story of Abraham's sacrifice of Isaac, when a ram in the thicket took the place of Isaac on the altar. The ram's horn reminds us, says the rabbi, of the readiness of Abraham to obey God's will even at the cost of the greatest sacrifice anyone can make. Think to yourself: Was Abraham really being tested during the Akedah? Or maybe it was God who was being tested! Was God actually going to go through with this cruel act? In our story, explains the rabbi, both God and Abraham passed the test. . . . There was to be no more human sacrifice. It was now forbidden for all time.

Think to yourself, Am I being tested too? . . . Have I been tested during this past year? In what ways? . . . Were the trials and tribulations which faced me in the past twelve months part of God's testing of my faith, my courage? Did I pass these tests? . . . In what other ways does God test us? . . . How do we test God?

If there is a Covenant, a mutual contract between God and us, can we not also demand that God fulfill the divine part of the agreement? Does God ask too much of me and others? . . . (Pause).

The blowing of the shofar is about to begin. The congregation rises. . . . The rabbi pronounces the blessing. **Baruch atta . . . ve-tzeevanu lishmo-ah kol shofar.**

"Blessed be God Who has commanded us to hear the blowing of the shofar."

Something inside you is deeply moved. More than all the words and prayers, the sermon and the Torah reading, the blowing of the shofar stirs you, awakens you, shakes you. . . . It takes you all the way back to Abraham, Sarah and Isaac, the Founders of our People. They had the courage to follow an unknown and invisible God. They thought of things which were never thought of before. . . . A new religion was founded four thousand years ago, and you are one of those who still upholds it, and transmits it to those who come after you!

The shofar blasts resound throughout your heart and soul. Will you be worthy to be inscribed in the Book of Life for the coming year? Will the shofar succeed in awakening you from your lethargy to become a better person, a more faithful servant of God?

Take some time to think about these questions. . . . (Pause).

The sounds of the shofar fade into the distance. The worship services continue. The questions remain inside you. . . . They haunt you, and yet they inspire you. . . . They prod you to be a better person, a better Jew, a more loyal child of your Divine Parent. . . .

It is time to return. This is the holiday of Return. Now we will return to this room, and the questions will continue to stir within you. . . . At the count of three you will be completely awake and refreshed, ready to greet another New Year. . . .One . . . Two . . .Three. ◯

ATONEMENT – AT-ONE-MENT

◯ *As we approach the last of the Ten Days of Repentance (**Aseret Y'may Teshuvah**), Yom Kippur, you think about the meaning of the solemn holiday. Yom Kippur is a day of reconciliation, between us and God, between us and our family, between us and our friends.*

Take a few minutes to think about being "at-one" on the Day of "At-one-ment" or "Atonement." In the course of life we get angry at others, and they sometimes get angry at us. At times our family and friends do things that cause displeasure in our heart, and we do the same to them. Most often it is not done intentionally, and Yom Kippur is a splendid opportunity to let go of these hurts and angers.

*When we repair a relationship, we call it in Hebrew "**tikkun**," meaning fixing or repair. Think of some of the people with whom your relatimnship is not* *completely whole, with whom you need to achieve some **tikkun**. . . . (Pause).*

*Can you resolve to approach these people before Yom Kippur and ask to set aside private time for a conversation together, in which both of you can work to achieve **tikkun**? Think about doing this with some people in your life. . . .*

*Now pick one individual with whom you especially would like to achieve **tikkun**. Take a minute to think about the one relationship in which you would like most to bring about **tikkun**. . . .*

*Now do the **tikkun** in your imagination. Do a "rehearsal" of this act of **tikkun**. See yourself making an appointment to meet with this individual. . . . You may want to start off by telling the individual how much you value your relationship, and why it is important to you to do **tikkun**. Explain that especially before Yom Kippur it is important to you to bring about a true act of **tikkun**. Now the two of you are talking together. Imagine how you will start the conversation. . . . Take some time to let the dialog proceed in your imagination. (Pause).*

When things have been settled, perhaps you may want to express your affection for the individual, and your joy in working together to make your relationship whole again. Imagine how a hug, or kiss, or handshake, would feel. . . . If you want to, try it now, in your imagination. . . . (Pause).

*Did you achieve the **tikkun** you wanted? If so, how does it feel? (Pause).*

Next, think about your relationship with God. Do you have any issues which you would like to straighten out in your relationship with God? If so, take all the time you need now to discuss with God some of these issues. Perhaps you have been hurt or angry at God, and you would like to "get this off your chest." Now have your one-to-one discussion with God. . . . (Pause).

*Is there anything else you need to do or say before completing this time of reconciliation and **tikkun**? If so, do it now. . . . (Pause).*

When you are ready, come back to this room, and slowly open your eyes. . . . ○

[Facilitators should be extra careful to design a grounding exercise that allows ample time for these matters—some of which may be very deeply felt—to be adequately processed. It is important to remember that anyone who so desires must be able to keep any parts of their experience confidential].

A SUKKAH TOUR

◯ *Get yourself very comfortable, take some deep breaths, and become very relaxed. . . . Let your eyes close, and feel very calm and serene, ready to enter a lovely guided imagery experience. . . .*

Together with a group of friends you are going on a "Sukkah Walk" today. You will walk around the neighborhood and visit four or five different sukkot which were built by neighbors and friends. . . .

As you walk you feel the light Fall breeze brushing your back, and you zip up your light coat to keep from getting chilled. . . . The sun is hidden partly by some white and gray clouds, but it is a beautiful clear day, and you are enjoying the walk. . . . Looking up at the trees you pass on the street, you see the Fall colors beginning to paint the leaves. You take a deep breath and feel the fresh October air fill up your nostrils and your lungs. . . . The aroma of fruits and vegetables waft by in the air. . . , perhaps from some of the decorated sukkot you are passing on the street. . . .

You now arrive at the home of the first family you and your group will visit. You walk around the back of the house to the yard, and cannot help but see the beautiful sukkah they have built and decorated. As you get closer you see a few other guests leaving the sukkah and saying good-bye. Greet your friends now, and approach the sukkah. . . . Look all over, inside and out, and see how they built their sukkah, and how they decorated it. . . . Notice the tall, proud lulav on the metal table inside, and the wooden etrog box next to it, containing the shiny yellow lemon-like fruit, used during this season. . . . Tell the hosts what you like about their sukkah. . . .

After tasting some honey cake and having a sip of sweet purple kiddush wine, you are ready to depart and visit the next sukkah on your walk. . . .

At the next house, you enter through the front door, and the hosts escort you through the house to the kitchen and out the sliding door to their deck, where they have built their sukkah. . . . It is built differently than the one you saw before. Go inside and take a careful look around. Admire the paintings which the children have done on large thick light brown paper, tacked up on the walls of the sukkah. . . . Have a conversation with the hosts about their sukkah, and tell them how it compares with others you have seen. . . . Compliment the children on their art work, and take a piece of fruit for the road. . . . Saying good-bye, you now leave and go on to the next sukkah on your walk. . . .

At the third house there are so many people it takes you a few minutes to find the hosts. . . . You make your way through the crowd, and go inside their sukkah.

It is much different than the other two. . . . Take a good look around, and see how they have gone to great labors to make their sukkah very beautiful and special. . . . Notice some of the ways in which this sukkah is totally different than any sukkah you have ever seen before. . . . Do you think you would ever want to build a sukkah like that? Share your thoughts and feelings with the people whose home you are visiting, and then walk around to see if there are other people you know. . . . Take a few minutes to converse with some of your other friends who happen to be there, and see how they like this family's sukkah. . . .

Finally, you begin to walk toward the home of the last stop on your sukkah walk. . . . You turn a few corners, and notice a few other sukkot on the way, in homes whose owners you do not know. . . . Then you arrive at the home of the people you planned to visit. Let them lead you into the sukkah, and go inside. It is a very small sukkah, and other people are waiting to enter, so you don't linger there too long. . . . Take a piece of chocolate candy, a few pretzels and a drink of diet soda, and walk outside onto the back lawn. . . . Taking a few steps back you look at the sukkah from a distance, and see that even though it is small, there is something very special and different about this sukkah. . . . Notice how they have done something to make their sukkah unique, unlike any of the others. . . .

When you and your friends are ready, begin to walk back home, and join in the discussion about all the different sukkot you visited today, and what a nice experience it was visiting with friends, sharing some food, admiring their hard work, and celebrating the Festival. . . . (Pause).

On your way home you begin to think about the last days of Sukkot, when Shmini Atzeret and Simchat Torah are celebrated, and the fun you will soon have during these special holidays. . . . When you are ready, come back to this room, open your eyes, slowly and gradually, and see how joyous and fulfilled you are. . . . ○

HANUKKAH – EIGHT GIFTS

○ *Close your eyes, and look at the Hanukkah Menorah, the Hanukkiah, sitting happily in the center of the dining room table. Stare at all eight lights and the shamash, the helper candle which lights the others, and find that you are becoming mesmerized. Watch the lights, and forget about everything else. Begin to be more and more completely relaxed. . . .*

For two thousand years the Hanukkah candles have symbolized religious freedom for our people. They rest on a table in every Jewish home during the winter festival of religious freedom, celebrating the Maccabee's victory over the

Syrian Greeks who wanted to destroy every vestige of the Jewish religion.

Jewish homes in every corner of the world light the Hanukkiah as a tribute to the brave Maccabee warriors who defeated a much larger army in their fight to maintain their own Jewish way of life. Stare at the burning lights and find yourself being filled with pride and joy. . . .

One of the ways we celebrate Hanukkah in North America today is to give gifts. Giving a gift is a way to show appreciation and to celebrate our pride in maintaining our Jewish identity, our right to be different. Think of eight different people to whom you would like to give something, as part of your Hanukkah celebration. . . .

For each night of Hanukkah try to think of someone who is dear and precious to you, and whom you would like to give a special gift that tells them how you feel about them. Think about the first person to whom you would like to express your affection with a special gift. . . . (Pause).

Now let your eyes move along the row of shining candles. For each night think of another special person in your life, and add a new candle and a new gift. . . . (Pause).

Have you thought of eight people yet? Take your time. . . . When you have thought of eight people whom you care about, and a special gift for each of them, let the image of the Hanukkiah fade from your mind's eye. . . . Replace the eight candles with an image of each of these special eight people. . . . (Pause).

When you are ready, come back to this room, and slowly open your eyes. . . . ◯

PESACH – FESTIVAL OF EMPATHY

Passover, like Hanukkah, is celebrated in homes all over the Jewish world, in Israel, in America, in Argentina, in Budapest, in London, in Kiev, in Tokyo. Each family Seder meal may have a different version of the Haggadah, the story book of rituals and tales about the Festival of Pesach, but in one form or another Jewish families celebrate the going out of Egypt. By doing so we empathize with our ancestors, and with all who are oppressed throughout the world.

◯ *It is customary for the leader of the Pesach Seder to sit on a pillow, and lean a bit, just as free people in Roman days leaned on soft-cushioned pillows. As you let your eyes close, picture yourself sitting on a soft, comfortable pillow, relaxing in the traditional Pesach way, and let your imagination begin to discover new thoughts about Pesach. . . .*

Pesach is a holiday in which we empathize with others, with people who are oppressed, such as the ancient Hebrews in the days of Pharaoh. As we were slaves, so we must not ever enslave others, the Torah commands. We must fight the battle for freedom and justice for every people, until all people are free.

Let your mind scan the Pesach table, set for the Seder meal, with a Haggadah at each place. . . . As you look at the table, with extra seats for many, many guests who will be joining your Seder this year, let your eye roam from symbol to symbol. . . .

Look at the **matzah**, the unleavened bread which reminds us that our Israelite ancestors did not have time to let their bread rise in their rush out of Egyptian bondage. Let your imagination focus on some person or group who are treated unfairly by some "Pharaoh." Who are they? In what way is their life flat like the **matzah** bread, the "bread of affliction" (lechem oni), and oppressed because of their race, ethnic group, or other minority status? . . .

Next turn your eyes to the **maror**, the bitter herbs. . . . This reminds us of the bitterness of slavery. We eat the bitter herbs during the Seder observance to identify with the bitter lives our ancestors endured when Pharaoh cracked the harsh whip of slavery over their backs. . . . Are there still slaves in the world? Who can we call enslaved, even though they may not fit exactly into the term "slaves?" What national, ethnic or religious group do you think of when we think of the bitterness of slavery? . . . What role do we have in trying to remove the stigma of slavery from the modern world? (Pause).

As your eyes scan the Seder table, turn next to the salt water, into which we dip our parsley, or other green vegetable. The salt water helps us recall the tears our Israelite ancestors cried because they could not find a way to live a normal life. People who are enslaved, physically, emotionally or spiritually, cry bitter tears, either inside their heart, or real tears of pain from their reddened eyes, when their life feels like it is caught in a vise. What person or group can you think of whose tears are ignored in the modern world, because of insensitivity, or cruelty, or discrimination? . . . What can modern nations, or civilized individuals do to lighten their burden, and relieve their oppression? (Pause).

There is another significant symbol on our Seder plate, the **charoset**, the strange mixture of apples, nuts, and wine, which stands for the mortar which the biblical slaves used to make bricks to build storehouses for Pharaoh. Their lives were devoted from early morning to late at night to the labor of Pharaoh and his henchmen. They had no time for rest, for leisure, for family. For them there was no Sabbath, no festivals, no chance to worship their own God, no life whatsoever, except to build, build, build, the empire of cruel Pharaoh. What last group *in today's world can we think of who suffers in a similar way? What group has no freedom, no say about their own life, no time to enjoy the quality of life of their cruel master? . . . How is society closing its eyes to the pain of these slaves of today's world? What must we do to put an end to this kind of slavery in the twentieth and twenty-first century? . . .*

We have tried to empathize with the forgotten, forsaken, oppressed and abused peoples of today through the Pesach symbols. Let us also try to allow our renewed empathy to extend to every day of the year, and be more caring and helpful in the ongoing struggle for human freedom and justice for all God's children everywhere. . . . ◯

TIKKUN LAYL SHAVUOT

Shavuot is a holiday with fewer home and synagogue observances than the other pilgrimage festivals, Sukkot and Pesach. It is the time of the giving of the Torah on Mount Sinai, and the establishment of the eternal Covenant between God and Israel. Its significance and meaning are no less important. If anything, an argument can be made that it is the most important festival on the Jewish calendar in its deepest meaning; namely, that freedom without law and restraint is license and has potential for danger.

In terms of ritual and custom, one of the few observances that has developed in recent centuries is called *Tikkun Layl Shavuot*, the coming together of Jews to study Torah. Since Shavuot is the Festival of Giving of the Torah, it is natural to celebrate it by studying words of Torah. During *Tikkun Layl Shavuot* people study Torah late into the night, sometimes all night long. Our next guided imagery exercise is based on this custom.

◯ *Imagine yourself sitting in a very comfortable chair, relaxed and serene, yet mentally alert. It is late, approaching midnight. You have been hearing lectures and studying Torah texts for several hours, and you feel deeply privileged and enriched. Feel the soothing warmth of Torah, and how it gives meaning, joy and understanding to your being. . . .*

You are feeling very secure and comfortable, having just listened to wise words of past sages. Let yourself become more and more relaxed as we enter this experience of learning and growth. . . .

The teacher sits in the corner in a lounge chair, holding an old, well-used book. The book appears as though it has been thumbed through and studied for decades, maybe even longer. . . . Look at the book as your ancestors have, holding it in great reverence. As the People of the Book, Jews have reverenced books and learning since the beginning of Judaism. . . .

Sitting around you are other people who have come to study Torah. Look around and see how wide-eyed and enthusiastic they are about what they are hearing. . . . The more everyone hears the wise words of Torah, the more enlightened and satisfied they are. Join in their feeling, and feel yourself becoming very happy that you are part of this learning group. . . .

When the lesson is completed, the teacher answers some questions, and there is a discussion about the themes in the book. People talk back and forth, and everyone feels happy and privileged to have been sitting at the feet of such a wise teacher. . . .

Next, another teacher takes her turn. She too holds a hoary and sacred book in her hands, and begins to impart of her wisdom, and of the wisdom of the book. . . . Listen to some of the wise things which the teacher and the book have to teach. (Pause).

You are learning new insights about how to live your life, and about how to treat other people. Notice how impressed you are by such great wisdom. How fortunate you feel to be part of the people that honors its books and teachers from the past. You are so happy to be part of this tradition of learning, and discussing; of teaching and reading and asking many questions. . . .

All through the night more teachers sit in the lounge chair, with new books, and new ideas, sharing their wisdom, and the wisdom of many men and women of past centuries. . . . The group listens, asks, and learns. The hour gets later and later, but no one is tired. Everyone is stimulated and alert, listening avidly to the wise teachings that pour out like a fountain, one after another. . . .

Think about some of the subjects you studied tonight. Perhaps you read the Book of Ruth and learned that wonderful story of loyalty and love. Maybe you delved into some Talmudic tractates, studying about the laws of reciting blessings (B'rachot) or of reciting the Shema or the Amidah. Maybe you studied some ancient midrashim about the personality of Moshe or Miriam, or about King David and Nathan the Prophet. Perhaps your studies included the works of Rashi or the Rambam, Yehudah Halevy or Yosef Karo. Your mind may have been enriched with writings of philosophy, poetry, liturgy, Hasidic lore or kabbalah.

What are some of the things you learned in this all-night study session? . . . What important discovery did you make? (Pause).

Think about how the whole world is sleeping, while you and your friends, and Jewish groups like yours in many other cities and lands, are studying words of Torah. How rich is our tradition! How fortunate you feel! Let yourself celebrate being part of a people that has recognized how much there is to learn about life from old books and wise people. . . .

Soon the morning sun begins to peak into the room. The light clears away the darkness, just as the light of Torah has swept back the darkness of ignorance and fear. The symbolism of the light entering the room reminds you that your life can be filled with study and learning, listening and reading, and you can become more and more enlightened as you continue to immerse yourself in the life-giving waters of Torah. You feel refreshed and renewed, and you are ready to have breakfast, to wash up, and begin the morning prayers. . . . ○

Chapter 13

THE JEWISH LIFE CYCLE— From Birth to Death

If a man could pass through paradise in a dream, and have a flower presented to him as a pledge that his soul had really been there, and if he found that flower in his hand when he awoke, ay, what then!

—Coleridge

May you be blessed to see this child study Torah, practice good deeds and stand under the chuppah.

—Traditional Baby-naming Prayer

ASK ANY JEW what is the most important characteristic of the Jewish People, and chances are the answer you will get is "the strength of the Jewish family."

An important part of the strength of the Jewish family, of course, is the beautiful tapestry of rituals created by the talmudic rabbis and their successors, which clothe the rites of passage from one stage of life to another with meaning and poetry. From birth to death there is a ceremony at every important Jewish milestone. These include baby-naming, bar/bat mitzvah, confirmation (for Reform and Conservative Jews), conversion, wedding, and funeral. New rituals are taking shape for other significant moments in life such as miscarriage or stillbirth, adoption, weaning, beginning menstruation, entering college, sanctifying gay/lesbian relationships, reaching midlife or menopause, more elaborate separation and divorce ceremonies, and aging (sometimes called *saging*). Two excellent resources for these rituals and their modern meanings and explanations are *Celebration and Renewal: Rites of Passages in Judaism* edited by Rela M. Geffen (Phila.: JPS, 1993) and *Lifecycles: Jewish Women on Life Passages and Personal Milestones* edited by Debra Orenstein (Woodstock, VT: Jewish Lights, 1994).

A NEW BABY

❍ *Permit yourself to enter a receptive mood, and sit or lie back comfortably. . . . As you become more deeply relaxed, let your eyes become heavy and the lids drop over them. . . . Let your mind be free of care and concern, and notice how refreshed and unencumbered you feel. . . .*

You are sitting in synagogue on a bright, sunny Shabbat morning, and the light is streaming in through the stained glass windows, bathing the comfortable cushioned seats with red, green, orange, yellow and tan. . . . There are several simchas in the congregation this morning, and the community rejoices together with each family, celebrating their lifecycle milestone. There are two couples getting married the following day, a bat mitzvah ceremony, and a family leaving for a pilgrimage to Israel who will receive a special farewell blessing.

The next aliyah honors a young couple who ascend the bema with their little baby girl, just three weeks old, Rachel Channah Goldstein. A sense of joy and spiritual satisfaction spreads through the congregation as the new parents and their baby come up for their aliyah. . . .

Take a moment to notice how you are feeling as you watch this young family beginning to recite the b'rachot before the Torah. . . .

After the Torah portion is chanted by the mother of the new baby, and the couple recites the closing b'racha, the rabbi pronounces a special blessing for the family and announces a Hebrew name for the baby. "May her name be called in Israel Rachel Channah bat Barukh ve-Avivah. May it be an honored name in Israel. May the parents raise their daughter to study Torah, to perform mitzvot, and may they be privileged to bring her to the wedding canopy."

The congregation then bursts out spontaneously in a traditional song, "Siman tov u-mazal tov," May this child's official naming ceremony and prayers on her behalf be a good omen and a sign of good luck. The worshippers clap their hands as they sing, and great joy is shared by all present. There is a feeling of family, even on the part of those who do not know the young couple. They are Jews, and the Jewish People is being augmented by the addition of a new life, the promise of another individual to carry forward the Covenant of Israel. . . .

Take a minute to think about the prayer the rabbi uttered for the baby. The first prayer was for the opportunity for Torah study. As if in a fast-forward mode, notice the child getting a bit older, and beginning the study of Judaism. Watch her as she continues to learn and study Torah each year more deeply and more intensely. . . .

Think about the growth of this young child in the ways of Israel. Watch her as she reaches the age of mitzvot (becoming a bat mitzvah), performs Jewish rituals and ethical laws, serves the community, and brings help to those in need. . . . Finally, project yourself ahead about twenty-five years and watch her stand under the wedding canopy, with these same parents, standing at her side. Perhaps the song "Sunrise, Sunset" is playing in the background, and you are watching this little baby, now grown up and standing under the chuppah. . . .

As the parents step to the side of the bema, making room for the next aliyah, you begin to let go of this fantasy, and think about returning to this room, and opening your eyes. When you are ready, bring yourself back to the present moment, shake your limbs and your body, and return to normal consciousness. . . .◯

CELEBRATION OF BECOMING A BAR/BAT MITZVAH

◯ *Let your breathing become slow and relaxed, and find yourself feeling totally clear and conscious, sinking into a deep state of tranquility. Uncross your arms and legs, and let your eyes become closed, as your body lets go of any tension. You feel very calm and serene. . . .*

Imagine that you are the parents of a young woman who is about to reach her thirteenth birthday, and will soon celebrate her becoming a bat mitzvah. What concerns do you have? . . . What feelings of joy and accomplishment do you find within you? . . .

You want the ceremony in the synagogue to have special and serious meaning, as well as joy and celebration. It is a rite of passage which marks your daughter's entry into adolescence, the step before full adult responsibility. It is time that you communicate to your daughter some important messages about human and Jewish values which are particularly important to you. Take a few minutes to talk with your daughter about life, and about the values you want her to live by. . . . (Pause).

If you have not included some words about what it means to become a Jewish woman, you may choose to add these words now. (Pause).

Tell your daughter about the obligations which Judaism teaches regarding caring for others, and about responsible and ethical personal behavior. Include in your conversation, if you wish, some things about your daughter's sexual growth, and her relationships with males and females her age, as well as about respect for people in authority, such as teachers and parents. . . .

Since your daughter wants to write a D'var Torah to deliver on the bema at her Bat Mitzvah celebration, talk with her about some of the ideas she might want to convey in this speech. Realizing that the D'var Torah should be hers, you just want to give her some very broad suggestions. . . .

Since your daughter will be receiving a considerable amount of gifts, including money, discuss with her the possibility of contributing some of her gifts to tzedakah. If she agrees, ask her to think of some charities which are personally meaningful and important to her. . . . Also discuss with her some possible ways for her to give extra time to community service in the months prior to, and perhaps after, her bat mitzvah celebration. . . . (Pause).

Now talk with your daughter about the kind of party she wants to have. Will it be a Shabbat kiddush luncheon in the synagogue? Will the entire congregation be invited? Will it be a lavish evening party with fancy clothing, a band and elaborate food? Discuss with her the connection between the meaning of the ceremony in the morning and the level of extravagance at the party. What conclusions do you reach in your dialog? . . . (Pause).

If there are any other issues you would like to discuss with your daughter about the bat mitzvah ceremony and its meaning or significance, do it now. (Pause).

When you have completed your conversation, you may affirm your daughter with words, and with a hug or kiss, thanking her for sharing her thoughts and feelings in an honest, forthright, and open way. Tell her how proud you are of her, and how she has grown into a beautiful young woman. . . . Watch how she responds. . . .

When you are ready, come back to this room, and slowly open your eyes. . . . ○

PRE-MARITAL INTERVIEW

A rabbi, counselor or facilitator in a pre-marital interview or marriage education workshop can use this guided imagery exercise. Both partners in a relationship can experience this imagery together, and share their reactions with each other, allowing the rabbi or counselor to assist them. (This exercise is based on a teaching of the Baal Shem Tov, eighteenth century founder of the Hasidic Movement in Eastern Europe).

○ Sit comfortably and find yourself becoming very calm and relaxed. Take a few breaths and let all the tension flow out of your body. Let your eyes close and take a few more very deep breaths.

Following our Hasidic tradition, notice that a light emanates from the top of your head, as it does from every human being. This pure, white light reaches all the way to heaven. Notice how this light binds you to God and to the highest spiritual ideals of our tradition. . . .

Paying attention to the light that flows from your head upwards, notice now that your two lights meet somewhere very high in space. This happens whenever two people who are destined to be together find each other. The streams of your two lights now join together to make a very powerful united stream of bright, pure light, rising all the way to heaven. It travels back and forth from your bodies to heaven, and from heaven back to you. . . . Notice how this divine light brings warmth and love to each of you, and to both of you as a couple. (Pause).

Watching the very bright stream of light that emanates from the two of you, see how it illuminates the environment around you. Wherever the two of you go that light shines on the space around you and brings wholeness and healing, joy and enlightenment. . . .

The light that will be created by your two lights joining together enables you to bring light to many others: to the Jewish community and to all humanity. Notice how your relationship brings extra light into the world. (Pause).

Pay attention to how your marriage (relationship) adds to our world, and how that makes you feel. What do you feel inside when you think about this? (Pause).

When you are ready, gradually come back to this room, and open your eyes. ○

The rabbi or facilitator can "process" this experience with the couple, and have them deepen their relationship through their sharing and dialoging about what they experienced in the guided imagery exercise. The counselor can tell them that they can repeat this imagery exercise on their own as often as they like, to help solidify their relationship, and bring a renewed and strengthened spiritual dimension to their lives whenever they wish.

MARCHING DOWN THE AISLE

○ *Find a comfortable position, and begin to let go of your tension by breathing out any tightness and anxiety inside of you. Find yourself becoming more and more deeply relaxed with each breath. After a few minutes you are very deeply relaxed and calm. . . .*

Imagine that you are a father or mother standing at the Sanctuary door, just before the wedding of your son or daughter. . . . The families of the bride and groom are all dressed and ready, the wedding party is lining up to begin the processional. . . . After all the others have entered the Sanctuary, you take your child's arm and walk through the doors. What thoughts and feelings are going through your mind and heart? (Pause).

You begin to walk down the aisle with your son (or daughter). . . . Both bride and groom are wearing white as signs of purity. The bride is in her traditional white bridal gown, and the groom is dressed in the traditional white kittel, draped with a tallit around his shoulders. . . . Perhaps the tallit is a family heirloom, passed down from the groom's grandfather, or even great-grandfather. . . . The bride and groom want to enter their new covenantal relationship with a new beginning, clear and clean as the white snow, putting behind them all other previous relationships and commitments, joining their lives and destinies. . . . The white they don is a symbol of their unsullied intentions. . . .

The parents of the groom begin to march with him down the aisle, and when they reach the bema, they take their places at the side, as the groom faces the rabbi and the holy ark.

On the bema stands a lovely chuppah, marital canopy, covered with beautiful flowers of many soft colors. All Jewish brides and grooms are married under the chuppah, symbolizing the Jewish home they are about to build together. As the groom stands facing the rabbi, he hears the music from the biblical Song of Songs, which means that his bride has arrived at the Sanctuary door, ready to enter. He turns and faces her. The harp plays the music to these words: "I am for my beloved and he is for me. . . ." Everyone looks as the groom faces the door and sees his bride. The parents of the groom enjoy looking into their son's eyes. What do you see in the face of the groom? (Pause).

Now the bride's parents escort her down the aisle. They walk slowly, gracefully, as the congregation sits quietly and solemnly, feeling privileged to share this holy moment with a couple who will in a minute be joined in a permanent, sacred relationship. . . . Many of the people in the congregation remember their own wedding ceremonies, and some tears begin to flow. . . . People who watched the bride or the groom grow up are now thinking about how a young child has blossomed into a mature adult, ready to begin his/her own family. . . .

When the bride reaches midway down the aisle, the parents gently lift their daughter's veil, give her a kiss, and move on to take their place under the chuppah. What are some of the things going on inside the heart of the bride's parents? (Pause).

The groom then steps down to the aisle, and marches toward the bride. When he reaches her, they look into each other's eyes for a moment. Then the two of them walk together the last few steps toward the chuppah. They stand beneath the chuppah, the symbol of their new Jewish home, together, as one person, in love and loyalty, in unity and devotion.

They now face the rabbi and the holy ark, and are prepared to exchange rings, listen to the prayers and message of the rabbi and the chanting of the hazzan. The ceremony is about to begin. Everyone in the room is filled with a sense of awe and holiness. . . . The cameras have stopped flashing, the harp has stopped its soft music. . . . An ancient ceremony is about to begin, which will change the lives of everyone present. . . .

We will close our fantasy now, as the bride and groom complete their commitment and become husband and wife. When you are ready, come back to this room, and slowly, open your eyes. . . . ○

ACCEPTING DEATH

The facilitator should use careful judgment in doing a guided imagery exercise about death and the funeral ceremony. In most cases there will be no problem. To avoid potential emotional difficulties, the leader should try to be aware of anyone who may not be ready to participate in such an exercise, such as one who has a fresh wound from a recent loss. The leader should also inform the group in advance that the next activity will be a guided imagery exercise about death and dying, and about a funeral, and that whoever does not wish to participate may step outside for a while. Of course no negative judgment should be attached to the person's absence.

On the other hand, in order to give reassurance to those who remain and participate, the facilitator should announce that the exercise will avoid any morbid depiction of death, and is designed to help participants understand and accept death as part of life. It may also give comfort to those who have suffered losses in their life, and to those who have experienced concern or worry about the loss of a loved one.

○ Become relaxed, sit or lie comfortably, and let us begin to enter an imagery exercise that will help us understand the process of life from beginning to end. . . . Breathe deeply and slowly. . . . When you breathe freely and fully, filling your lungs when you inhale, and emptying your lungs when you exhale, you will help yourself avoid fear and anxiety, and encourage feelings of confidence and security. . . .

Imagine a funeral service for an elderly person whom you do not know. This person has had a full and rich life, surrounded by loved ones, and has achieved many worthwhile things. Before the funeral service begins, people are sitting in the sanctuary and you hear them whispering to one another: He had a good life, and a long life—we should all be so blessed! His death came quickly, and he did not suffer. Others say: I hope that when my time comes, it's just like that. . . .

We shall not imagine an entire funeral service, but only the beginning. At funeral services the rabbi will choose selections to read from the biblical psalms, some traditional prayers, and sometimes words from modern writers that bring comfort to the mourners.

All is very quiet now as the rabbi steps up to the podium, and begins to read a few selections from ancient Jewish literature, all of which bring comfort to the mourners present. Then he reads the following selection, an adaptation of an article that Rabbi Morris Adler of Detroit wrote just three weeks before his own death in 1964:

Shall I cry out in anger, O God, because your gifts are mine but for a while?

Shall I forget the blessing of health the moment it gives way to illness and pain?

Shall I be ungrateful for the moments of laughter, the seasons of joy, the days of gladness and festivity?

When tears cloud my eyes and darken the world and my heart is heavy within me, shall I blot from my mind the love I have known and in which I have rejoiced?

When a fate beyond my understanding takes from me friends and kin whom I have cherished, and leaves me bereft of shining presences that have lit my way through years of companionship and affection, shall I be ungrateful for their support when it was there?

Shall I grieve for a youth that has gone once my hair is gray and my shoulders bent, and forget days of vibrancy and power?

Shall I in days of adversity fail to recall the hours of joy and glory You once granted me?

Shall I in turmoil of need and anxiety cease blessing You for the peace of former days?

Shall the time of darkness put out forever the glow of the light in which I once walked?

Give me the vision, O God, to see and feel that imbedded deep in each of Your gifts is a core of eternity, undiminished and bright, an eternity that survives the dread hours of affliction and misery.

The youth that once was mine continues to course in memory and thought and remains unspent even in age. . . .

Those I have loved, though now beyond my view, have given form and quality to my being, and they live on, unfailingly feeding my heart and mind and imagination.

They have led me into the wide universe I continue to inhabit, and their presence is more vital to me than their absence.

What You give, O Lord, You take not away, and bounties once granted shed their radiance evermore.

Within me your love and vision now woven deep into the texture of my life live and will be mine, till You call me hence to another realm, where these moments of eternity shall be joined together in unbroken sequence to form eternal life.

Sit quietly for a moment and think about the words of Rabbi Adler. . . . What does he think about death, and about life? . . . (Pause). What message is he attempting to convey to those gathered at this funeral? (Pause). Do you agree with what he wrote? . . . In what way does this prayer, and other parts of the funeral service, serve the process of healing for a person in mourning? . . .

In a moment, when you are ready, come back to this room so we can discuss your feelings about this experience. . . . Take your time, and gradually and slowly open your eyes, and sit quietly for a moment. . . . ○

Chapter 14

THE JEWISH FAMILY – Backbone Of Jewish Life

Let not your eyes envision beauty;
let them envision rather the family!
—Talmud Yerushalmi, Taanit 4,7

W E HAVE already stressed the importance of the Jewish family in several previous chapters—on Shabbat, the Jewish Festivals, and the Life Cycle. However, given the overwhelming significance of the Jewish Family in the process of transmitting Jewish values, assuring Jewish continuity, and strengthening what Virginia Satir calls "Peoplemaking"—the growth of healthy, mature and spiritually developed children for a whole society, it is helpful to look at the Jewish family in the normal context of its daily and weekly activities, aside from the special events of holidays and peak experiences.

Thus, we shall turn, through a few guided imagery exercises, to other ways in which the Jewish family plays a crucial role in Jewish life.

VISITING THE "IDEAL JEWISH HOME"

❍ *Begin to think of the word "relax" on the movie screen in your mind. Let the word disappear, and then imagine that you are outdoors staring at the sky. See some white clouds and stare at them. Pay close attention to every detail of the beautiful, large white clouds, until you find yourself mesmerized by them. Soon you will feel very deeply relaxed and comfortable. . . .*

Since you were a little child your parents have told you about your cousins in Montreal whom you have never met. Your family described this family to you as an "ideal Jewish family." You never quite understood completely what an "ideal Jewish family" was, but you have always wanted to visit them and spend time with them.

During winter break this year your family decided to drive (or fly) to Quebec Province in Canada to visit your cousins, the Abramsons, in suburban Montreal. For weeks before the trip your excitement builds, and finally the day arrives. You drive to their home, and are welcomed with smothering hugs and kisses. After an hour or so of introductory conversation, you are invited to take a tour of the house. The Abramsons take in their stride the many tangible expressions of their commitment to Judaism and Jewish life. As you go from room to room, you are amazed at how many ways the Abramson family has made their home a place where being Jewish is felt at every turn. . . .

Before leaving the family room, you look around and see some things hanging on the wall, and sitting on the mantle. What are they? . . .

You now pass through the dining room, and you peer inside the large, beautiful hutch with glass doors, and see some fascinating Jewish objects. What do you see? . . .

Entering the kitchen, you notice a mezuzah on the doorpost, as in every other room. Inside the kitchen are many large cabinets. The Abramsons open the doors of the cabinets, and you look with careful eyes to see what's inside. Then you look around on the walls, the shelves, the table, the sink, the appliances, and it is easy to see what makes their kitchen very Jewish. . . .

Sam and Adele Abramson, the parents of the family, take you next into their study on the first floor. You marvel at how large the room is, and immediately let your eyes focus on the two large desks, one for Adele and one for Sam. Notice the picture frames, and other objects on the desk. Notice the large number of books covering the walls from floor to ceiling. Some of the books you recognize, and some you don't. Notice the titles of some of the books. . . . What else do you see in the study? . . .

Then you are led into the living room. There is a distinctly Jewish flavor to this room. Look all over the room, and notice carefully how the room is filled with signs of the Abramsons' commitment to Judaism. . . . Take a moment to gaze around the room and notice every detail. . . .

The Abramsons now want to take you upstairs. Their spacious home has many bedrooms, since they have six children, and each child has his/her own room. Before entering any of the bedrooms you notice the hallways and the pictures hanging there. What do you see? . . .

You then go from room to room, and see how each child has a room that is different, in decoration, in furniture, and in other ways. Each room expresses the personality of its resident. What do you see in the rooms as you go from room to room? . . . (Pause).

After the tour, you unpack your suitcases for your three-day stay, and rest up after your long trip. When you come down to dinner, you sit around the large dining room table, and talk about many things. First you catch up on the news of other family members. . . . Then you talk about your own lives, what each person does in their vocation and avocation . . .what hobbies and interests each person is involved in . . . what friends each has made . . . where you travel on vacation . . . what exciting things in your lives are happening soon. . . . From this long dinner conversation you discover many interesting things about why your family has always thought of the Abramsons as an "ideal Jewish family." What are some of them? (Pause).

Over the next few days spending time with the Abramsons, you notice many other interesting things about their family—the way they talk to and treat each other, the newspapers that come to the house, the telephone conversations you cannot help but overhear while you are there, the hospitality they show you, the people who visit them, the places they take you to, the kind of meals they serve, the rituals they perform, the prayers they recite, the way they observe Shabbat, and so many other daily details that help give you a complete picture of this "ideal Jewish family."

Think about all the things you learned concerning the Abramsons and their Jewish feelings and commitments. . . . (Pause). What makes them worthy of being called an "ideal Jewish family"? . . . (Pause). In what ways would you like your family to be like the Abramsons? . . . (Pause).

When you are ready, return to this room, and at the count of three open your eyes and be fully present. . . . One, two, three. ○

HANUKKAH GIFTS

○ *Let yourself become very relaxed. Take a few deep breaths, and watch how all your worries and anxieties melt away. . . . Let your eyes close and become more and more deeply relaxed. . . .*

It is the Festival of Hanukkah, which has become an important time for family gatherings and gift-giving in America. On the first night of Hanukkah you have invited several close relatives to celebrate with you. You are all seated in the dining room, finishing dinner, wiping clean the large serving plate of delicious latkes and cinnamon-covered apple sauce.

The children go into the other room to play dreidel and other games, enjoying each other's company. The parents linger a while at the table, and chat together about family, about past Hanukkahs and other holiday celebrations. . . . What are some of the memories that are being spoken about? (Pause).

There is a very warm feeling in the room. Look around and see what relatives have come to be with you this Hanukkah. . . . Think about the important role each of these people plays in your life. (Pause).

In the forest of your memory, review some of the times, both long ago and more recently, when your family was there for you when you needed them. What did it feel like? . . .

It is time to light the Hanukkiah, recite the b'rachot, sing the songs, such as "Mee Ye-malel," "Sevivon," "Maoz Tzur," and others. Your family loves to sing, and everyone joins in to make this a very special time together. . . .

Now it is time to exchange gifts. This year your family decided to give specifically Jewish gifts—gifts that would help you deepen your Jewish lives. Things which fit each person's special interests in Judaism. For one relative it may be a new book that was just published on Jewish history. For another it might be a necklace with a "chai" symbol hanging from it. For another perhaps a new hand-woven tallit from Israel. For some of the younger family members it might be a ticket to visit their grandparents next summer for a long stay.

Begin now to exchange gifts. Open some of the gifts you received, and see what your relatives thought would be a special gift which would enrich your Jewish life. (Pause).

Now watch as the other members of your family open the gifts which you bought them. Watch each one of them as they open your gift, and appreciate what thought and preparation went into your buying a gift that would be meaningful and special for them, and would help them live fuller Jewish lives. . . . (Pause).

When all the gifts have been opened, and the family is feeling very good about each other, notice what things are said, such as when they will get together again, how much they enjoyed this Hanukkah celebration, and anything else anyone might express. (Pause).

Think about the evening, and what good fortune you have to know special people like the ones who were together with you tonight celebrating the Festival of Lights. . . .

When you are ready, return to this room, and gradually open your eyes. . . .○

FIFTIETH WEDDING ANNIVERSARY

❍ *Go inside yourself and find the place where there is peace and harmony. . . . Stay there for a while, and enjoy the feeling you have. . . . Some soft and gentle feelings wash over you, and you feel even better and more calm . . . Find yourself very relaxed and at ease. . . .*

Some cousins of yours are celebrating their fiftieth wedding anniversary, and you and your family attend. After a beautiful dinner and a wonderful hour of Israeli and Yiddish folk singing and dancing, the daughter of the celebrating couple stands at the microphone and asks everyone to be seated for a while. She announces that several people in the family will pay tributes to the elderly couple in honor of this special silver wedding anniversary.

First, some close friends come forward and speak about their friendship with the couple that goes back to elementary school and Cheder (afternoon Hebrew School) in the Bronx. They tell some interesting and some humorous tales, and everyone enjoys listening. What are some of the things you hear them say? . . .

Next comes another cousin, a bit younger, who was at their wedding, as a very young child, but remembers only parts of their wedding ceremony, and relates the memories he has. Everyone tries to picture the couple standing under the chuppah and being married, what the rabbi said to them, and the wonderful celebration that followed. . . .

After that each of the couple's three children gets up to speak, and relates memories of growing up, the kind things their parents did for them, what wonderful, nurturing and loving parents they were during those crucial grow- ing-up years. . . . What kinds of things are they saying? . . .

Some other relatives then go up to the microphone, one after another, and tell special memories and stories which characterize what kind of warm and caring people this couple has been throughout their lives. Listen to what they are saying. . . . (Pause).

Next, a representative of a Jewish organization stands up and speaks about the important work this couple has done, each in his/her own way, for this organization. How they helped raise funds, and volunteered their time, and brought great service and assistance to the organization. . . . What are some of the things this person says? . . .

Last, the rabbi of their synagogue, now rabbi emeritus, who has known them for almost the entire fifty years of their marriage, gets up to speak about the kind of menschen this couple has been in their relations with the schul, with their friends, with the community, and what a model of Jewish commitment and loyalty they have been. He tells of traveling together with them to Israel several times, and some of the experiences they had together in Jerusalem and other places. . . . He concludes by repeating the marriage ceremony, and asking them to recommit their marriage vows to one another. . . . (Pause).

Finally, the celebrating couple each gets up to tell some favorite family stories, to thank their large and loving family for coming and celebrating with them, and for sharing such wonderful stories with them. They express their gratitude to their children who made the party, to their loving grandchildren, to the rabbi, and to all their dear family and friends who helped make this unforgettable evening so special. What were some of things they said which made a special impression on you? (Pause).

When you are ready, take your time, say goodbye to this couple in your own way inside yourself, and let go of this imagery experience. . . . Open your eyes and return to this room. ○

SHABBAT FAMILY BLESSINGS

○ Let yourself sink into your chair, or the floor beneath you, and stop supporting yourself. . . . Feel yourself sinking deeper and deeper, until you find that you are totally relaxed and calm. . . . Withdraw your mind from your surroundings, and be a peace with yourself. . . . The relaxation you feel spreads all over your body, and you feel very secure and calm. . . .

Every Friday night in the Shapiro family home Shabbat is observed with all the beautiful customs and rituals. All the prayers are said over the Shabbat candles, over the wine in the shiny silver kiddush cup, over the golden braided challot, and Shalom Aleichem is sung. The other ritual performed at the Friday night table is the family's blessing each other.

Each person in the family has a chance to bless everyone else. The father begins with a song of praise to his wife, taken from the thirty-first chapter of the biblical book of Proverbs. Some men chant it in the original Hebrew. Others read it from the Tanakh, and others read a modernized excerpt. This poem is called "Ayshet Chayil," Woman of Valor.

Listen as Bill Shapiro reads the Ayshet Chayil poem to his wife, Doris. "A good wife is a special treasure! Her worth is far above precious jewels. . . . Her husband trusts in her, and he lacks nothing. . . . She gives generously to the needy, she is clothed with dignity and splendor. . . . Her mouth is filled with wisdom, and her tongue with teachings of kindness. . . . Her husband and children praise her by saying 'Many women have done well, but you excel them all.' Grace is deceiving and beauty is vain, but a good woman fears Adonai. . . . Let her works be her praise. . . ."

Watch as Bill and Doris share this tender moment of sharing their affection and respect for each other. . . .

Next, the wife responds with a prayer of her own. Since tradition did not prescribe a specific prayer, there are many different customs that have developed. Some women read selections from the Book of Psalms, and others read a modern poem, or write their own song of praise for their husband.

Listen as Doris Shapiro reads a prayer of praise and affection to her husband, Bill. What kinds of things do you hear her saying? . . .

Next the parents join in blessing their daughters, Joan and Beverly. The parents rise from their seats, stand behind the girls, and place their hands on their heads. Then they say together: "May God bless you as the Matriarchs of Israel, Sarah, Rebecca, Rachel and Leah. May Adonai bless you and keep you. May God's face shine upon you kindly. May God always be with you throughout your life and give you shalom." They then kiss the girls, and continue their blessing by saying some nice things to them. They tell them how much they appreciate the things they did this past week in school, at home, and in the neighborhood. . . . The girls enjoy their parents' blessings, and look forward to it each week. It is a special time in their life which will stay with them forever. . . .

The final blessing is one in which the entire family joins. They say together: "May the Almighty bless this family with the special blessings of love and devotion, with a home filled with peace and harmony, always open to guests and friends. May our family show affection to each other, and celebrate happy times such as this beautiful Shabbat dinner. Amen!"

What thoughts and feelings might be going through the hearts of different members of the family during these blessings? (Pause).

Take a mental snapshot of this family at the Shabbat evening table, celebrating together with all the traditional prayers and rituals, taking time to talk and share what happened during the week, the low points and the high points. . . .

When the meal is completed several hours later, and all the final songs and Birkat HaMazon have been chanted, it is time to go to bed. Everyone in the family has a special feeling of warmth and satisfaction deep within their heart. ○

Chapter 15

TRANSMITTING JEWISH VALUES

If you have built castles in the air, your work need not be lost; that is where they should be. Now put foundations under them.
—Henry David Thoreau

We can make the dream more important than the night.
—Yiddish Proverb

MUCH INK has been spilled about transmitting Jewish values. This is a sign that no one knows exactly how it is done most effectively. Jewish religious and educational leadership is very creative in trying many new and innovative techniques and programs, and yet rampant assimilation continues to spread its dangerous virus.

Having said that we have not been as successful as we would like, it is also true that there are large pockets of success in many quarters. The best we can do at the present time is to capitalize on our successes, try to replicate them, and continue experimentation.

In the guided imagery exercise below we utilize some success stories about a variety of people who have been "turned on" to Jewish life for one reason or another. These personal stories and testimonies come mainly from a series of well-executed advertisements placed over the last few years in the New York Times by the American Jewish Committee. The particular selections quoted were made by Rabbi Richard Plavin, and the chronological sequence of the quotes is a fictionalized creation by the author of this book. (With apologies to the authors for any unintended distortions). This exercise is somewhat longer than others in the book, and sufficient time should thus be allocated for its use.

JEWISH VALUES

◯ *Take some time for yourself now by sitting or lying down and becoming as relaxed as you possibly can. . . . Scan your body and see if there are any parts that are tense or tight, and if so, let the tightness go. Let yourself be very comfortable and serene, allowing your breath to bring you life-giving oxygen, and exhale any impurities inside you. . . . See how good you feel now. . . .*

In this guided imagery exercise you will hear voices of different people, speaking about what their Jewish identity means to them. It is best if you try to listen as intently as possible to each voice, trying to picture the person speaking, watch them in your mind's eye, and identify with them as far as you can. . . . Consider perhaps that there is a stage in front of you. The chairperson comes forward and announces that the theme of today's program is: "What Values Are Important To You In Shaping Your Jewish Identity?"
Each of the respondents comes forward to the front of the stage to say a few words, articulating his or her reply, and then walks off so that the next person can take his/her place. . . .

The first voice is that of the famous novelist and Nobel Peace Laureate, Elie Wiesel. Try to picture Elie Wiesel talking directly to you as you listen to him. He talks about the importance of the ethics of the biblical prophets:

"To be Jewish today is to recognize that every person is created in the image of God and that our purpose in living is to be a reminder of God. . . . A Jew must be sensitive to the pain of all human beings. A Jew cannot remain indifferent to human suffering, whether in the former Yugoslavia, in Somalia or in our own cities and towns. The mission of the Jewish people has never been to make the world more Jewish, but to make it more human."

What thoughts and feelings go through your heart and soul as you hear these words? (Pause).

A similar voice, also stressing the importance of Jewish ethics, comes from Connecticut's Senator Joseph Lieberman, an observant and dedicated Jew and a credit to the Jewish People as well as to America. He now stands up on our imaginary platform. Listen to his words:

"To me, being Jewish means having help in answering life's most funda-mental questions, such as 'How did I come to this place?' and 'Now that I am here, how should I live?' My faith, which has anchored my life, begins with a joyful gratitude that there is a God who created the universe and then, because He continued to care for what He created, gave us laws and values to order and improve our lives. God also gave us a purpose and a destiny—to do justice, and

to protect, indeed to perfect, the human community and natural environment."

On the same theme of Jewish values are lesser known people whose words are no less eloquent or important. First are those of David Finn, the CEO of a prominent public relations firm in New York City. Feeling somewhat guilty about his father's having changed his name from Finkelstein to Finn, David tried to compensate by placing Jewish values as the highest priority in his life. Here are his words:

"When weighing the moral consequences of business decisions . . . the Ethics Committee of our public relations firm seeks knowledgeable counsel to guide our thinking. I will always remember how some years ago a professor at the [Jewish Theological] Seminary helped us make the decision to resign the sizable Greek tourism account after three colonels seized power and installed a military dictatorship."

The next voice we hear on Jewish ethics is from Rosalyn Yalow, a Nobel Laureate in the field of physiology. Here are her words:

"As a Jew, I share a strong commitment to the Jewish intellectual tradition. That tradition places emphasis on learning—learning for the sake of under-standing and perfecting our world, and learning for its own sake. . . . In a world which is too often concerned with instant pleasures and self-gratification, Jews have long believed in the importance of scholarship and disciplined learning."

Sit for a moment, and think about the words you just heard. . . . How do they apply to you and your own life? . . . What things can you do to instill these same values into your own life in a more deep and intense way? (Pause).

We turn now to a different set of speakers who focus on a second Jewish value, that of Jewish study and learning. The first of these is Morris Smith, the former manager of the Fidelity Magellan Fund, who left his firm some years ago, along with his enviable position and salary, to study for a year in Israel. His talk on Jewish values emphasizes traditional Torah study:

"The practice of Judaism and the study of our religious tradition have provided me with the guidance I need in conducting my personal and profes-sional life. Our Torah, given to the Jewish people as a sacred trust more than three millennia ago, has preserved and protected us throughout our wanderings and persecution and will always remain the foundation of our people in the future."

Anne Roiphe, the famous novelist, concurs with the previous speaker, and gives her own perspective on Jewish learning:

"I was ankle-deep in middle age, wading down the waters of assimilation when I discovered being Jewish was more than I had ever dreamed. . . . I've learned the whole story. I learned where Chelm, the town of fools, lies on the map. I can tell you wild tales about Jewish gangsters in Chicago and Jewish soldiers in the Czar's army. I expanded my family. Freud and Einstein are cousins of mine, so are Rashi and Maimonides. Once I knew only about Jewish catastrophe, now I can tell a Jewish joke (not so well) and I have seen Torah pointers, cups for Elijah and menorahs made of clay. . . . Today I frequently argue with a God whose existence I question, but I think that the Jewish people has a purpose, a destiny, a reason for being. . . . I have a past, present and future among my people. Am I ever surprised!"

Sit comfortably and relax, as you ponder the words of Morris Smith and Anne Roiphe. . . . Think about how you too can enrich your own existence by turning to the sacred books of Jewish learning to enhance your knowledge and your perspective on life. . . . What special message can you take away from these two speakers? (Pause).

After hearing all about Jewish ethics and the Jewish intellectual tradition, some of our respondents wish to talk about another Jewish value. The chairperson turns to the group and asks them: Who would like to share your thoughts about the importance of the State of Israel in your Jewish value system? Several of the same speakers come forward, as well as a new speaker. We will introduce them as they come up to the platform. . . .

Anne Roiphe steps up again, and says:

"I have seen tomatoes growing in the Negev and can imagine the Baal Shem Tov dancing in the forest. I am no longer the child who asks what has this to do with me. I was proud at Entebbe, my heart skipped beats when the Scuds flew over Tel Aviv. When Russian Jews and Ethiopian Jews arrive at Ben-Gurion Airport, I feel like a child at a birthday party. The survival of Israel, its difficult, quarrelsome, glorious bark, soothes me."

It is difficult to hear words so eloquently and passionately spoken, and then listen to the next respondent without a brief minute to catch your breath. Sit and let Ann Roiphe's words roll around inside you for a bit, and then sit back and listen to some other testimony. (Pause).

At this point, three of the participants jump up to the microphone together, insisting that they be able to share their own strong feelings about Israel.

Elie Wiesel speaks about rejoicing "in the renascence of Jewish sovereignty in Israel." David Finn adds his feelings about "the electric sense of homecoming I feel on visits to Israel as I look out the airplane window and catch my first glimpse of the biblical landscape below."

If you have also witnessed that biblical landscape, as David Finn describes, you will resonate with his strong feelings, and know what a thrill it is, no matter how many times you repeat the experience.

After Wiesel and Finn take their seats, a younger participant takes her turn. She is Jodi Padnick, and has recently graduated from Georgetown University. She speaks:

"This past summer I made my first trip to Israel. Some images linger: The family I met in a synagogue in Eilat that welcomed me warmly and lovingly into their home for the Sabbath meal. . . . Lake Kinneret at sunset, proof of the beauty of Israel and the Jewish people's bond to it. . . . A concert violinist on a Jerusalem street corner, recently arrived from Russia and playing for small change, sure that things would improve."

Think about the words of Anne Roiphe, Elie Wiesel, David Finn, and Jodi Padnick, and the powerful magnet that Israel has become in their lives. Has it yet become that for you? In what ways? How do you react when you think about Israel reborn? Take some time to think about your connection to Israel in its struggle for survival, freedom, justice, and renewing the Jewish spirit. (Pause).

The last Jewish value which our panel of speakers addresses is the importance that ritual has in their lives. First, Senator Joe Lieberman returns to the podium:

"I am helped by daily prayer and religious rituals such as observance of the Sabbath—a time to stop and appreciate all that God has given us. I also find strength and humility in being linked to something so much larger and longer-lasting than myself."

Another voice is now heard from, that of Dr. Barbara J. Wachs, a family and adolescent consultant at the Auerbach Central Agency for Jewish Education in Philadelphia. Dr. Wachs steps up and says:

"Sociologists and anthropologists have long known that rituals function as powerful tools to define family roles and to pass on the values of the family and group. The rituals also build group cohesiveness and mark important life-cycle events and transitions. Rituals also provide the mechanisms for expression of emotions, such as love and joy as well as grief and sorrow. In addition, rituals provide a sense of stability for families and groups. Their regularity provides an anchor and a sense of order in times of stress and change. . . . [Educators recog-

nize that rituals] not only help define us in our families, but also link us verti-
cally to our people in the past, as well as horizontally to our peers in the present.
As such, they represent powerful educational tools."

Pause for a moment, and think about the role of rituals in your own life.
What role do they play? How can we strengthen the power that rituals exert
over our lives, which Barbara Wachs speaks about so authoritatively? . . .
What Jewish rituals might you like to add to your life? (Pause).

We have been enriched by the thoughts and ideas of some intelligent,
sensitive and well-spoken individuals: Elie Wiesel, Senator Joe Lieberman,
David Finn, Rosalyn Yalow, Morris Smith, Anne Roiphe, Jodi Padnick, and
Dr. Barbara Wachs. They spoke about their commitments to Jewish ethics, Jewish
study, the centrality of the State of Israel in our lives, and the importance of
rituals in endowing our lives with the glue, the poetry, and the structure, which
help us endure in a shaky and confused world.

Let their words stay with you as we complete our symposium, and return to
our normal wakeful state. . . . ○

Chapter 16

THE UNITY OF THE JEWISH PEOPLE

A great people cannot live without an ideal.
—Max Nordau, Zionist Congress, 1915

Imagination is the beginning of creation.
You imagine what you desire; you will what you
imagine; and at last you create what you will.
—George Bernard Shaw

A POPULAR talmudic saying tells us that "Every Jew is bound to every other Jew," *Kol Yisrael Arevim Ze La-Ze.* Golda Meir once told an American audience, "We are all one family." B'nai B'rith, the international order of Jews which has been an important part of Jewish life for a century, means "Children of the Covenant." All Jews are tied by our Covenant to God made at Mount Sinai. The Torah states clearly that all Jews, including those who were present then and Jews to be born in any future generation, are all considered to have been present at Mount Sinai when the Covenant was established between the People of Israel and God.

The theme of the United Jewish Appeal some time ago was "We are one." This theme rings true, since Jews feel connected and responsible for one another in a multitude of ways. It is one of the privileges, joys, as well as responsibilities of being a Jew.

The exercises in this chapter will focus on the theme of the unity and solidarity of the Jewish People.

YOUR JEWISH FAMILY ACROSS THE GLOBE

❍ *Find a comfortable place to sit or lie, and stretch your limbs, wiggle*
around a bit, until you feel completely at ease. Take a big yawn, and find your
eyes drooping from fatigue. Remain mentally alert and yet physically relaxed and
comfortable, as you become more and more deeply relaxed. . . .

Imagine yourself taking a trip through Europe. Traveling can be a very broadening and enriching experience, as you see new places, meet new people, and do new things. Naturally, among the places you would like to visit are some Jewish sites, such as synagogues, museums, kosher restaurants, the Jewish Quarter (neighborhood) of various cities, etc.

After traveling through England and France, you come to the city of Geneva, Switzerland. It is a most beautiful part of the world, and you enjoy the restaurants, the culture, and other tourist sites. The added dimension of being far away adds to your excitement. Seeing many old buildings, you feel as if you have been transported to the Middle Ages. It is as if you have traveled not only in space but also in time. . . .

It is Shabbat morning, and you decide to visit the prominent synagogue in Geneva, to see what religious services there are like, and how they compare to the ones with which you are accustomed at home. You enter a large, stately, medieval building, go through some corridors, up some stairs, and into the Sanctuary.

It looks a bit strange, and you feel somewhat out of place. The people are dressed differently, more formally. Sitting in one of the back rows, you feel very far from the bema. There is no microphone and you have difficulty hearing. The women are sitting upstairs, and the men are absorbed in their prayers on the main floor. People begin to look in your direction, and you wonder if you have done something strange or wrong, to offend anyone. . . .

Soon the Torah service begins, and you begin to feel a bit more comfortable, seeing the Sefer Torah removed from the Aron Kodesh, and hearing some of the same melodies used as the ones you enjoy back home. . . . After some preliminary prayers, the first aliyah is called. After the Torah is read for the first aliyah, an official-looking worshipper walks over to you and asks if you would like to tie and dress the Torah. You are surprised! See what other feelings you now have. . . .

When the aliyot are completed, the Shamash calls out "Ya-amod ha-magbee-ah, ya-amod ha-golel." The usher motions to you to ascend the bema and fulfill your role. You are now beginning to feel even more comfortable being in the synagogue. After the Torah is lifted, and the magbee-ah holds it high, showing parts of three columns to the congregation, as is traditional, he sits down on a chair at the edge of the bema, and you are handed a piece of cloth to tie the Sefer Torah. Then you receive the mantle, which you carefully place over the Torah. Next you place the silver breastplate and the yad over the spindles, slip on the polished silver finials, and stand next to the person holding the Sefer Torah while the next prayer is recited. As time goes by you are feeling more and more relaxed and comfortable. . . . Things are beginning to sound more familiar, and you are enjoying yourself. . . .

Toward the end of the service, you hear some melodies that are exactly like the ones you use at home—the ones for Ein Kelohenu and Adon Olam. . . . You are simply delighted. . . .

At the end of the service, in addition to the normal announcements in Swiss German, the Rabbi says a few words in English, inviting all foreigners and guests to the Kiddush in the social hall. You are delighted, and look forward to meeting some members of the congregation. . . .

At the kiddush, a young couple in their forties approach you, and you find out that they too come from North America. You chat in English for a while, talking about all the places you have been on this trip, and about others you are planning to visit. You even make some plans to have dinner together later in the week at a restaurant in Geneva. This makes you feel so happy. . . .

A few minutes later the gentleman who gave you the honor of g'lilah walks toward you, together with another couple, perhaps in their early sixties. In a slight accent, they speak to you in English. They welcome you to their congregation, and ask you about your travels, where you are from, and other things about yourself and your background. Then they ask you where you plan to have Shabbat lunch. You are taken aback, and after a moment, feel a sense of warmth and delight. You accept the offer, and walk back with them, about three fourths of a mile, to their home. . . .

Together you spend a few hours eating and talking, and then singing some songs which everyone knows, followed by the chanting of the traditional Birkat HaMazon (grace after meals). Though their melody is a bit different, still you relish the idea that they recite the very same prayers, with some minor alterations, in the same Hebrew language, which you and all Jews throughout the world use. It is a very special feeling. . . . Take a minute to enjoy that feeling, and see what other feelings or thoughts come to you at this time. (Pause).

At about four o'clock you bid farewell, thanking your hosts, and taking with you a card on which is printed their names, address and telephone number. You are certain that you will be in touch with them again, to thank them for their gracious hospitality, and to know that far, far away in the heart of Europe, you have friends, who share a heritage with you, and who are part of the same Covenant with God that you are. They too stood at Mount Sinai, along with you, and Moshe, and the entire Jewish People. . . . ○

A TRIP TO BEN GURION AIRPORT

❍ *Imagine that there is a small spigot near the top of your head. . . . Open the spigot and let all the noise and turmoil flow out, as your mind becomes empty of interference. As the last drops of confusion and static fall from the spigot, you feel very, very relaxed and comfortable. Let the spigot disappear, and just take a few deep, slow breaths to deepen your relaxation. . . .*

Imagine that you are in Israel on a special mission conducted by the United Jewish Appeal (UJA). As one who is concerned about the welfare of Jews throughout the world, you are involved in learning more about Jews in places like Eastern Europe, Yemen, Syria, Egypt, and the former Soviet Union. During this UJA Mission to Israel, together with other Jews from all over North America, you travel to many interesting places where new immigrants in Israel are able to adjust to their new life.

You just returned from a small restaurant on a side street in downtown Jerusalem, where new immigrants from Atlanta, Georgia, with the help of the "Jerusalem Business Development Center" have just opened a lovely gourmet eatery. While there you learned that the Jerusalem Business Development Center helps new immigrants from countries which are both free and those where Jews are, or have been, oppressed in recent years, to establish new entrepreneurial endeavors.

Another interesting stop on your bus tour is an "incubator," a building where new immigrants from Russia and other countries are given a small room, capital, equipment and professional advice to follow through to completion their own scientific inventions. You learn that Israel is doing everything in its power to assist people coming from all over the world to make a new life in the Homeland of their ancestors. Besides re-establishing themselves in a new, free, democratic country, they are beginning to contribute to the technological development of Israel and providing new technological advances in world science.

After a long day of touring and visiting UJA-supported facilities and agencies, you finish a late dinner, and chat for a few minutes with your companions. The group leader tells you that there is a possibility that you may be awakened during one of the next few nights to witness a very unusual experience. The UJA leaders are not certain when, but want to forewarn the group so that if they are awakened by a phone call in the very early hours of the morning, they will not be frightened. You say goodnight, and everyone looks forward to a good night's sleep after a long and exhausting, though exhilarating day.

As luck would have it, you receive your telephone call at 4 a.m., in the midst of a deep sleep. "Hello," says the voice on the other end, "this is Yosef, your tour guide from UJA. We are getting up now to take a bus ride to somewhere very interesting. I apologize for awakening you, but I think you will thank me after we have returned."

With eyes half opened you drag yourself out of bed, throw on some clothing, bring your camera and a valise with your notebook and pen, and stumble down the hallway to the elevator, down to the lobby and into the bus. You try to sleep on the bus, but the bouncing and noisy conversation makes it impossible. . . . You are truly exhausted. "This better be worth it," you mumble to yourself.

About five minutes before you arrive at Ben Gurion airport you finally fall asleep, only to be awakened again at arrival, and your system jolts into a semi-awake stupor. There is a tiny sliver of reddish yellow light coming up on the horizon, and it is about 5:30 a.m. now. You are taken through the airport, and then outside to the tarmac. Everything is fairly quiet so early in the morning, as no planes are either arriving or taking off.

Yosef then calls the group together and informs you that a 747 El Al jet from Moscow will be arriving in the next twenty to thirty minutes carrying 250 new immigrants. On it will be Jews from all over Russia who have chosen to throw their lot in with the burgeoning Jewish State. You have heard stories about friends who have met other arriving groups at Ben Gurion airport, but you are hardly in the mood to be excited at this moment, having lost most of your night's sleep.

Five, ten, fifteen minutes go by, and you begin to get a bit impatient. "Maybe the flight was canceled," you begin to worry. "Maybe there will be a delay of an hour or two. . . . Oh, my God, did they have to drag us out this early in the morning for nothing?"

Suddenly you see everyone pointing to the sky, as dawn in breaking, and there in the distance is a little speck which looks like it might be an airplane. As it gets closer, you recognize the logo of EL AL, in Hebrew and in English intertwined, and the large blue Magen David (Jewish Star) painted on a white background on the tail.

The plane sets down, and a musician with a guitar stands at the bottom of the stairway from the plane to the tarmac. The group begins to sing, "Hayvaynu Shalom Aleichem,"—A Hearty Welcome to All! The plane door slowly opens, and a flight attendant helps a few elderly people march down the steps. . . . Next comes a young family with two small children, and a baby in arms. . . . After them is another couple, then a few teenagers,—and more and more and more. Their eyes are bright, and there are gigantic smiles of relief and looks of excitement on their faces. . . . One of the older men takes out a handkerchief, and wipes away some tears. When he reaches the bottom of the steps, he stands on Israeli soil for the first time, bends over on his knees and kisses the ground. You walk over to him, and without even thinking about it, you reach out and give him a big hug. Now both of you are crying, and laughing, and you begin to dance. . . .

The whole group then joins arms and makes a large circle. The musician plays "hava nagila" and you all start to dance the hora. . . . Your group waves Israeli flags toward the windows of the plane for those who have not yet disembarked. After the hora, all the members of your UJA group spontaneously form a double line, just like a receiving line at a wedding or bar mitzvah, and as each passenger walks through, you greet them, welcome them, shake their hands, hand them a small bouquet of flowers, hug them and kiss them. . . .

You begin to think to yourself: I have never had an experience like this in my life! I have never met these people before, and here I am, reacting to these total strangers as if I have known them all my life. . . . I cannot believe it!

Everyone in your group feels the same way, and there is singing, dancing, rejoicing, celebrating, and an incredible feeling that some kind of divine redemption is taking place, almost like Moshe and the Israelites when they passed through the Sea. . . . It reminds you of the feeling you had when the Six Day War came to an end, and every Jew in the world felt an enormous sense of relief, joy and exhilaration.

For a minute you step aside and go inside yourself. You take just a moment or two to imagine what kind of life these people have had for the last several decades. For some of them their entire lifetime has almost gone by, living under a repressive, cruel regime of tyranny and discrimination. For most of their lives they were not able to live as a Jew. Now they have been freed from exile and are at home. Finally, at last, free. . . . (Pause).

You walk over to Yosef, and thank him for waking you up in the middle of the night. "This is truly an unforgettable experience. One that will influence my life as long as I live. . . ." ○

THE SCUDS ARE FLYING

❍ *Imagine yourself sitting on the beach, watching the waves. It is late in the afternoon, and most bathers have left the beach. It is quiet and the sun is setting. You are sitting quietly and staring at the soft waves coming in and out. With each wave you become more and more deeply relaxed. . . .*

See yourself at home, doing a few chores around the house, and you hear a flash over the news program on TV. It is during the American invasion of Iraq in January, 1991, and the announcer reveals that a scud missile just fell over Tel Aviv, and landed in the crowded residential area of Ramat Gan. Reports so far are that there has been some damage done to a few homes and office buildings, but no one has been hurt.

Immediately you rush to the telephone to talk to relatives and friends, to see if they have heard, and find out if they have any additional information. . . . Panic is beginning to set in, and phone wires in the Jewish community are burning.

For the next several days, you continue to listen to the radio and watch television as often as possible. At night, after work, the TV doesn't go off. CNN gives minute by minute live reports, and you and your family are glued to the TV set every second. Your fears and concerns for the welfare of the Jews of Israel is mounting. . . .

Next you hear that the American government has asked Israel not to retaliate or become involved in the war with Iraq, lest other Arab allies decide to drop out of the multi-national alliance. You feel terribly frustrated, and wish Israel could get in there and bomb Iraq out of existence. Israel is exposed to danger like a sitting duck. The Israel Defense Forces are forced to remain passive with their hands tied behind their back. All agree that for the moment Israel must cooperate with the U.S. Government, and let the American armed forces handle the battle with Iraq.

You hear on television that Israelis are prepared for chemical and biological warfare, going to the highest floor in the house to their specially prepared "sealed rooms," where gas masks and injections of chemicals to fight deadly nerve gas are readied, and everyone in the country is frustrated, waiting for the next "shoe to drop."

The entire Jewish world becomes as one people, focusing its total attention on the danger to their precious, hard-earned State, the refuge of Holocaust victims and other survivors of oppression. Is it possible that Jews from all over the world came together in one place from over one hundred countries, to the State of Israel, so that a vicious and well-armed enemy can destroy greater numbers of Jews in one spot more quickly and with greater effectiveness? How could God let such a terrible thing happen to our people again? Jews everywhere find themselves worrying, praying, hoping, and keeping themselves informed at every minute about the latest developments.

At synagogues, Jewish federations, Jewish Community Centers, and other Jewish agencies throughout North America and in Europe, phones are ringing off the hook with callers asking how they can help. They want to know if they can send money, travel to Israel to help, do anything they can to prevent this new, terrible scourge. Meetings and rallies are held at the United Nations, at every local synagogue, at Jewish Federation offices, and at Jewish Community Centers. No effort is too great to prevent another Holocaust. The fear and anxiety in the Jewish community is continually building. . . .

Pause for a moment, and pay attention to your body. Are there any physiological reactions from reliving these frightening events of a few years ago? Is your heart beating faster, or your stomach churning, or are you having other bodily responses to these unsettling events? (Pause).

Think to yourself, this is what happens in the world when there is a crisis in the Jewish community. Notice how the Jewish world closes ranks as one family. Go inside yourself and see if there is some comfort and security for you in your deep emotional response. . . . What is it that makes every Jew concerned when another Jew is in trouble? . . .

Perhaps it is this profound emotional reaction, and the call to arms, that reminds each of us how much our people and its survival and security mean to us. Perhaps a reminder like this helps us to understand the high priority we give to our Homeland, and our people living there. It helps to remind us that having a Jewish state in the world is such an important part of who we are. Think for a moment about these ideas, and see how you react. (Pause).

When you are ready, come back to this room, and gradually open your eyes. . . . ○

Chapter 17

AN IMAGINARY PILGRIMAGE TO ISRAEL

Everything you can imagine is real.
—Picasso

Toward the Eastern corners of the world Jewish eyes envision . . . : The Land of Zion, Jerusalem!
—*Hatikvah*, The Jewish National Anthem

A VISIT to the Holy Land, Eretz Yisrael, has been the dream and hope of Jews ever since the destruction of the Temple by the Romans, and the exile of the Jewish People from their Homeland two thousand years ago.

Anyone under the age of fifty was born after Israel's resurrection in 1948, and probably too young to be aware of the miracle of the Jewish State reborn in our century. While it is easy enough to travel to Israel today, some four-fifths of North American Jewry have never been there. Those who have relish their memories of the pilgrimage, and long to return. A visit to Israel today, while obviously much easier than it was fifty to one hundred years ago, is still in a sense a dream of a lifetime.

In these imagery exercises, participants will be able to experience the next best thing to visiting Israel—a visit in our imagination. It can be used to motivate people to travel to Israel, to prepare for a coming organized tour, or to review the experience for those who already went. An imaginary visit can be a very powerful educational tool for the classroom, youth group, adult Federation, congregational or other Zionist-focused classes or groups.

TRAVELING TO ISRAEL

❍ *We are about to fulfill the dream of Jews for four thousand years, to make a pilgrimage to Eretz Yisrael, the Homeland of our People. Sit back in your El Al seat, buckle your seat belt, listen to the instructions of the flight attendants, and begin to relax. Take some deep breaths and get ready for take-off. Whether you are a good traveler or not, this trip will be easy and exciting, better than any you have ever had. You will be more relaxed and comfortable in your large, roomy seat than even sitting at home in your favorite easy chair. . . .*

Being aboard El Al gives you a special sense of security and calm. You feel as though you were already in Israel, and the sense of being at home has already begun to cause you to feel elated, excited, and at the same time very inspired. Your sense of elation makes every part of your body feel energized and ready for a unique experience. . . .

Sitting in your extremely comfortable, soft-cushioned and wide-spaced seat, you stretch your legs forward, yawn and rest your eyes for the long trip ahead. As your eyes close you begin to review the many weeks of preparation you made for this unbelievable voyage. You recall sending away your application for the visit, getting your passport and plane tickets in order, carefully reading through the itinerary when it came in the mail, and reading through some articles and books about the people, places and history you are soon to encounter. . . .

You recall packing some gifts for friends or relatives in Israel, which you carefully selected and wrapped, placing them securely under some thick clothing in your suitcase to protect them. You bring a watch for one special person, a camera for another, and an English technical book for a scientist who couldn't find it in any of Israel's bookstores. . . .

You begin to think about all the exciting places you are about to see, and unusual people you will meet . . . [Specific names and places can be inserted here by the facilitator].

After a few hours of sleep, the captain announces that dinner will soon be served. It is so wonderful to hear the announcement both in Hebrew and in English. Just the thought of Hebrew being used as a modern language, like French, Spanish or Italian, gives you a special feeling inside your chest. . . . You straighten up the back of your chair, place your earphones on, and listen to some popular Israeli folk songs. See how you feel hearing these songs on an El Al plane, about to set foot on the holy soil of Eretz Yisrael. . . .

After several hours of dozing off and awakening, you hear over the loud-speaker that the plane will land at Ben Gurion airport near Tel Aviv in just fifteen minutes. The excitement begins to build. . . . You look out the window and see Israel's coastline. . . .

When the El Al Boeing 747 sets down, you hear one of your favorite songs, "Yerushalayim Shel Zahav," playing, and you ignore the little bit of bumpiness that accompanies your landing. . . . You gather your belongings, exit the plane, and step foot on the ground of the State of Israel. It feels so much like coming home. There are no words to describe the feelings you have inside. Just pay attention to your feelings for a minute, before you go any further. . . .

After going through Passport Control and exchanging some dollars for Israeli shekels at the bank window in the airport, you board your bus for Jerusalem. It is like a dream. . . . You can hardly believe you are here. . . .

When the bus begins to climb the Judean hills and approaches Jerusalem, the driver stops, and the guide tells everyone to get off the bus for a moment, for a special surprise. It is an old/new custom to walk into Jerusalem, so you take a few steps as you enter the Holy City, and everyone receives a small cup of wine for a blessing. You recite the proper blessing for wine, and then the "She-he-che-yanu" prayer. "Bountiful are You, O God, Ruler of the Universe, who has kept us in life, and sustained us, and enabled us to reach this unique and holy moment in our lives." You look out over the city in the distance, and savor the moment, one which you will surely never forget. . . . (Pause).

After checking into the hotel, and resting for a while, you board the tour bus again, and begin to see some of Jerusalem's highlights. You pass some sidewalk cafes and watch Israelis on their coffee break, sitting in the bright sunny Jerusalem outdoors, seeming to be arguing about politics, religion, or something very important. . . .

Next you pass lots of stores and marvel at the Hebrew writing everywhere you look, trying to make out the words you see. . . . One long word is very difficult, but you finally figure out that it says, in Hebrew letters, "Sup-er-market." You laugh loudly and fully, mixing your joy and excitement at noticing how unique and yet "normal" Israel is. . . .

You pass the large, impressive, stately Knesset building with its beautiful giant Menorah out front. . . . You go to Hadassah Hospital and see the chapel where the famous Chagall windows dazzle your artistic tastes. . . . You walk through an Arab shuk *(market), and enjoy the Middle Eastern feeling you get from the sight of Arab* kafias *(headdresses), stalls for nuts and fruit, tourist gifts, little wooden statues, religious icons for all faiths, leather jackets and pocketbooks. More than once you notice an Arab merchant haggling with a customer over the price of some trinket. . . .*

You arrive now at the Kotel, the Western Wall. It is so awesome. No words can possibly begin to describe it. . . . Take a few minutes to rest after this deeply emotional experience, and then walk into the Jewish Quarter (the "Rova") where you buy some postcards with pictures of Israeli sites to mail to friends at home. . . .

The next day you spend time walking around Yad Va-Shem, Israel's main Holocaust Memorial, and feel in your bones the reason why there must be an independent Jewish State so that there will never again be a Holocaust against the Jewish People. Israel will always be a haven for persecuted Jews. . . .

You walk through the stirring Valley of the Lost Communities, the chilling Children's Memorial, the small, dark and eerie prayer room where names of concentration camps are etched in stone with a memorial candle over each of them. In the far corner of the room you hear a cantor with another touring group chanting the memorial prayer, the El Male Rachamim. . . . What thoughts and feelings are going through your mind as you hear that prayer in this place? (Pause).

Part of your cultural tour of Jerusalem includes the large, sprawling Israel Museum, with its modern art, ancient archeological artifacts, and a gift shop where you purchase some beautiful gifts with which to adorn your home. . . . Nearby is the Bible Lands Museum, with objects from thousands of years ago, preserved from the days of the Tanakh, coming from all over the Fertile Crescent.

Next on your itinerary is an electronics laboratory where Israeli scientists, many from Russia and other countries, are creating inventions that will establish Israel as one of the world's leaders in science and technology. . . . You stop in an Absorption Center and meet with new immigrants who arrived in Israel from the former Soviet Union, Eastern Europe, Ethiopia, Yemen, Syria and other countries. With the help of a translator you talk to some of these people whose lives have been redeemed by escaping their former places of oppression and now are living as free and proud Jews. . . .

It is nighttime now and everyone enjoyed dinner at the hotel. Your tour guide reviews the itinerary for the next few days, and you sit with awe and amazement when you realize that you will be experiencing so much in such a short visit. You will be climbing Masada, floating in the Dead Sea, getting a healthy mud-bath and relaxing in the nearby spa, visiting Ben Gurion University and Kibbutz Sde Boker where Ben Gurion lived his last years and is buried. At this kibbutz, and others you will visit, you will see the most modern agricultural techniques and irrigation pipes, orchards and trees, animals and family life, and all kinds of hi-tech industries for domestic and overseas consumption. . . .

You will visit schools where Israeli children are imbibing the heritage of their past, and the heroic history of their own State for half a century.

After Jerusalem and the South, you will travel northwards, visiting Israel's major metropolis, Tel Aviv, and then Haifa, the large, beautiful port city, with huge ships coming and going bearing cargo from all over the world. . . .

In the North you will see Safed, the medieval mystical city where Rabbi Joseph Karo's famous synagogue is still a holy place of prayer for residents and pilgrims. You will walk down the narrow cobblestone streets where artists display their paintings and beautiful crafts, including menorahs, Shabbat candlesticks, etrog holders, mezuzot, and other religious objects. . . .

You will be spending one night in Tiberias and visit the grave of the famous sage Maimonides (1135-1204) who was born in Cordoba, Spain, and because of persecution was chased with his family to North Africa and later to the Egyptian village of Fostat, a suburb of Cairo. To see the grave of one of the Jewish People's most famous scholars is just one more moment that is beyond description, and helps you understand that there is nothing in the life of a Jew that is precisely comparable to a trip to Israel. . . .

In Tiberias you will also see people fishing in the nearby Sea of Galilee (Yam HaKineret), a calm and beautiful body of water resembling the shape of a harp.

You rest overnight in Jerusalem, have one day off for some shopping, where you buy some more gifts—some silver key chains with the Hebrew names of friends hanging from them, a kiddush cup and challah cover for your own Shabbat observance back home, and even a T-shirt with a phrase from a Grateful Dead song, translated into Hebrew. . . .

After having visited all those wonderful places, you and your group dine on the last night of your visit at a well-known Israeli restaurant in the Jewish Quarter called the Culinarium. The Culinarium is modeled in every detail on the eating places, decor, utensils, musical entertainment and menu of the ancient Romans who occupied the Land of Israel two thousand years ago. Around the table, each person tells about his or her highlight during the past two weeks of your incredible tour. . . .

Think of what you might say when it is your turn. . . . (Pause).

You are sorry to leave, but exhilarated by the experience, and promise yourself that you will return at your first opportunity. Unlike other promises you make to yourself, this one you know you will keep! . . . At the end of your group meeting and dinner, you all stand and sing together Hatikvah ("The Hope"), the Jewish National Anthem, and depart for your bus ride back to the airport. . . .

Your sacred pilgrimage to Eretz Yisrael has come to an end. . . .
How does it feel? (Pause).

Knowing that you can always come back to Israel, in your imagination or for real, you are comforted, and begin to let go of this trip. . . .

When you are ready, begin to return to this room, stretch your limbs, shake out your body, and open your eyes. . . .slowly and gradually. . . . ○

LEAVING AND RETURNING

○ *Take time to stretch your arms and legs. . . . Yawn a few times, and let go of any tightness or tension in your body. . . . Breathe slowly and deeply several times. . . . Focus on your breath. . . . If other thoughts enter your mind, let them enter and pass through. . . . Pay attention only to your inhaling and exhaling. . . . Let yourself be more and more deeply relaxed. . . .*

Find yourself wandering the streets of Yerushalayim about two thousand years ago. It is the late spring of the year seventy C.E. Your people have been at war with the Romans, and their tenth legion is now getting closer and closer to the Holy City. . . . You and your family are frightened of what may be coming soon. . . .

As early summer arrives your worst fears are fulfilled. The walls of the city have been breached. You and your family are told to leave Yerushalayim, so you pack up your belongings, put them in a wagon, and begin to march to the nearby hills. . . . You can see the walled city from the distance. . . .

On the ninth day of Av, you and your dear ones are sitting under a tree, watching from a distance, and you see a fire lit. It looks like it is close to the Temple Mount. The fire spreads, and the city is engulfed in flames. . . . You begin to shake, and cry, and everyone joins you in tears. . . .

Someone takes out an old parchment with the Book of Lamentations written on it. This holy book, thought to be inspired by God and written by the prophet Jeremiah when the first Temple, built by King Solomon, was burned to the ground by wicked King Nebuchadnezzar of Babylonia. . . .

The book is read in a minor key melody, with a sad, haunting chant, in its original Hebrew. . . . In English translation it says something like this:

"Alas, lonely sits the Holy City, once teeming with people. She who was once powerful among nations has now been turned to a widow. . . . The princess among states has become a slave.

"Bitterly she weeps throughout the night, her cheeks soaked with tears. None comforts her. . . .

"Judah has gone into exile, in misery and oppression, wandering without rest. . . . Zion's roads are in mourning, empty of festive pilgrims. Her gates are deserted. Her Kohanim sigh in sadness; her maidens are without joy. She it totally inconsolable. . . . Her infants have gone into captivity. . . . Gone from Fair Zion are all that was her glory. Her leaders are like horses without pasture. . . . They walk feebly away from their pursuers.

"Zion is in shame. . . . The majesty of Israel is cast down from heaven to earth. . . . The inhabitants of Jacob are destroyed in anger. . . . Fair Judah's strongholds are brought low in dishonor. . . . The altar is disdained, the Sanctuary is despised. . . . The walls of the citadel are given over to her enemies, who shout in God's own house. . . . as if it were a day of rejoicing. . . .

"The elders of Zion sit on the ground, their heads covered with dust. . . . Their loins are girded with sackcloth, their heads bowed to the ground. . . . My eyes are empty of tears, my heart is in tumult, my whole being melts from pain. . . . Babes and sucklings languish in the city squares. . . .

"O Zion, Fair Maiden of Yerushalayim, how can I comfort you? Your ruin is so vast, it is as the sea. Who can heal you from your illness? . . . All who pass by clap their hands in scorn, they hiss and shake their head in sadness and disgust. . . . Is this the Holy City that was called Perfect in Beauty, Joy of the whole world?"

The reader stops for a moment, now turning to a passage of comfort:

"But I will not give up my hope—Hatikvah. . . . The kindness of Adonai has not ended. . . . God's mercies are not spent. . . . They renew themselves each morning. O God, Your grace is bountiful! O how I hope in You, Adonai. Adonai is good to all who trust. . . . Rescue comes from Adonai. . . . I call upon Your name, Adonai, from the depths of the pit. Hear my plea, shut not Your ear to my groan and cry! In times past You have championed my cause, and redeemed me. . . . Let not our home be given to strangers, who see our disgrace. Let not our heritage pass to aliens, and let us not remain orphans, bereft of mother and father. . . . Our hearts are sick and our eyes dimmed, because Zion lies desolate, and jackals prowl upon it. . . .

"Take us back, Adonai, and let us return. . . . Renew our days as of old. Take us back, Adonai, and let us return. . . . Renew our days as of old!" (Pause).

Sit for a minute, as you mourn for fallen Zion, and rely on the goodness of Adonai. . . .

Jump ahead now, centuries and centuries. . . . The year is 1967 C.E., almost 1900 years later. It is late Spring again and the enemies of Israel once again are trying to destroy Israel restored and rebuilt. . . . Yerushalayim, the old city, inside the ancient walls, are in the hands of the enemy. Neighboring nations join together to attack again, as they did in 586 B.C.E., and 70 C.E. This time Israel is strong. Her armies are trained and armed. She will never again permit her sons and daughters to suffer humiliation and exile. . . . This time she is ready.

When war comes on June 5, 1967, Israel takes the advantage. Monday morning, in several hours, Israel destroys the air force of Egypt. In the next day Israeli troops advance toward the Walls of Jerusalem. By Wednesday, the twenty-eight day of Iyyar, June 12, 1967, Israeli troops break through the gates of the Old City, and advance toward the Temple Mount. Within hours the city is recaptured, and in Israeli hands once again. . . .

There is joy, excitement, and tears among Israel's mighty soldiers. . . . A general takes the microphone and announces to the country: Har Habayit be-yadenu. "The Temple Mount is in our hands." We have retaken the Kotel, the holy Western Wall, and all of the Old City. . . .

Citizens of Israel listen closely to their radios. . . . They cannot believe the good news. It is like a miracle. God has fulfilled the Promise of Old. Adonai has not forsaken the People of the Covenant forever. It is the beginning of the time leading to Redemption. . . .

Old men and young, grandmothers and babies, all hear the good news and weep with tears of joy. The attacker has been pushed back. Yerushalayim, a city that is united in glory, will never be divided again. . . . Yerushalayim is ours, never to be lost. . . . The eternal, undivided capital of the State of Israel, of the Jewish world. . . .

After several days, the area around the Kotel is cleared, and stones are laid to create a large plaza for the massive throngs who come to visit, to pray, to cry, to rejoice. . . . Brave soldiers, with an Uzzi on their shoulder, hang their heads against the ancient stones. . . . Old men in black coats and white beards stand so close to the Kotel, there is no room for even a breeze to pass by. . . . All who love Yerushalayim rejoice in her. Rejoice ye with Yerushalayim, sing with her. Rejoice with her all you who love her. She is a city united, never to be divided again!

On your ramparts, O Jerusalem, City of David, we have placed guards to protect you. . . . You are ours. . . . You are one. . . . Forever. . . .

Sit quietly with your feelings for a moment. (Pause).

*When you are ready to let go of this dream of fulfillment, slowly say goodbye to Yerushalayim, knowing that you will soon return, in your heart or with your feet. Soon you will return.... Say **lehitraot—au revoir**—soon I will be back. ... (Pause).*

When you are ready, come back to this room, and slowly, gradually, open your eyes, and be present again in this time and place. ○

Chapter 18

IMAGERY FOR MORAL DEVELOPMENT

By logic and reason we die hourly;
by imagination we live.
—J.B. Yeats, father of William Butler Yeats

The Torah is a beautiful crown upon your head.
—Midrash, Vayikra Rabba 12:3

If you see the Book of Psalms in a dream,
you may hope to gain wisdom.
—Talmud, Brachot 57b

WINSTON CHURCHILL wrote that "Jewish ethics is incomparably the most precious possession of mankind, worth in fact the fruits of all other wisdom and learning put together."

Rabbi Abraham Joshua Heschel, Professor of Jewish Mysticism at the Jewish Theological Seminary until his death in 1972, once said that it is our job to make human beings into Jews, but also to make Jews into human beings. That is the task of character education.

We could devote this chapter to any one of thousands of passages in Jewish literature which foster a heightened awareness of improved moral behavior. We could focus on Leviticus 19, on Psalms 1, 15, 24, or 146; on Isaiah 11 or 58, etc. We could deal with almost any of the statements in Pirke Avot, or some of the wonderful passages in the Midrashic collections or in the Talmud. Character development in Judaism is a silver thread that is woven through the entire warp and woof of the tapestry of Jewish history and literature.

The exercises we suggest will be merely samples of others which any teacher or group facilitator can construct out of their own Jewish learning and growth.

ROLE MODELS

Rabbi Louis Finkelstein, late Chancellor of the Jewish Theological Seminary, frequently told the story about the time he was interviewed to become a student at the Seminary. He was interviewed by Solomon Schechter, one of the great theologians of this century. Schechter asked young Finkelstein why he wanted to study at the Seminary. Finkelstein answered "to study great books." Schechter was disappointed. "Great books," he said, "can be read in a library. You don't need to become a student at this Seminary to study great books. If you want to study at the Seminary, it must be because you want to be exposed to great people."

In modern parlance, exposing ourselves to great people is one way of choosing "role models."

○ *Place your hands on your eyes. There is a healing power in hands. Let your hands bring warmth and healing to your body and spirit. Let the healing power of your hands bring relaxation and security to all your muscles, bones, nerves, and every other part of you. . . . You are feeling whole, calm, and relaxed. . . .*

Think now about a special person in your life, someone whose moral character is or was exemplary. Think of a person whose behavior was above the crowd, and whom people respected. . . . (Pause).

What are some of the things you admire about your special person's character and values? (Pause).

Do you remember some of the things this person said or did? Try to recall them in as much detail as possible. See if you can reconstruct on the movie screen in your mind some specific times when your special person acted in an exceptional way. When and where did it happen? Who was there? Try to experience inside yourself all the sights, sounds, smells, and other senses that were present when this happened. . . . Why did it make such an impression on you? . . . What did you learn from it? (Pause).

Think of a situation in your life which presents an ethical dilemma. . . . What would your special person say to you or advise you about this problem? (Pause).

Now focus your attention on some issues that are facing you in your family, your work, your school, or some other important place in your life. . . . Ask your special person how he/she would handle this problem. . . . See what the answer is. (Pause).

What are some of the qualities which you would like to emulate in the life of your special person? . . . How can you begin to achieve these? . . .

Say some words of appreciation to this special person, and explain in detail what it is that you respect and admire about him/her. (Pause).

Ask your special person if he/she has anything to say to you before you say goodbye. . . . Listen carefully to what the answer is. . . . (Pause).

Your special person would like to give you a gift, to remember your conversation together. Reach out your hand, and accept it. Look and see what it is. . . .

It is time to part now. Remember that you can always talk to this special person again for advice, to help you solve problems, answer questions, figure out difficult ethical dilemmas and other matters. . . .

When you are ready, come back to this room, and slowly open your eyes. . . . ○

MORAL & SPIRITUAL SELF EXAMINATION (*CHESHBON HA-NEFESH*)

The facilitator may explain to the group that the practice of *Cheshbon Ha-Nefesh* (literally, taking an accounting of the soul, or measuring the soul) has been an important practice in Jewish moral growth. It is especially common around the period beginning with the month of Elul, thirty days prior to the High Holidays, and during the *Aseret Yemay Teshuvah*, the Ten Days of Repentance (between Rosh Hashanah and Yom Kippur). However, it is practiced by serious Jews all throughout the year.

There are many imagery exercises which can help a person do an accounting of his/her moral growth (*Cheshbon Ha-Nefesh*), and we shall select just one by way of example. Many others can be designed by using some of the ideas found in Yitzhak Buxbaum's splendid collection, *Jewish Spiritual Practices* (Northvale, NJ: Jason Aronson, 1990).

○ *Imagine that the music of a harp is playing softly and beautifully very close to you. . . . The music begins to relax you very deeply, and the more it plays, the more your attention is turned inward. . . . Let go of any distractions from the outside world. You feel as though you are floating away on soft clouds, as the music of the harp penetrates all the parts of your body and mind, and makes you feel good and calm. . . .*

It is a time-honored custom in traditional Judaism to constantly search for ways to make yourself a better person. This practice is known as **Cheshbon**

Ha-Nefesh, or examination of the soul. The soul is a metaphor for our moral and spiritual self. We are now going to engage in a guided imagery exercise which will help us take an accounting of our moral selves.

Remember to be very gentle and loving to yourself as you carry out the instructions in this exercise. We are not here to be judgmental or critical. We are doing this exercise to help ourselves, not to make ourselves feel bad or inadequate. The practice of **Cheshbon Ha-Nefesh** is a caring and helpful act, not a punitive or critical one. . . . Feel in your heart how fortunate and blessed you are to be engaging in **Cheshbon Ha-Nefesh**. . . .

Imagine that you are watching a movie screen in your mind, and a wise, hasidic master appears in front of you named Rabbi Levi Yitzchak of Berditchev (Poland), who lived at the end of the eighteenth century. Rabbi Levi Yitzchak is known in Hasidic literature as a kind, gentle and loving teacher, who always wanted to find ways to become and to help others become better human beings. As you look at Rabbi Levi Yitzchak's face, see in his eyes, and in the lines of his smiling face, the desire to help himself and you to be better human beings. . . .

Now we will engage in a practice which Rabbi Levi Yitzchak did each night before going to sleep. He wanted to do a **Cheshbon Ha-Nefesh** for the day that just ended, so he reviewed all his actions for that day. Imagine that you are going to sleep now, and you review all the things you did during the day that is now ending. . . . Think of where you went, with whom you spoke, projects in which you were involved, meetings you may have attended, what you did at work, or school, or home. As you review each conversation and each action, see if there were any blemishes in any of them. . . .

Perhaps you got angry too quickly. Or maybe you held back from telling the entire truth in another instance. Perhaps a financial mistake was made in your favor, and you neglected to bring it to the attention of the party involved. Perhaps you overlooked calling a sick friend. Maybe you wanted to bring some food to a shut-in, and decided you just couldn't make time to do it. Think of any other blemishes which may have intentionally or unintentionally entered into your day's schedule. (Pause).

Now comes the important part. After reviewing his day, and taking an accounting of his soul, Rabbi Levi Yitzchak would say to himself, as if talking about another person: "Levi Yitzchak will not do that again." Now, following Rabbi Levi Yitzchak's practice, say to yourself, using your own name: ". . . will not do that again!" Look inside your heart and make sure that you are sincere in saying this to yourself. . . . Repeat it again, with even more sincerity. ". . . will not do that again!" (Pause).

See how pleased and content you are after having promised to make yourself a better, more morally conscious person. . . . Make sure you do not burden yourself with heavy guilt, but just a desire to be even better than you are now. . . .

Now picture yourself encountering a similar situation, just like the ones which had a blemish in your review of your day's activities, and see yourself acting differently, and not repeating the same mistakes as before. Do this for each activity in which you found a blemish. . . . (Pause).

Congratulate yourself for having worked so hard to achieve a higher level of moral awareness. . . . Affirm your willingness to change, and to engage in the strenuous practice of **Cheshbon Ha-Nefesh**. . . .

Try to remember to return to this imagery exercise often, as Rabbi Levi Yitzchak did, so that you can always be climbing higher and higher on the ladder of moral growth. . . .

When you are ready, slowly and gradually open your eyes and return to this room. . . . ○

AWARD FOR MENSCHLICHKEIT

○ *Let your eyes close, and picture yourself walking down a long flight of stairs. As you descend, count back from twenty to one. . . . Each time you take another step, you become more and more deeply relaxed. . . . By the time you reach the bottom step you are feeling very calm and serene. . . . You are totally relaxed.*

Imagine that it is ten or twenty years from now, and your synagogue has decided to present you with their special annual award called the "Menschlichkeit Award." This award is presented to someone in the congregation who has done exemplary things in the area of social justice, moral education, acts of compassion and kindness, or other related activities.

When you receive the telephone call from the president of the synagogue, you are very flattered and honored. You are not certain why it is you whom they have chosen, but still there is a wonderful, warm feeling of joy and satisfaction inside your heart. Take a minute to go inside and see how it feels. . . .

When the evening of the award's presentation comes, watch the proceedings as if you were a "fly on the wall." As the chairperson calls your name to come forward, you receive a standing ovation from the audience of hundreds of relatives, friends and members of the congregation who have come to honor you.

The chairperson begins to read a long list of accomplishments in the realm of being a "mensch": a truly moral, compassionate, and spiritual person. Listen carefully as the long list is read. . . . Some of the ways in which you merited receiving the Menschlichkeit Award have to do with your service to the synagogue. . . . Listen as they are read. . . . (Pause).

Another group of activities is connected with your service to the general community: serving on committees, boards, and special service projects. . . . Listen to them. . . . (Pause).

Then the chairperson talks about the way you have served in helping the poor, the homeless, and minority groups. . . .

The chairperson also mentions several quiet, unannounced projects of tzedakah in which you have participated anonymously, which cannot be mentioned specifically. . . . But you know what they are, and you think about them to yourself. . . .

Listed also are some of the conflicts you helped resolve with your kind and gentle ability to listen to both sides of an argument, and bring a creative solution to a seemingly insoluble problem. . . .

Finally, the award presented mentions some of the ways that you have shown kindness to members of your own family, more than most other people would have done. . . .

You feel very embarrassed by some of these things, which you considered just part of your daily obligations of living as a Jew. But it seems that others appreciate them even more than you would have realized. . . .

You overcome your embarrassment, and let yourself take satisfaction and joy in the fact that others are inspired by your example. . . . You think of all the good that will come out of this award presentation, because other people will try to emulate the high standards of menschlichkeit which have been ascribed to you in the presentation. (Pause).

At the end of the evening, you receive another standing ovation as the award is handed to you. . . . You feel especially good and have a nice warm feeling inside. . . . Spend a moment taking in this good feeling and enjoying the good you have brought to the world. . . .

As we conclude our imagery exercise, remember that you have the opportunity in the next ten or twenty years to live up to many or all of the things that you heard in this award presentation. You are excited about the prospects of trying to achieve these high standards in your moral and spiritual life in years to come. . . .

We will now count to three, and when we reach three you will be completely awake and alert, back in this room, opening your eyes, and feeling good in every way. . . . One . . . two . . . three. . . . ○

AFFIRMATIONS

○ *Imagine that you are sitting in a favorite place, such as the beach, or in a garden, or in the middle of a beautiful forest. . . . The warm sun begins to shine on you and bring you a very comfortable feeling. . . . It is not too hot, just the way you like it. . . . The light and warmth of the sun have a very soothing effect on you, and you begin to feel very relaxed and calm. . . . The warmth penetrates your skin, and begins to enter your heart and other organs, bringing healing and tranquillity to all parts of your body and mind. . . . Let your eyes be closed, and notice how good and relaxed you feel. . . .*

In this guided imagery exercise, we will follow a custom described by the pious hasid, Rabbi Aharon of Zhitomir. Rabbi Aharon recommended to his students to place signs all over the house to remind them about their religious and spiritual obligations.

Think of some area of your life that you would like to improve. . . . Perhaps you would like to develop more patience, or a calmer temper, or be more punctual in your appointments. Maybe you would like to devote more time to study, or to prayer, or to your spouse or children. . . . Maybe you would like to be less arrogant, or less of a perfectionist, or less fearful. . . . Perhaps you would like to develop more faith, or try to practice meditation in your life. . . . Select one specific trait you would like to improve now. . . . (Pause).

The next task is to create or select a sentence which will help remind you of the trait you would like to develop. You can write one if you wish. Or if you know some verse in the Tanakh, or some saying from rabbinic literature, which will remind you of the trait you would like to acquire or develop, then that is preferable. Write a sentence now in your imagination, or select a quotation which you may know. . . . This is called your "affirmation."

Following the advice of Rabbi Aharon of Zhitomir, imagine that you are making many signs of different sizes and colors, and place them all through your house. You need not be embarrassed about doing something so unusual. Consider this a very admirable and desirable action on your part to help make yourself a better human being and a more worthy servant of God. . . .

In your imagination walk around your house and see how many different places you have placed these affirmations—in your study, in the living room, kitchen, dining room, bedroom, on the doors, and any other places you can think of.... Just be careful not to place any quotations from holy books, or sentences with God's name, in the bathroom, which is against Jewish practice....

Watch yourself walking around the house in the course of your normal daily routine, finding these affirmations in so many different places, and being reminded about the trait you would like to develop.... Find yourself remembering and practicing this trait in your life more and more frequently as a result of these affirmations, which serve as constant reminders....

When you are content that you have achieved your goal in this area, you may choose another affirmation. Perhaps consult some books, or your rabbi or other teacher, to help you find a verse or quotation which can serve as your affirmation for this new trait.... Continue throughout your life writing notes, signs, and reminders to yourself, to constantly develop new ways to follow the spiritual and moral teachings of Judaism.... ○

Chapter 19

BOARD TRAINING FOR JEWISH AGENCIES

Synagogues, Federations, Jewish Community Centers and Other Jewish Groups and Institutions

Vision looks inward and becomes duty.
Vision looks outward and becomes aspiration.
Vision looks upward and becomes faith.
—Rabbi Stephen S. Wise (1874-1949)

PART OF the purpose of the ongoing education of lay leaders in Jewish organizations such as Jewish Federations, synagogues, Jewish Community Centers, Jewish Family Services, Bureaus of Jewish Education, and volunteer organizations such as Hadassah, ORT, B'nai B'rith etc., is to enhance their Jewish self-awareness.

The following guided imagery exercises are designed for people who, by volunteering to serve on the Board of Directors of such organizations, have accepted upon themselves the responsibility of making decisions for their agency or organization, and ultimately for the entire Jewish community.

JEWISH CONTINUITY

❍ *Imagine yourself taking a short voyage, floating in the sky on soft white clouds and feeling very comfortable and relaxed. . . . You feel no pressure or tension anywhere in your body or mind. . . . The color of the sky, the softness beneath you, and the cool, comfortable breeze gives you a sense of total well-being. . . . Let your eyes close and enjoy the feeling. . . .*

In your imagination let yourself view what life will be like a few generations ahead. You are looking down and watching the lives of your grandchildren or great-grandchildren, now adults and with families of their own. . . .

Look at them and watch them for a while. (Pause).

What kind of Jewish lives are they living? . . . Are they members of a synagogue? . . . Do they belong to other Jewish organizations? . . . Do they contribute to Jewish charities? . . . Are they and their children involved in Jewish educational activities? . . . In what ways are they involved in Jewish learning? . . . (Pause).

Have a look at the Jewish community in which they live. . . . Where is it? . . . What type of community is it? . . . How does the community support an active Jewish lifestyle? . . . What types of programs, activities, cultural and religious events are held in the community? . . . (Pause).

You now have an opportunity to talk with your descendants. . . . Ask them how they feel about being Jewish? (Pause).

Ask them what they are doing to see that their own children and grandchildren will help preserve the Jewish People . . . the State of Israel . . . Jewish education . . . the Jewish community . . . the Jewish heritage. (Pause). Are you satisfied with their answers? . . .

As you are about to leave, say anything else you would like to tell your descendants. (Pause).

Thank them now for the opportunity to communicate with them across the generations. Affirm them for any choices they have made which please you. Perhaps you wish to ask them if they would join you in a brief prayer together. . . . If you would like, say whatever prayer is in your heart now. (Pause).

When you are ready, slowly come back to this room, and gradually open your eyes. ○

JEWISH SELF-ESTEEM

○ *Find a comfortable place to sit or lie, and become very relaxed. . . . Imagine that the light of the menorah is shining on you. . . . The light grows brighter and stronger, and begins to envelop your entire body, bringing you healing and security. . . . As each second passes, the light offers you more and more inner peace and spiritual joy. . . . You are feeling a sense of divine protection and a canopy of shalom surrounds you. . . .*

Imagine yourself walking through a busy thoroughfare. . . . There are people all around you, walking in different directions. . . . You have a Hebrew book in your hands. . . . People around you begin to look at the Hebrew letters on the book, and then start to look at you. . . . They look at your face, your body, your clothing. . . . What are they thinking? . . .

You reach into your pocket and take out some Jewish garment, such as a kippah or tallit. Place it on yourself now. What kind of reactions do the people around you have? . . . How do you feel inside? . . .

You begin to walk down the street, passing many shops and offices. . . . All kinds of different people pass you as you walk. Tall people, short people, skinny people, heavy people. . . . People of different ethnic backgrounds— African Americans, Latinos, Asians, and others. Some are wearing native costumes of various sorts: hats, shirts, scarves, headdresses, Arab kafias, some with long smocks. . . . See how you react to these sights. . . . (Pause).

Next you pass a group of three Hasidim with fur hats and long blacks coats, long black curls of hair hanging from their ears, carrying a large oversized copy of the Talmud. . . . Pay attention to how you feel inside. . . .

As you continue to walk, you see a large billboard on top of a six-story building. It has a picture of Russian Jews coming towards Ellis Island. The legend on the bottom says: "Help us help our brothers and sisters start a new life of freedom. Support the United Jewish Appeal." What are you feeling or thinking inside? . . .

As you go further up the street, you notice a kosher butcher shop. Look inside the large store window and glance at the people inside. What do they look like? . . . Turn your gaze toward the merchants behind the counter, and the other things you see inside the store. . . . What do you see? . . . . How do you feel? . . . .

You enter a coffee shop for a brief break, and sit at the counter for a few minutes, enjoying a drink and something to eat. On the counter are a few charity cans, one for the Magen David Adom (the Israel Red Cross), another for the Jewish National Fund, a third for the United Way, and yet another for a talmudical yeshiva. . . . Notice how you react when you see these cans. . . .

On the street you see a group of teenagers. Around their necks most of them are wearing chains with various pendants. Some have a cross, others a Moslem star. Some have a Magen David (a Jewish star). . . . What reaction is taking place inside you as you see this? . . . (Pause).

You have passed a street of shops, and now you are on a residential street. You notice that every third or fourth house has a mezuzah on the door. What are you thinking when you see them? . . .

After a few more blocks you pass an old, decaying building. Some of the windows are broken and the wooden frame desperately needs a coat of paint. There are ugly graffiti on some of the wooden panels. You notice a sign over the door that says "Anshe Emeth," and you realize that this is a synagogue. . . . Again, pay attention to any reactions you have inside. . . . (Pause).

You continue walking, and on the next block is another Jewish building. It looks like a Jewish community center. On the corner of the building, painted in black over a sign in front of the building is a swastika. Notice what reactions you have upon looking at it. . . .

As you walk a bit further, you are reach the end of your trail, and you slowly return to this room, opening your eyes whenever you are ready. . . . ○

The facilitator should take ample time to allow for participants to share their reactions, and process this exercise. Encourage candor and openness, letting people become aware of and share their honest reactions to the various visual and other stimuli in this exercise. Some of the participants openly admit to having some embarrassment at their Jewishness in certain instances. It will also be interesting to compare reactions to non-Jewish symbols to reacting to Jewish ones. (Participants may accept public displays of non-Jewish symbols, and yet feel embarrassed at people "showing off" their Jewishness in public). The facilitator can explain that these are sometimes normal reactions which members of a minority group have. Without any attempt to create a sense of guilt or shame, the facilitator can help participants understand the inevitable experiences of low Jewish self-esteem that occur as a result of living as a minority culture. There is probably no one who does not harbor some degree of self-hatred living outside a majority Jewish population. A healthy discussion following this exercise might involve suggestions regarding ways to help raise people's Jewish self-esteem. Self-awareness, paying more attention to one's internal process when encountering such experiences, and intensified Jewish education are all part of the path towards greater Jewish self-esteem.

JEWISH LOYALTY

○ Let yourself find a very comfortable place to sit or lie, and imagine that you hear some very soft music playing inside your head. . . . The music is just the right kind to make you feel at ease and tranquil. . . . The more you listen to the music, the more relaxed and serene you feel. . . . You are becoming more and more deeply relaxed. . . . Take a deep breath, and let your eyes gently close. . . .

Imagine that you are sitting at home in the evening, feeling good in every way. . . .

Reach over to the coffee table in front of you and pick up a copy of **The New York Times**. *Glance through and find some very interesting articles on a variety of political, cultural and other topics. . . . The first article is about a group of Russian mafia who have penetrated New York and New Jersey and who have taken control of some gambling rings. Many of the names are Jewish. Notice how you react when you read this article. . . .*

Next notice in the international news that Israel has been criticized by Amnesty International for its treatment of Palestinian prisoners. . . . Early that same day you heard about a Palestinian farmer who was shot by an Israeli settler whose brother was killed a few months ago in a Hamas suicide bombing. . . . Pay attention to how you feel when hearing that some Israelis do not always behave in a completely humane way. . . .

At that moment, your telephone rings, and it is the solicitor for the United Jewish Appeal. You tell the person that at this particular moment you have reservations about maintaining the previous level of your contribution to the UJA Campaign. . . . Listen to what the solicitor responds to you. . . . (Pause).

Share your reaction to what the solicitor says, and, if you like, have a fuller dialog on the subject for a while. . . . (Pause). As you bring your discussion to a close tell the solicitor that you will call back tomorrow with your final decision. . . .

Pick up your newspaper again and continue to read. You come upon an article about a neighboring rabbi who owned slum housing. The story relates that in one of the homes owned by the rabbi there was a fire in which someone was killed yesterday. Notice how you react when you read this. . . . Sitting in your chair, remember how your mother was in the Home for the Jewish Aged before she passed away last year, and no one from the synagogue or the entire Jewish community outside the Home came to visit her. You begin to get annoyed, and you are distracted for a few moments from your newspaper.

The telephone rings again and now it is the president of the synagogue. She would like you to serve on the Board next Fall, as chairperson of an important committee. Notice that you feel somewhat resistant, and at the moment prefer not to get involved in the politics of the synagogue. . . . Tell the president how you feel, and see what she says. (Pause).

Return to your paper and read some more articles, then sit back and relax, yawning and thinking that you will soon retire for the evening.

At that moment there is a knock at the door. Your non-Jewish next door neighbor just returned from a trip and tells you that his family is back home now. . . . In the conversation tell your neighbor some of the things you have been reading in the paper about Israel and the synagogue. Your neighbor is an active member of his church, and he gives you his point of view about your feelings. . . . Listen to what he says. Your neighbor gives you some new ideas on the issues you have been thinking about for a while. . . . (Pause).

After a few minutes of conversation your neighbor leaves. You are now ready to end this exercise, and come back to this room. Open your eyes, and feel very enlightened and pleased with everything that happened. ○

The facilitator may follow this exercise with a discussion which emphasizes the point, preferably expressed by group members in addition to the facilitator, that every social group, organization, country and culture has faults and moments of failure. Part of the discussion might focus on the question of whether a person who is disappointed with the actions of a group will let his/her ultimate loyalty be shaken by periodic incidents of failure and mistakes. Are one's ultimate convictions and loyalties able to weather temporary lapses and transcend the events of the day? The facilitator will have to balance a sense of non-judgmental openness in the discussion, while sharing his/her own personal views about the importance of the mission of a particular organization and the Jewish People as a whole. While being open to hear other opinions, it is not necessary for the discussion leader to hide his/her own views that being part of the Jewish People and its glorious historical past should not be forsaken because things are not always as they should be ideally.

JEWISH ACTIVITIES – PRIMARY AND SECONDARY

○ *Think of one of your very favorite places to be in the whole world . . . some place where you feel very much at peace and calm inside and out. . . . Sit or lie back, and imagine yourself totally enjoying being in your favorite place. . . . See how good and comfortable you feel. . . . Everything is just the way you want it. . . . You are feeling very rested and peaceful, just the way you love to feel. . . . Let your eyes close and enter a receptive mode. . . .*

As one who is deeply involved and committed to the Jewish community, think of all the many ways in which your being Jewish influences your life. (Pause).

Think of the organizations to which you belong. . . . Think of the life cycle events you celebrate in your family. . . . Think of the sense of community which being Jewish brings to you. . . . Think of the ties you have to the Jewish past, present, and future. . . . (Pause).

See yourself involved in some Jewish activities, and notice how you feel when you are doing them. . . . Think about some times in the past few years when you attended Jewish functions, such as meetings, political advocacy campaigns, fundraising projects, perhaps a baby-naming ceremony, a bar/bat mitzvah, a wedding, or a funeral. . . . Think of some worship services you attended on Shabbat or festivals. . . .

Think about a Jewish book you read, or a Jewish painting you saw. . . . Think about a trip you took in the past few years, perhaps to Israel, Europe or some other places of Jewish interest. . . . Think about a Jewish museum you visited, or other tourist sites. . . .

Think about a Jewish lecture you heard, or a class you attended. . . . Think about some action you took to help another Jew, or group of Jews, somewhere in the world. . . .

As a member of the lay leadership of your organization, think about the many responsibilities you have undertaken. . . . What are some of the things you want to do because you hold this position? . . . Think about the meetings you attend, and the decisions you make . . . about the funds, time and energy which you contribute . . . about the leadership you provide in so many different ways. . . . (Pause).

Think about some times when you chaired an event or activity, a project you helped implement. . . . Think about how you contributed your expertise to enable your organization to flourish and succeed. . . .

Shift gears a bit now, and think about your relationship to God. . . . Think about how much time you have given to spiritual activities such as prayer, study, observance of Shabbat and holidays. . . . Think about any other mitzvot you have performed. . . .

Take a minute to see if you there are any areas of your Jewish self which you would like to enhance or improve. . . . Ask yourself if you are pleased and satisfied with the way you live your Jewish life. . . . What might you add to make yourself a more involved Jew? . . . (Pause).

When you are ready, return to this room, and gradually, slowly, open your eyes. . . . ○

The facilitator may lead a discussion dividing all the Jewish involvement which participants thought of into two categories: primary and secondary Jewish activities. The primary ones are the direct Jewish involvements which help one become a more dedicated Jew in one's personal life, and which are vital to the preservation of the

Jewish religion and culture. These include such activities as prayer, study, giving charity and helping to fix our unredeemed world, doing some of the mitzvot, practicing Jewish rituals and customs. Secondary activities are more geared toward supporting the primary activities, such as institution building, fund-raising campaigns, serving on committees and in other leadership roles.

By making the distinction between primary and secondary Jewish activities, some Jewish leaders may see that more of their time is devoted to secondary rather than primary Jewish involvement. It might be suggested, without being judgmental, that the ultimate purpose of all of the secondary activities is to support and assist the primary ones (study, prayer, observance, mitzvot, acts of charity and direct human service). Let participants decide, after doing this analysis of their own Jewish involvement, if they are pleased with the balance of primary and secondary Jewish activities in their lives. The results of this exercise and the discussion following may enlighten participants as to where they may want to shift the balance of their Jewish involvement: from more heavily in secondary, or support, activities, to more direct, or primary activities. If this is the facilitator's agenda, it should be clear and forthright, without, of course, making anyone feel diminished for disagreeing. Nor should anyone feel that support activities are unimportant or unappreciated. The ultimate decisions regarding commitment of time and energy must be left to the individual participant. The exercise should be geared toward heightening awareness, and sharing the views of the facilitator, not toward being judgmental or critical.

Chapter 20

TEACHER TRAINING

Imagination is more important than knowledge; for knowledge is limited, while imagination embraces the entire world.
—Albert Einstein

To know is nothing at all; to imagine is everything.
—Anatole France

I N A SENSE this entire book is a manual for teacher training, assuming that we define the word "teacher" in its broadest framework. From the introductory chapters which explain the methodology of guided imagery, to the scripts provided in the rest of the chapters, a teacher, facilitator or group leader of adults or children, will learn how to use this exciting and innovative methodology inside and outside the classroom.

The purpose of this chapter is to provide a trainer in a teacher training workshop with specific scripts for doing guided imagery exercises. By selecting the types of exercises we shall suggest below, we will have focused on the some of the critical and crucial issues which the teacher in today's classroom has to face. Most of all, we have tried to foster the importance of creativity and innovation in teaching. In the words of Robert and Isabel Hawley, two prominent humanistic educators, "Perhaps the single most important skill for living which can be fostered in the classroom is the habit of flexible and creative thinking. This is the ability to remain open and tentative in gathering and organizing information and in solving problems rather than submitting to a static and limited view of the possibilities in a given context." It is our hope that it is exactly this kind of creative thinking which will emerge from involvement in the following guided imagery exercises.

HELPING TEACHERS BE CREATIVE

○ *Imagine a beautiful bouquet of flowers. Look at the rainbow-like design of the variegated colors. . . . See the unusual shapes of the different flowers. . . . Imagine that you are lightly touching the soft texture of the flowers. . . . Smell the soothing aroma of the bouquet, and see what a calming influence it has on you. . . . Gaze at the flowers for a moment or two, and as you do so, find yourself becoming more and more deeply relaxed, serene and comfortable. . . . Let your eyes close and settle in to a position that feels just right. . . .*

Search through the forest of your memory and recall some very creative teachers with whom you were privileged to study over the course of your life. (Pause).

Create in your imagination as much detail as you can about the kinds of things these creative teachers did to engage you and your peers. . . . See the sights, looking around to see who else is there with you. . . . Get in touch with the sounds, smells and scenes of these experiences. . . . Focus your attention on some of the specific things which your teacher, or teachers, did to make your learning experience different, exciting, engaging. (Pause).

Think for a moment about how you can be like that teacher, or those teachers. . . . In what way are you like them? In what way can you try to emulate some of their creative traits? . . .

See yourself in the classroom, or leading whatever group you are accustomed to lead, and being very creative. . . . Notice how everyone sitting in the room is deeply interested in what you are saying and doing. . . . Your creativity is shining through very brightly. . . .

After class, or at the conclusion of whatever session you led, notice how many of the students come up and thank you for sharing your self, your personality, your ideas, your thoughts, your feelings, your soul, with your group of students. (Pause).

Feeling very affirmed and satisfied with your achievements, begin to return to this room, and open your eyes, slowly and gradually, whenever you are ready. . . . ○

TEACHING JEWISH WISDOM

❍ *Imagine yourself sitting on the beach at the edge of the ocean. . . .
There is a soft, gentle breeze blowing on your face, keeping you cool and comfortable. . . . You begin to stare at the waves coming in to wash the shore. . . .
Direct your eyes toward the waves as they roll in and out, in and out. . . .
Keep watching the water as it comes toward you and rolls back, toward you and
rolls back. . . . Your attention is captured by the mystery and beauty of the waves
as they continually go back and forth, back and forth. . . . As you become very
relaxed, let your eyes close and feel very calm and comfortable. . . .*

*As a teacher of Judaism, you are filled with a love of your Heritage, and are
proud to be among those chosen to impart some of its knowledge and understanding to those who sit at your feet to drink in the wisdom of the past. Feel the
power for good, and the positive influence you are capable of imparting. . . .*

*Knowing that Judaism has helped you deal with many difficulties in life,
you want to share with your students how helpful the wisdom of Judaism can be
to act as a beacon of light through the shadows of life. . . . Think of one important
idea which you especially respect and admire in the wisdom of the Jewish tradition. Perhaps it is a sentence in the Torah or Talmud, perhaps a hasidic story,
maybe a line from the siddur, or maybe the message of a story from the vast
storehouse of Jewish literature. . . . Take your time and select just one idea.
(Pause).*

*Imagine yourself sitting in your favorite comfortable chair in your study at
home, and thinking about the lesson plan for your next class. . . . As you sit there,
quietly, fully relaxed, let your creative mind wander a bit, and think of an
innovative way to present this idea that has helped you so much in the past. . . .*

*After you have selected one idea, think of a few others, so you will have the
choice of presenting this important idea in an alternative way in case you change
your mind while you are teaching. . . . (Pause).*

*Now that you have a few good ways to present your important idea in a
variety of creative ways, see yourself presenting this idea to your class, or group,
and see how they become excited and inspired by your teaching. . . . You are very
pleased with your presentation, and are determined to spend ample time preparing your lessons so that you will be satisfied with your preparation. In this way
you can very often come up with new and unusual ideas for presenting the
material you would like to teach. . . .*

Feeling very warm inside, with a deep sense of spiritual satisfaction, you are ready to conclude this exercise, and return to this room, gradually and slowly opening your eyes, and feeling very good in every way. . . . ○

BLOSSOMING OF THE ROSE

The following exercise is adapted from a modality in humanistic education known as psychosynthesis, originated by an Italian psychiatrist, Roberto Assagioli, in the middle decades of the twentieth century. As with many guided imagery exercises, appropriate music in the background providing a sense of peace and calm is helpful to achieving maximum results.

○ *Imagine yourself looking down from a balcony over a beautiful garden. . . . The beauty of the garden brings you a sense of calm and peace. . . . Everything around you is very quiet and hushed. . . . Only the sound of a few birds chirping and the wind blowing break the stillness of the garden. . . . With all the beauty and majesty of the garden below, lying quietly without disturbance, you find yourself becoming very calm and relaxed. . . . Let your eyes close, and allow yourself to give your imagination free reign. . . .*

As you gaze upon the beauty of the garden below, let yourself pretend that you are a rosebud on one of the rosebushes below. . . . Look around and see what other plants are nearby, and what kind of area the rosebush is growing in. . . .

Take your time and let yourself smell the scents around you—the grass, the earth, the other flowers and bushes. . . . Look up at the sky and see how beautiful the white puffs of clouds look against the blue background. . . .

Feel the weight of your body resting on the rosebush which supports you. . . . Let your consciousness be one with the rosebud which you have become. . . . Feel what it is like becoming this budding rose. . . . Feel the flow of life energy inside you. . . . As a rosebud you are part of the ever-growing world of nature, and you feel the desire to blossom and grow within yourself. . . . You feel the inner longing to expand and fulfill your destiny as a rose. . . . (Pause).

Now become aware of the warmth of the sun shining down from above. . . . Let the warmth of the sun's rays awaken your cells and all your inner parts. . . . You feel yourself gradually beginning to unfold. . . . Slowly imagine the green sepals around the bud starting to open. Now the color of the petals within is more clearly visible. . . . One by one the petals continue to unfold. . . .

Beneath you, in the earth that is supporting you, experience the flow of life energy ascending from the roots of the plant and flowing through the stem, leaves and flowers. . . . Just as all living beings, plants, flowers, trees, animals and humans, share in the flow of energy moving through nature, so do you as a rosebud feel this rising energy within yourself. . . . Feel how you are linked to the fabric of the universe. . . .

As the life force flows through you, your petals continue to open until the rose is full-blown. Now you can experience yourself as a fully opened rose. You are a radiant center of beauty and joy, always growing and expanding. . . . Experience the bliss and perfection of your own true nature. . . . Experience the wonder and glory of the fully opened rose. . . .

Now be aware of the scent of your perfume. Feel how this sweet scent is your love flowing out into the world. As you are filled with the warmth of the sun and the flow of life energy, you radiate this as love into the world, longing to share it with all creatures. You are an important source of caring and nurturing to all who are near you. . . .

Remain with this feeling as long as you wish, letting yourself open and grow as you feel yourself connected to the one great universe of which the flower is just a part. (Pause).

Whenever you are ready, begin to return to normal consciousness. Remember that whenever you wish you can return to the essence of this experience and allow it to inspire you in your quest for fulfillment of your true Self. . . . ⭘

The trainer can use any of the grounding exercises listed in chapter three to complete this guided imagery exercise. Following the grounding part of the exercise, and leaving sufficient time for participants to share their experience of blossoming as a rose, a discussion may follow on how this exercise applies to the calling of teaching and education. Some of the ideas which may emerge in a sharing period after the exercise are: 1) the teacher should always continue to grow as a person and as a teacher, 2) life is always filled with opportunities for learning, and we fulfill our best true nature when we continue to learn and grow, 3) the best way for a teacher to help a student is by modeling the life of a growing, learning person, who is flexible, open, and continues to follow a life-long pattern of growth.

The "Blossoming of the Rose" exercise can be used in other contexts besides teacher training, including leadership development, moral education, prayer and spirituality, etc.

THE EVER-FLOWING FOUNTAIN

In the talmudic tractate *Pirke Avot* a metaphor is use to describe a scholar, or a learning Jew, as "an ever-flowing fountain" (6:1). This is an apt metaphor for one who loves to learn and teach, and it will be the basis of the next exercise.

❍ *Imagine yourself sitting in the middle of a large fountain in the middle of a park, with water pouring over you, bringing you purity, wholeness and relaxation. . . . The temperature is just right, the sun is shining warmly on your skin, and the air is fresh and invigorating. . . . As the water pours over you it brings you a sense of renewal and refreshment, cleansing you and healing you. . . . As you begin to feel more and more deeply relaxed, let your eyes close and allow your imagination to be free. . . .*

In many passages in the Tanakh and throughout the rest of our Tradition, we find that the image of water represents Torah and knowledge, enlightenment and inspiration. Imagine to yourself that the water coming out of the fountain is the water of Torah and of wisdom. . . . The fountain is none other than the eternal fountain of wisdom. . . .

In many ways the wisdom flowing from the fountain brings you a sense of renewal and awakening. . . . As the water cascades over your shoulders and your body, you feel its power to make you feel clean and clear. . . . The water washes off any impurities from your body, and its essence washes through your soul and makes it pure and whole. . . .

When you get thirsty, raise your head and allow the fresh, clean and pure water to roll down your throat, giving you nourishment and refreshment. . . . It makes you feel alive and energized, bringing life to all the cells, muscles and nerves in your body. . . . After drinking, you feel more alert, more energized and more empowered. . . .

As you stand and let the water pour over you, and drink from it to refresh and renew your body and soul, you realize that there is a never-ending source of this fresh, clean and pure water. . . . It comes from the earth, and it is part of God's plan to feed and sustain the universe. . . . You share your thirst for water with all living beings, and you feel connected to the world of nature in a deep and spiritual way. . . .

Knowing that you can always return to this fountain of wisdom, you begin to conclude your visit and return gradually to this room. When you are ready, slowly open your eyes, and feel invigorated and strengthened in body and soul. ❍

Participants may be asked to think of things in their profession which are represented by water, and be given time to ground their experience in one of the ways listed in chapter three. Perhaps a text can be introduced, such as Isaiah 40:28-30, or Pirke Avot 6:1, in which the power of spiritual strength is demonstrated in the life of individuals. A classic text comparing Torah to water is found in the midrash of Shir HaShirim Rabba 1:2 (found in English in *The Book of Legends* by Bialik and Ravnitzky [New York: Schocken, 1992], pp. 404-5, paragraph 22).

APPLYING FOR A TEACHING POSITION

○ *For the next while you will find yourself becoming more and more still and quiet. . . . Listen to the quiet, and see how calming it is. . . . As you sit or lie very quietly, your mind slows down, and you begin to become centered and relaxed. . . . Take a few deep, slow breaths, and let yourself become very comfortable and confident. . . .*

Imagine that you are sitting in the office of a director of education in a large, prestigious school. You are applying for a position to teach in that school, and you find an immediate rapport with the director. . . .

Your personal warmth and charisma is very evident, and all the wonderful qualities about you which make you a special person are being felt by the director. . . . You can feel the warmth between the two of you. . . .

The director begins to ask you questions about yourself and your background. Begin by telling the director why you wanted to become a teacher. (Pause).

Next tell the interviewer about your previous successes in teaching. Tell about some special children or adults whom you influenced, and the impact you have had on other educational institutions in your previous years of teaching experience. . . .

The director asks you now to talk about the areas of teaching in which you excel. Talk freely and without inhibition about these areas. . . .

Next, the conversation moves to the subject of you as a person. What kind of qualities make you a good teacher? What parts of your personality help you influence the people you teach. . . . Tell about this unabashedly and without reservation. . . .

The director now asks you what things you will bring to this school which it may not have now. . . . How will your presence here make a difference—among the faculty, the parents, the students, and the community. . . . Speak with confidence and experience. (Pause).

The director now asks you in what ways would you like to become an even better person and a better teacher. What are the parts of you which you are working on to grow, as a person, a Jew, and a human being. Again, talk fully and without hesitation. . . . (Pause).

The director now asks you if you would like to add anything about yourself which you may have omitted so far. Say whatever you would like to add now. . . .

The director thanks you for sharing your time, and expresses delight in having met you. . . . Thank the director for the opportunity to share all the wonderful parts of yourself, and say goodbye, with your usual friendly and warm manner. . . .

When you are ready, slowly and gradually come back to the present, feeling confident and joyful, with an abundance of good feelings exuding from every part of you. . . . Stretch your body and open your eyes. . . . ○

THE COUNCIL OF SAGES

○ Sit down at a table with a pen or pencil and a notebook. Sit comfortably and become very relaxed. . . . While in most guided imagery exercises participants close their eyes and sit or lie passively, this one will be different. I will ask you to take some notes while you are in the process of using your imagination.

[Facilitator: an alternative to this approach would be to indeed conduct the exercise with eyes closed and ask participants to jot down the ideas that came to them when it is completed].

During this guided imagery exercise you will have the opportunity to meet many very wise and experienced teachers. They have taught in classrooms, were advisers to groups of adults and youth, were guides in family education, were involved in day school as well as supplemental education. They are master teachers, recognized throughout the world for their successful teaching experience over many decades. They are now all close to retirement, and would like to share their experience with teachers who have had fewer years pursuing their vocation.

Enter a large stone building with a medieval look about it. Its windows are arched, and its ceilings high. . . . It has the look of an academy of scholars. Or, if you wish, it may appear to you as a yeshivah from the Eastern Europe of several centuries ago. . . . Inside there are ten large classrooms.

During this exercise you will enter the building and have a chance to talk with each of the ten sages inside. Each wise teacher is sitting in his or her classroom at the desk in front of the room. When it is your turn, go to the sage, and ask a question about teaching and learning.

You may want to ask some of them what is the secret of their many years of successful teaching. . . . Go to the first classroom where one of the sages is sitting, and ask your question now. . . . (Pause). When you hear the answer, write it down. (Pause).

Now proceed to the next room where a second sage sits. You may want to ask something about the teacher's approach to teaching various subjects, or where the sage learned the material that they taught. . . . Or you may want to ask about their own education throughout the years, what courses they took, what books they read, what experiences they sought out to enrich their teaching credentials. . . . Ask any questions you like. Listen to the answers. (Pause). Now write them down. (Pause).

It is now time to approach the classroom of the third sage. Enter and have a conversation with the sage. Ask the wise teacher something about how to handle different kinds of students, some who are motivated and some who are not; some who have a thirst for learning and some who do not want to learn; some who are deeply concerned about developing their Jewish identity, and some who are not. Ask any question you wish related to approaching a wide variety of students in your classes. . . . Now listen to the answer, and write it down. (Pause).

As you approach the fourth classroom, begin to formulate some questions you may want to ask. Perhaps this time you may want to inquire about the future of Jewish life and education in the city where you live, or in the Diaspora in general. Perhaps this question will be a much broader one. . . . Ask it now, listen for the answer, and write it down. (Pause).

Now you are entering the fifth classroom, and begin to talk with the next sage. This person looks and sounds like the kind of individual who may be able to answer some deep theological question you have. You have searched for an answer to this question from many books and scholars, and have never received an adequate response. Ask this sage that question now. Listen for the answer, and then write it down. (Pause).

As you begin to chat with the next teacher, you have on your mind some questions about the profession of Jewish education and Jewish community service. Think of some of the things that have perplexed you about this issue, and ask your expert any question about this subject. When you have your answer, write it down. (Pause).

You may continue to go to all the other four classrooms, or you may just want to go to one or two more. Go into any of the classrooms you have not yet visited, and select any question on any subject that you wish to inquire about. Have any discussion you like with any or all of the remaining wise teachers. . . . (Pause).

Now jot down anything else you may have forgotten to write before, and any additional thoughts which may come to you as you conclude your visit. (Pause).

You are about to conclude your visit to the learning academy, and you feel very confident and joyful. Your mind and soul are full and refreshed. You are feeling very fortunate to have met these wise people, and they have enriched your life in many ways.

When you have finished all your notes, bring yourself back to normal wakefulness, and begin to stretch, take a long yawn, and find yourself alert, inspired and content. Take your time. (Pause). At the count of three you will be ready to end this exercise. One. Two. Three. ○

Chapter 21

LEADERSHIP DEVELOPMENT

The Imagination is the only truth.
—Bertolt Brecht

Only the inward vision can reach that heavenly goal.
—Yehudah HaLevi

EVERY GROUP and organization should be concerned about its future leadership. If things are running smoothly, programs are successful, membership is growing, finances are strong, and all is going well, it is easy to assume that it will always be that way. It will not unless provision is made for new people to ascend the ladder of leadership in the organization. Such new leaders must have the requisite training and experience to take over the helm of the important committee chairs and board positions in a year, or in five or ten years from now.

In a Jewish organization leaders need two kinds of skills. First, they need Jewish knowledge and loyalty, so that they understand and are committed to the mission of the institution. Second, they need group and organizational skills such as group process, group development, strategic planning, team building, communication skills, administration, goal-setting, time management, supervision, evaluation, conflict resolution, dealing with volunteers, etc.

Some of the issues subsumed under Jewish knowledge and loyalty are included in chapter nineteen of this book on the subject of "Board Training." In this chapter we shall focus more on organizational skills, although when dealing with Jewish organizations, the Jewish component is almost inevitably included in one way or another.

(For leadership training activities and suggestions other than through guided imagery exercises, see the author's *Organization Development For Jewish Institutions* (Princeton, NJ: Growth Associates, 1980).

The following guided imagery exercises may be used for leadership development programs in any Jewish organization.

QUALITIES OF A GOOD JEWISH GROUP

○ *Close your eyes and let yourself imagine the flame of a candle. It may be the flame of a Shabbat or festival candle on the dining room table; or perhaps the flame of a Hanukkah menorah, a yahrzeit candle, or another candle that has meaning to you. . . . As you stare at the fire of the flame, let yourself become deeply relaxed. . . . The more you focus on the flame, the more the external environment will fade away, and permit you to become more and more deeply relaxed. . . .*

Imagine that you are a veteran leader in the Jewish community, with thirty to forty years of successful experience in every possible leadership capacity. You have been chairperson of important committees of such organizations as your synagogue, the JCC, the Federation, B'nai B'rith, the Home for the Aged, the Jewish Family Service, the Bureau of Jewish Education, and a national college for training rabbis, hazzanim, religious educators, teachers, and community workers.

Due to your vast amount of experience in dealing with Jewish organizational life, and with professional and lay leaders, you receive an invitation to deliver an address to the national biennial convention of a prominent Jewish movement. Your topic is "The Five Ingredients of A Successfully Run Jewish Organization." Present in the audience of some several thousand people will be lay and professional Jewish leaders from all over North America and other countries.

Take a few moments to think about what you want to say. (Pause).

Imagine yourself now jotting down an outline of your talk. The first thing you do is to list in short form the five ingredients you want to talk about. In your imagination jot down now these five ingredients. . . . (Pause).

Look over the list and see if there is anything you omitted. . . . Next, make an appointment to visit a colleague of yours who has the same kind of successful experience of many years of leadership in Jewish groups. Show the list to your friend, and see if this person has any suggestions for you. . . . Perhaps there is one your friend wants to add or subtract, or to modify. . . . If you like, have a discussion with your friend, and come to an agreement about which ingredients you want to address in your talk. (Pause).

[The facilitator may bring the exercise to a close here, or continue, as desired].

Imagine now that you have completed your talk, and you receive a standing ovation from the audience. Several people come over to you and tell you which of the things you said were most helpful to them. Listen to what they say. . . .

Think about the reactions you have received, and consider what additions or modifications you may want to make the next time you may be invited to give this talk. (Pause).

Now we are ready to conclude this guided imagery exercise, so slowly begin to return to this room, and gradually open your eyes. . . . ○

The facilitator may wish to permit participants to take a few minutes to write down the five most important ingredients of a Jewish organization which they came up with. Alternatively, it is possible to have them do the writing during the exercise, as long as the writing does not interfere with their ability to be engaged in the guided imagery.

Another possibility is to have the group create a consensus among themselves, or among smaller groups of four to six within the larger group, as to what are the five most important ingredients.

A MODEL JEWISH LEADER

○ Find a position in which you feel very comfortable and relaxed. Shift your weight around so that your body is completely supported. . . . Take a few deep, slow breaths to bring a sense of cleansing and healing to your entire body. . . . Breathe out any tension you have in your body, and see how calm and serene you feel. . . .

Your Jewish organization has invited you to join a day-long workshop at national headquarters at which a very prominent leader will be the leader/ speaker/facilitator. You have heard the name of this well-known Jewish leader, but have never had the opportunity before to see or listen to the person face to face. You are excited to have been chosen for the honor to participate in a national workshop such as this. Since you know that you will come away with many new ideas and insights for your own leadership skills, you are looking forward very much to this as a personal and professional learning experience.

The day arrives, and you are now sitting around a large table in an attractive paneled conference room together with fifteen other national leaders chosen to participate in this unique workshop.

Before the workshop begins, beverages and fruit are served, and you happen to be standing next to the guest facilitator. Tell the person how you feel about being selected to join in the leadership training experience. (Pause).

When the workshop begins the facilitator asks the participants what kinds of things they would like to derive from the training experience. Listen to what some of the people say. . . . Now it is your turn. Tell the leader and the group what goals you have for yourself for the day of training. . . .

During the morning of the workshop you notice some very interesting and highly skilled actions which the national expert does in moving the group process along. You think to yourself how you can apply these same skills in your group back home. What skills did you notice? . . .

Before you break for lunch you think to yourself about several important learnings you acquired during the first half of the workshop. Take a mental note as to what these learnings are. . . . Later you will be given a chance to write them down.

At lunch you sit with people from other parts of the country who belong to different branches of the your organization. What kinds of things are you discussing with these other people? (Pause).

At the beginning of the afternoon session of the workshop, the facilitator asks everyone to state one learning which they derived from the morning session. Listen to what some of the others say. . . . Now you raise your hand and volunteer to share what you learned. What is it? . . .

You thought the facilitator could not possibly surpass the successful activities and lectures of the morning session, but find that the afternoon half of the workshop is even more interesting and useful than the morning part. What are some of the things which you learned in the afternoon session? (Pause).

It is about five o'clock now and the workshop is about to conclude. The final task assigned to each person around the table is to mention one way in which he/ she will be a better organizational leader after returning to their home communities. Listen to what some of the other participants say. . . . Then take your turn and share with the group how you think you will change now that you have participated in this very inspiring, exhilarating and informative workshop. . . . (Pause).

The facilitator thanks everyone for their active participation, and for the things which this expert learned from the group. Say goodbye to your new friends

*and to the leader. Thank them all for letting you share in the day's experience,
and for the things you learned from them. . . .*

*When you are ready, come back to this room, and slowly open your eyes and
return to normal consciousness. . . .* ◯

The facilitator may wish to post on a chalkboard or poster paper some of the learnings the participants in the guided imagery exercise derived from their imaginary experience. Other grounding experiences can be chosen from chapter three of this book.

ASSISTING A YOUNGER COLLEAGUE

◯ *Imagine that you are enjoying a wonderful vacation, and waking up
from a very restful sleep in a luxurious bed. . . . See how rested and comfortable
you feel. . . . Look out the window and see the magnificent view of nature. . . .
You are feeling extremely calm and at peace in every way. . . .*

*Imagine that you have worked your way up the ladder of leadership of your
organization over a period of many years. You served on many committees, on
the Board of Trustees, were elected an officer, and now after many successful
experiences in a wide array of capacities, you have been chosen to be president.
This makes you feel very honored and respected, and you are very pleased with
the course of your years of service to your organization.*

*In a community a few miles from you another organization exists which is
part of the same national movement as yours. You receive a telephone call from
the young president of that organization asking for your advice. This individual
is less experienced than you, and would like to ask you several questions.*

*The first question this young president asks you is about getting new
members. What advice can you offer on this subject? . . .*

*After sharing your answers, your colleague then asks about handling financial affairs. It seems that they have a large deficit, and would like some ideas on
how to reduce it. Share some of your ideas on this subject with that person. . . .*

*Next you are asked about recruiting new volunteers to serve in leadership
roles. In today's world many people are over-committed and are not easily
convinced to take their limited free time for voluntary organizations.
What ideas can you give this person for conscripting new, fresh blood for the
organization? . . .*

*Then the young president tells you that there is a problem in the organization. Many people complain about a wide variety of things, and it is difficult to
handle all the discontent. The phone is constantly ringing, there is an abundance*

of complaints that come in the mail. The president sometimes feels overwhelmed by all the unhappy members. What advice you can offer about dealing with dissenting and complaining people in the organization? . . .

Finally, tell the president that you have time for only a few more minutes of conversation right now, and if there is one final question, you will try to answer it. See if there is another question, and if so, answer it. . . . Conclude your discussion now with the other president. . . .

You can decide if you wish to continue giving advice at another time, and if so tell the person that you will be happy to talk on the telephone or meet on another occasion for further coaching sessions. . . .

Now say goodbye, and get ready to return to this room. Slowly and gradually open your eyes, feeling very good and alert. . . . ○

A RIDE IN THE SKY

○ *Imagine that you are floating in the sky on a very comfortable and light mattress. . . . You are floating along, looking all around at the many beautiful sights above and below. . . . You feel very good, and everything is just the way you want it . . . the temperature, the wind, the sunshine. . . . You feel very content and pleased. . . .*

Since we are using our imagination it is possible for you to do anything you want, and go anywhere you would like, up or down, fast or slow. . . . You are very safe, and are enjoying yourself in every way. . . . Your magic mattress will do anything you want it to do. . . .

Right now you are flying over the building which houses the organization to which you belong. Sail down a bit and get close enough to see and hear anything you wish. . . .

The people in your organization are meeting in different rooms. Some are sitting on a committee to plan an event. Others are trying to work out various organizational problems. In another room there is an educational program going on. In still another room some young people are having one of their regular programs.

With your magic mattress, travel above the building over each room. Since you have the magic power to see and hear everything going on inside, you will be able to observe everything very easily. Fly over now and watch how successful your organization is. . . .

First you fly over the room where a committee is planning an important event several months later. See how well the meeting is going, and pay attention to what it is that makes everything work so well. . . . (Pause).

In another room the strategic planning task force is convening, and making some long range concepts for the next five to ten years. Observe what they are talking about. . . . (Pause).

In still another room, you watch a group of people who are planning the calendar for the coming year. See what exciting new programs they are devising. . . . (Pause).

In another room there is a group that is evaluating the progress you have made in different areas of the organization. Everyone in the room seems very pleased and satisfied with what has been going on. Pay attention to some of the positive comments and other creative ideas that are emerging from this discussion. . . . (Pause).

As you continue to float over room after room, you next come upon several people who are talking about some important structural changes that are being suggested to make your organization more streamlined. . . . Pay attention to the ideas that are being outlined. . . . (Pause).

In yet another meeting room there is a planning session of the membership recruitment committee. They are excited about some new ideas to attract many new people to become part of your group. What ideas do they have? . . . (Pause).

In one of the offices of the building you see the leading staff member of the organization meeting with some of the top lay leaders. They are pleased because of the way the staff has been working together, and are discussing some new methods put into place recently to help create a warmer and more supportive atmosphere for the staff. What ideas are they most excited about? . . . . (Pause).

Take your time and visit any other areas of the building you would like. . . . (Pause).

When you are finished, bring your magic mattress back down to earth, and return to this room. Open your eyes, stretch, and be fully alert. . . . ○

For a variant of this exercise, cf. *Organization Development For Jewish Institutions*, edited by Dov Peretz Elkins (Princeton, NJ: Growth Associates, 1980), p. 47.

Chapter 22

GUIDED IMAGERY FOR YOUTH GROUPS

Imagination and fiction make up more than three quarters of our real life.

—Simone Weil

GUIDED IMAGERY can be utilized with people of all ages. It is an effective educational tool for a wide variety of age groups, including very young children and very sophisticated adults. This innovative educational technique can be part of a formal lesson plan in a school classroom, part of an adult or family education program on serious themes, or it can be used with school-age children in informal youth groups.

The guided imagery exercises which follow are designed specifically for informal youth education, such as meetings of groups like BBYO, Young Judea, NFTY, USY, and NCSY, including such settings as summer camps, weekend retreats, etc. As with many of the scripts in other chapters in this book, there is no reason why many of these exercises cannot be used in other places as well, even though they are designed specifically for one setting. Most of the exercises in this book can be used in almost any setting. The decisions as to which script fits which setting, and what modifications are made in the script, depend largely upon the discretion and judgment of the facilitator. Such a decision will be made by the leader based on the size, age and maturity level of the group, the goals of the session, time available, and how this exercise fits in with the overall program of the group. An important factor always, of course, is the facilitator's level of comfort and familiarity with a particular group.

The introductory exercise in this chapter is designed to demonstrate what guided imagery is. It is for groups which have not had an experience with this method previously, to show them that it can be both educational and fun to learn how to better use the God-given gift of our imagination. The first exercise, "Put Your Magen David on the Ceiling," is adapted from a wonderful book written by Richard de Mille (son of the famous movie director Cecil B. De Mille) titled *Put Your Mother on the Ceiling*. De Mille's book is designed to introduce children to the notion of the fantasy world, and to help them realize that it is a useful and playful part of their brain's capacity to be creative and intelligent. Guided imagery should be presented in a fun-oriented fashion, while at the same time explaining that the same technique involved in this exercise is one which adults use for very serious activities for learning, growth and discovery.

PUT YOUR MAGEN DAVID ON THE CEILING

The group leader should introduce this exercise with a brief explanation about different parts of our brain. There are parts that help us memorize important things, like our telephone number, address, and those of our friends and relatives. There is another part of our brain which helps us to discover new ideas and make valuable inventions, such as creating new medicines to cure sick people, new computer games, writing novels and poetry, and discovering ways to make cars safer, planes faster, etc. In this exercise we shall be using the part of our brain (usually referred to as our "right-brain") which is the creative part of us. To use this part of our brain we need to utilize our imagination, and let ourselves loosen up a bit and be playful with our minds. The facilitator may suggest to participants that they try not to permit too much "reality" to block their usage of fanciful guided imagery. By explaining that this is a "mind game" the participants will be freed to let their imagination reign free without the blocks which normally surface in our thinking, such as "This does not ring true," or "I could never do this is the real world," or "Such a thing would never happen in reality." This is not reality, but imagination and education. In the end it can be very useful and growthful.

Anyone who is not in the mood, or for whatever other reason does not wish to participate, may just sit and watch the others. It is counterproductive to pressure someone to participate in this kind of activity. Time should be left for questions and discussion, if desired by participants, before the exercise begins. It is important that anyone who so wishes has a chance to talk about the experience at the conclusion of the guided imagery exercise.

Now let's begin.

❍ *We are going to do an activity called "imagining." To use our imagination effectively it is helpful to close our eyes, and feel relaxed. Take a deep breath, and when you breathe out pretend that all the tension and tiredness inside you is going out of your body with your breath.*

Imagine that there is a Magen David (a Jewish star) hanging on a chain around your neck. Pretend that the Magen David flies off your neck and begins to twirl around in the air. Let it now attach itself to the ceiling. . . . Have the Magen David move around the ceiling in circles. Let the Magen David become twice its former size. . . . Now see how it turns a bright red color, and let it come down from the ceiling and hang on the wall. . . .

As it hangs on the wall, you see six smaller Magen Davids all around it, each a different color. . . . Let the Magen Davids all turn into velvet now, as you walk over and touch them, and see how smooth they are. . . . Let the Magen Davids join together on the wall and do a dance. . . . While they are doing that you hear the Jewish National Anthem, Hatikvah, playing in the background. . . . Out of each of the seven Magen Davids there is an Israeli flag which pops out from its center. . . . All the Magen Davids now turn into wood, painted with blue and white stripes, and they march out the front door onto the lawn. . . .

Watch how the Magen Davids on the lawn become double their size, and join together dancing a hora. Behind them is a Klezmer group playing Hatikvah. . . . Look at the houses on your street. From all their doors come more Magen Davids, and they all walk toward your front lawn and join in the hora. . . . The hora becomes so exciting that the Magen Davids jump high into the air as they dance. . . . As the hora continues you see a squadron of El Al planes flying overhead in the sky. . . .

The planes begin to form a large circle in the sky and jump up and down as if they are dancing the hora. Out of each plane come thousands of paper Magen Davids dropping all over your city, blanketing the entire area with paper Magen Davids in all colors. . . . Now these thousands of Magen Davids turn into wood and become thirty times their size. . . . They join together and dance the hora, so that there are horas all over the city, and dozens of more klezmers come to play Hatikvah for them. . . .

Each Magen David turns into a delicious cookie, and they stop dancing. . . . Watch as all the people in the city go outside and find thousands of cookie Magen Davids, wrapped in cellophane. They pick them up and eat them. . . . When they bring them into the house, the Magen Davids turn from cookies into different kinds of food. Some of them become chicken, and some potatoes, some vegetables and others bread. . . . Everyone has enough food from the Magen Davids for the next year. . . .

Now turn yourself into a Magen David, and go outside onto your lawn. . . . You find there all the neighbors who are also Magen Davids, and you all join in dancing the hora. . . .

We will now bring our imagination exercise to an end. Very gradually allow all the pictures and sounds in your mind to fade away. . . . Return to this room, open your eyes, and take a big stretch. . . . You are feeling good, and are pleased with the results of your mental exercise. . . . ○

During the discussion which follows the leader should allow the participants, without being judgmental, to express any reactions they have. Explain to them that there is no "right" or "wrong" way of doing such an exercise in our imagination. There is no "better" or "worse" way to use fantasy. Whatever each person did was fine. There is no grading or evaluating when it comes to the imagination. Imagination is a very private matter. We may compare our reactions to doing a guided imagery exercise with seeing a painting or listening to music. Each person reacts in her/his own fashion, differently and individually, and no one's reaction is superior in any way to that of another. The results of the discussion may show what a wide variety of reactions participants had, and how each is in its own way legitimate and interesting. It will also be a good opening for participants to be willing to do other guided imagery exercises. They may express the idea (or the leader may) that this is one more way to expand their ability to be creative in life.

IMAGINATION CALISTHENICS

The facilitator can begin this exercise, or any guided imagery exercise (especially at beginners' levels) with some brief explanations about the use of fantasy and imagination. Scientists and educators compare our power to imagine with the power of muscles in our body. When we use our muscles we strengthen them and make them more supple and flexible. Just as muscles that are not used become weaker, so too our imagination is not in its full ability to be creative and innovative when it is not exercised. Our power to be creative is related to our capacity to develop our spiritual selves, and thus, when we develop our creativity, we also develop our spirituality. (These explanations should be tailored to the age and maturity of the participants).

○ In this exercise we will try to use our imagination muscles the way we would our body muscles. We can call it doing "imagination calisthenics." To do this well it helps to try to relax and close our eyes. . . . Take a few deep breaths, and see how you can control your own sense of relaxation. . . . A yawn or two, and some stretching, will also help you relax. . . .

We are going to practice with writing implements. In your imagination take a pencil in your hand, and write a sentence. . . . Now let the pencil turn into a red felt pen. . . . Use this red pen to write in other languages. Since we are imagining, you don't need to worry if you know the language or not. Write a word in Greek. . . . Now write one in French. . . . Now write a whole sentence in Hebrew. . . .

Let the pen turn into a paint brush. Go over to the wall and paint a design on the wall. What design did you paint? . . . Now walk outside and notice some homeless people sitting on the ground. . . . Take your paintbrush and paint a new set of clothes on them. . . . See how nice they look. . . . Let your paintbrush turn into a sponge, and with one whisk over their heads they suddenly are clean as a whistle, smelling like a fancy cologne. . . . Invite the homeless people to walk with you for a few blocks to an empty lot. . . . Now each of you has a paintbrush in your hand. . . . Paint a house in the air. As you paint it let it become real. . . . Go inside the house with your new friends and paint some furniture, drapes, carpets, and television sets. . . . Paint some computers and other office equipment such as telephones, fax machines, and anything else you want. . . . As you paint it, it becomes real. . . .

Ask your friend to sit down and show him how to type on the computer using a word-processing program with which you are familiar. . . . Print out what the person wrote and take it to a large publishing house in New York City. The few pages turn into a three-hundred page novel, and the publisher agrees to put it on the market. . . . It becomes a best-selling book, and both you and your friend become very wealthy. . . .

Now go to the bank, open an account and deposit the large sum of money you have earned from the famous novel. Go to a builder and tell him to build several large apartment buildings to house the homeless. Write a large check to pay for the new buildings. . . . Use your paintbrush to bring new furniture to every new apartment in the building. . . .

Take out your checkbook and write another check to establish a job placement service. A director and staff are hired, with spacious, well-appointed offices. See that everyone in all the new apartment buildings has a new job, and can support themselves. . . . Notice how happy all the people living in the buildings are, and how their lives have improved so much through your efforts. . . .

Go to the newspaper in your city and place a full page advertisement. Sit down at their computer and compose the text of the ad. In it you publicize the obligation of giving Tzedakah, and helping everyone climb out of poverty and homelessness. Write a check and pay for the advertisement. . . .

The next day you receive many phone calls from all over the state from people who want to help in your program to eliminate poverty. They write large checks, and you build counseling centers, health centers, job training facilities, and everything that is needed to help many thousands of people establish new, constructive lives. . . .

Since this project was so successful, go back to the newspaper and place another full-page advertisement about another problem, such as drugs, or violence. Sit down at the computer and compose the advertisement. The responses to your ad have helped ease the problems in great measure. Watch how these problems are eliminated from society after you initiate new ideas for the community. . . . (Pause).

Having done so many good things, you now can take a rest, and end this exercise. When you are ready, gradually bring it to a close. When I count to three, you will open your eyes, stretch, and come back to this room. . . . One. Two. Three. ○

Allow ample time to discuss this exercise, without being critical or judgmental in any way. Talk about the differences between reality and imagination. Discuss also some notion of how imagination cannot solve problems, but it can often lead to solutions, and to new ideas about how to solve problems. You may ask participants to offer ideas on how our imagination works in helping us to find new ideas and new solutions to many of our personal problems and often to some of the world's problems. Keeping our imagination skills in tune will accomplish many things for us and for those with whom we live.

WRITING A SHORT STORY

○ *We are going to write a short story in our imagination. First find a comfortable place to sit down and relax. . . . Let your eyes gently close, and take a slow deep breath. . . . As I count down from five to one you will find yourself more and more deeply relaxed. Five. Four. Three. Deeply relaxed. . . . Two. One.*

In your imagination you observe a pious Jewish family in a small town in Poland in the late nineteenth century. Watch this family for a while and find out more about them. . . . How many people are in the family? How many children, grandparents, uncles, aunts, and cousins are there? Who else lives in this small house? . . . What kind of people are they? . . . What does the father do for a living? . . . How does the mother spend her time? . . . Where do the children go to school? . . . What Jewish topics are they studying? . . . Who are their friends? . . . What is their neighborhood like? . . .

It is Friday morning and the father tells his wife disappointedly that there is not enough money to provide for their normal delicious Shabbat meal. . . . They come up with a plan to obtain the money they need. What is their plan? . . .

The sun sets in the sky, the Shabbat candles are lit in the home. Watch the family around the Shabbat table. . . . Notice some of the things they are doing. . . . How do they look? Are they happy or sad? What kind of conversation are they having? . . .

Suddenly there is a knock at the door. One of the children answers the door. Notice who it is, and what the person is saying. . . . The family quickly finishes the meal, cleans up the kitchen, and then goes out of the house. Where are they going? . . .

About an hour later they return and there is great relief on their faces. . . . Everything seems to be OK now. The father tells the family some important news. What does he tell them? . . .

The next day in synagogue people seem distracted from their prayers. There is a great deal of talking and buzzing all through the synagogue. . . . What are they talking about? . . .

At the end of the Shabbat the family begins to do some things which they have not done in a long time. . . . What are they doing? . . . Notice the expressions on the faces of the members of the family. . . . What emotions do you notice as you watch them? . . . What is the mood in the house? . . .

The next day the family's situation has changed dramatically. All kinds of new things are happening, and they must prepare for some major adjustments in life. What is going on in this family's life? . . . (Pause). Pay attention to your own emotional reactions as this story plays itself out in your imagination. What feelings are you experiencing? . . . What thoughts are going through your mind?

We are about to conclude our story now. . . . Bring your story to an end. (Pause).

When you are ready, return to this room, relaxed and refreshed. Gradually open your eyes and be ready to proceed to our next activity. ○

In all likelihood each participant has a completely different scenario in their imaginary story. The leader can ask the group to share their stories in many different ways. Each person can find a partner and tell about the family and its adventures which he/she "created." Or small groups of four or five can join together to share each member's creations. Instead of small group discussions, or in addition to them, each participant can be given about thirty to sixty minutes to write down their story in as many details as possible. Encourage the participants to include the thoughts, feelings, and actions of each person in as much detail as possible. Their fantasy thus becomes the basis for a short story. Alternatively, the leader can ask the group members to write the story at greater leisure at home, and bring it to the next meeting. This has the advantage of giving them more time. The disadvantage is that some may not find the time to complete the "assignment."

The leader can explain that this is the process used in many creative acts; i.e., first the artist conceives of the idea(s) in her/his imagination, and then proceeds to plan and execute the artistic creation—a short story, a painting, a sculpture, a poem, etc.

At the end of this guided imagery exercise and whatever follow-up it may have, a general discussion may be held about the variety of uses and benefits of exercising our imagination, and how guided imagery can be a vital method in fostering these benefits.

SERVING THE JEWISH COMMUNITY

To introduce this guided imagery exercise, the leader can conduct a brief discussion regarding Jewish leadership. Ask the students what it takes to have a thriving, well-organized Jewish community. Part of the answer will inevitably be that there must be competent leaders, both lay and professional. Explain that this exercise will help the participants understand the importance of helping the Jewish community survive, with the assistance of qualified Jewish leaders.

❍ *As in all guided imagery exercises, it is important first of all to become relaxed. Please find a comfortable position, sit back, and begin to feel very calm and serene. Imagine that you are sitting or lying on the beach on a very beautiful day. There are no clouds in the sky, and the sun is strong, but not too hot. The warmth of the sun penetrates your skin and warms your entire body, inside and out. Your heart feels very warm and loved. You feel strong and confident, and very calm and relaxed. . . .*

Think of someone in the Jewish community, in your organization, or anyone you know whom you admire. . . . This may be a teacher, a rabbi, a synagogue president or other lay leader, a respected figure in the community, a generous contributor, or anyone for whom you have special regard and respect. . . .

After you have someone in mind, think of the things which this individual does to contribute to the vitality of the Jewish community where you live. . . . (Pause).

In your imagination go through a typical day of this person. What does she/ he do in the course of the day to strengthen Jewish life? (Pause).

What are some of the things which you would also like to do when you become older and a full adult member of the Jewish community? . . . What are

some of the things your special person does from which you might benefit were
you to do some of these things? Think of how you might enjoy and derive special
satisfaction from doing them. . . . (Pause).

What is one specific activity which this person does, or has done recently. . . .
Now picture yourself, as an adult, doing the same thing. . . . How do you feel?
. . . What contribution do you think you are making by accomplishing this? . . .

Imagine some other things which you may want to do as a future Jewish
leader. . . . These ideas may come either from what your special person does, or
from some things you have seen or noticed other people doing. . . . See what joy
and satisfaction you are bringing to others as you do these things. . . . Imagine the
good that will come from these acts, and how you feel doing this. (Pause).

Sit quietly for a while and think about the things you have just imagined.
. . . How do you react to this exercise? . . . What meaning might you derive from
this experience? . . . Knowing that you will have many more opportunities to
think about these issues in the future, prepare to set this topic aside for now, and
consider returning to think some more about it at a later time . . . whenever it
feels right.

When you are ready take a big yawn, stretch your arms and legs, shake your
body a bit, and slowly open your eyes. ○

Many different kinds of follow-up experiences can be designed permitting young
people to consider Jewish community service, either as a career or in a lay capacity.
They may want to interview lay or professional Jewish leaders based on their own
guided imagery exercise. They may want to plan a career day in which Jewish community service is one of the options. They may want to go through a number of values
clarification exercises to help sort out their thoughts and feelings about Jewish community service, and about being a Jewish leader in a lay or professional capacity.

One such exercise would be to have one of the participants stand at the head of the
group and conduct a "pretend" interview, responding to questions from "pretend" news
correspondents about having served for fifty years as a servant in the field of Jewish
communal service. (Let the one doing the role play interview suggest the career which
he/she chose). Other kinds of role playing activities are also possible.

(For suggestions of values clarification exercises see this author's *Clarifying Jewish*
Values, Jewish Consciousness Raising and other titles listed in the back of this book).

Chapter 23

HEALING WITH GUIDED IMAGERY

Take two meditations and call me in the morning.
—Holistic physician to patient

Moshe cried to Adonai: "O God, heal her now!"
—Numbers 12:13

THE TECHNOLOGY of guided imagery began in the realm of transpersonal psychology, that branch of psychology which approaches the healing of the mind through a spiritual dimension. Once experimentation in mental health through the exploration of fantasy life, imagination, and guided imagery had begun, the next area of exploration undertaken was the healing of the body through imagery. After using this technique, mental health practitioners began to notice the marked effect of a positive attitude on the entire organism, not just the mind. A person's ability to control the images in his/her mind became a potent tool to strengthen the immune system, and prevent and cure physical and mental illness. Thus, in the mind of many people guided imagery is a method of healing—healing the mind and the body.

As noted in chapter one, guided imagery is now used in many other settings, including religious and spiritual development, education, sports, etc. As we have increased the focus on the uses of this new technology in education, religion and spirituality, we recognize that healing is a process that involves more than emotional and physical health. Healing is not merely for people who are ill. In an unredeemed and broken world we all need constant healing to cure the ordinary pains and hurts of daily life, and to raise the level of human wellness so that psychological, physical and spiritual health can be constantly maintained and improved. At the same time, while working to raise the level of general human wellness, we prevent illness and disease.

By using educational and spiritual methods to cure the body and soul, we are returning to the biblical understanding of a human being as an organic whole, not separated into material and spiritual, mind and body. In the Bible the Kohen (priest) was the healer of both the spiritual and the physical maladies of the community. In the modern science of holistic health practitioners are teaching us that many components, including diet, exercise, a positive attitude, meditation, prayer and other psycho-physical-spiritual approaches, all work together to produce a unified organism that maintains good health on every level.

In this chapter we shall include some guided imagery exercises that can help bring healing by utilizing the influence of the mind and soul on the health of both the body and the spirit.

HEALING HANDS

The leader may explain to the group that prayers for health are included in many parts of the traditional Jewish liturgy. Such healing prayers are found in the daily Amidah, in the prayers recited during the Torah service (*Mee-she-bayrach*), and other places. This exercise can be considered a silent prayer through the use of our imagination.

It may also be wise to mention prior to the first exercise that the touching used in our imagination will be non-sexual and purely an act of deep love and affection.

○ *Imagine lying on your stomach and having someone rub your back slowly and softly. The warm healing hands of your friend bring you a feeling of calm and relaxation. You notice your breathing becoming slower and deeper, your heart beating more slowly, and your entire organism becoming more relaxed and serene. . . .*

You continue to enjoy the healing hands of your friend, who brings you affection and caring in a non-sexual way. As your friend's hands go up and down your back you enjoy the sense of touch and the feeling of being cared for. . . .

The hands of the person bringing you deep caring and love have a special healing power. Every cell, muscle, nerve, and bone in your body feels warm and nourished by the touch of these warm, comforting hands. . . .

As you are lying peacefully and happily on a soft surface, you begin to feel the special quality of healing that these hands bring to you. . . . The warmth of the healing hands begins to penetrate deep inside your body to all its parts. . . .

Your friend's hands start at the top of your head and give your scalp and hair some soft rubbing, while all through your head you feel the impurities and imbalances being swept away. . . . Then the hands move down towards your neck and shoulders, and they feel stronger and healthier. . . . Then your back and ribs feel the nice sense of warm relief and relaxation moving down across your body. . . . The same good, healing warmth spreads downward through your lower back, your buttocks, and your thighs. . . . All the muscles, nerves and bones in your entire body are beginning to feel a new wholeness and strength. . . .

Next the backs of your knees, your lower legs and feet also experience a sense of renewal and health, warmth, caring and healing. . . .

You feel especially blessed by these warm, healing hands, and your entire organism feels better and better as each minute passes. . . . You know that God has sent this pair of healing hands to help you become stronger, healthier and more whole. . . . Every part of you is relaxed and strengthened. . . . Inside your heart you feel a deep sense of gratitude for this blessed gift of healing. . . .

Thank your friend for helping you feel better than you have ever felt in your entire life. (Pause). Now thank God for allowing you to experience these moments of warmth and caring, of good health and inner calm. (Pause).

Remember that you can bring these wonderful healing hands back to help you again any time you wish through the use of your imagination. . . . Begin to conclude this exercise, and gradually return to this room and open your eyes. . . . ○

COMMUNITY HEALING

○ *Imagine that you are lying in your comfortable bed at home, ready to retire for the evening. . . . Some parts of you are very tired. In some ways you feel very weary and worn out. . . . How wonderful you would feel if somehow you could receive some special healing at this moment. . . .*

As you lie in bed imagine the faces of some of your caring friends with whom you work, study, pray, or enjoy times of recreation. . . . These are all people who care about you and your welfare. . . . Look into their faces and notice the caring eyes that are looking at you with full attention and affection. . . . See how good it makes you feel to know that you have people in your life who care about you so deeply. . . . (Pause).

Above all the people whose faces you have placed before you is the Presence of God, Who is also looking down toward you with a great deal of warmth and caring. . . . Notice how some of the tiredness and tension begins to leave your body. . . . Slowly you are beginning to feel better and better as all your friends, along with God, send you their glances, smiles and shining faces. . . .

These dear friends help create a sense of security and steadiness inside your heart. . . . You feel the firm support under you and above you that you know you can count on at all times. . . . The love of your friends and of God are always there for you. . . . Whenever you feel a sense of despair or hopelessness, you can bring these faces into your imagination and let yourself feel their warm affection and healing blessings. . . .

As time passes you feel stronger and brave-hearted, supported and secure. . . . You realize that any time you want to be remembered, your friends are there to look upon you and bring you healing. . . .

You are feeling so much better and stronger now. . . . As you lie on your comfortable bed, all the tightness and tension, the weariness and frustration, are lifting. In their place is a feeling of love and affection, of security and strength, of health and wholeness. . . .

While looking up at your friends and at God, see a strong light coming from their presence. . . . The light moves towards you and surrounds you, making you feel even stronger and healthier than before. . . . The light begins to penetrate every part of your body, mind and soul. . . . It brings even more purity and lightness. . . . Feel more protected with this special light than you did before. . . . Its rays of shining light and brightness bathe your entire being in a holiness that uplifts you and raises your spirit. . . .

Breathe in this pure light. . . . It travels all through your body. . . . The light radiates stronger and stronger as your friends and God smile upon you with more love and caring, more protection and nourishment. . . . The light enters all the small spaces inside you and seeks out any unhealthiness and fatigue, all the places where you are sore and aching, sad or angry. It brings its healing power to every part of your entire body and soul, and helps you rid yourself of anything harmful and unhelpful. . . . The love your body receives from this caring light from your friends and God makes you feel healthier and stronger in every way than you have ever felt before. . . .

See how comfortable, strong and healthy you feel. . . . Enjoy the ease and comfort, the strength and security you are experiencing. . . .

Turn your eyes in the direction of your friends and toward God and thank them for this deep and moving experience of joy and healing. . . . Remember that you can always return to these supportive beings, and slowly begin to return to this room. . . . Open your eyes and see how strong and healthy every part of you has become. ◯

THE RIVER OF EDEN

❍ *Find yourself sailing slowly along a very lazy and narrow river with beautiful trees, bushes and shrubs on both sides. . . . You are sitting or lying very comfortably in a rowboat, moving down the river very gradually on a warm, sunny and cloudless afternoon. . . .*

Some parts of your body are not feeling exactly as you wish them to. . . . There are places within you which you would like to heal. . . . You would like to rid yourself of any aches or pains . . . any rough spots or sores . . . any tightness or stiffness. . . . Perhaps you have some bones or tissues that are not as healthy or as strong as they might be. . . . Perhaps there is a part of the inside of your body which needs healing . . . your intestines or lungs, your liver, kidney or your heart . . . your blood, your chest, your stomach, your sexual organs. . . . Anything in your body that is not working as well as you would like or has some malfunction or disease. . . . You would like to bring some healing and relief to some of these parts of yourself. . . .

See yourself continuing to sail along this special river with lush verdure surrounding you on both sides. . . . This is a natural and untouched corner of the planet which seems to you to resemble the biblical Garden of Eden. As you sail down the river you feel more and more as if you are rolling along a river in the Garden created by God for Adam and Eve. . . . How fortunate you feel. . . . (Pause).

In this blooming garden on the banks of the river on which you are traveling you go from one bank to the other simply by shifting your weight. It is so easy to go from side to side. You can smell the flowers and sniff the fruits that are growing all around the river as you continue to glide along. . . .

Reach out your hand and touch the soft surface of some of the colorful flowers, and find how healing and soothing they are to your body. . . . Sniff the aroma of the pedals and feel a healing power race through your entire body as the air carries a healing potion all through you. . . .

This unusual river on which you are moving in your comfortable boat is surrounded by plants and flowers and fruit which have a divine healing essence. Each small gift of nature has its own ability to heal a different part of you. . . . With unusual insight coming from your inner wisdom, you know exactly which smells and tastes will bring healing to the parts of you that need strengthening and restoring. . . .

Think about the various parts of your body, and how you would like to fix them: your skin, your bones, your muscles, your organs, your extremities. . . .

Whatever part of you which needs the most healing will receive the curative powers of the divine plants and flowers first. . . . Reach over to the bank on one side of the river and pull off a lovely flower which has an aroma which will help cure the part of you which you want healed first. . . . Breathe the smell in deeply and see how much better you feel, and how quickly it brings healing to you. . . .

Next go to a plant, pick off a fruit and take a small bite from it. . . . See how it heals another part of you very quickly and totally. . . . Reach up to a bush and pull off a large fruit whose juice drips down your throat and travels to yet another part of you that wants to feel stronger and healthier. . . .

Now sail under a special tree that casts its shadow over a large section of your body that you would like to heal. . . . Let the shade of that tree send a healing mist over your entire body, which helps bring renewal and refreshment to a large part of you. . . .

Over on the other bank you pull off a few leaves and chew them up slowly, until they travel all through your body. . . . Notice how yet another part of you is being healed and fixed, so that you are feeling stronger and stronger, healthier and healthier, every moment. . . . This mystical River of Eden is bringing new health and well-being to so many parts of you that have longed for more vibrancy and vitality. . . .

Travel further down the river and continue to find different herbs and fruits, leaves and flowers, which bring a sense of renewed power to all the parts of you which you would like improved and strengthened. . . . Take your time as you continue to find more healing and more wholeness in every part of you. . . . (Pause).

We are reaching the end of this trip now. Remember that you can always return and find more healing whenever you want by sailing down the River of Eden in your imagination. . . . All you need do is close your eyes and return here at your will. When you are ready, come back to this room, slowly open your eyes, and continue to feel the power of your renewed self. ○

THE HEALING OF THE KOHANIM

The following exercise is adapted from the author's *Jewish Consciousness Raising* (Princeton, NJ: Growth Associates, 1977), p.60. This exercise can be especially effective when used in a setting of people who know each other and are part of an on-going community.

❍ *Find a comfortable position, take some deep breaths, and become very relaxed. With each inhalation bring life-giving energy into your body. With each exhalation let go of some tension and tightness. . . . With each breath find yourself more and more deeply relaxed. . . .*

Think of someone you know who needs healing, physically, emotionally or spiritually. Have an image of that person's face in your mind's eye. . . . Look upon that person with feelings of care and deep warmth and concern. . . . Deep in your heart feel a desire to bring healing and repair to all the parts of that person. . . .

Begin the process of bringing healing to your dear friend by rubbing your palms together. This has the effect of bringing energy into the hands. . . . After doing that for a moment or two, feel the special healing energy in your palms. . . . Now hold your palms up in the same way that the ancient biblical Kohanim did when blessing worshippers who approached the altar in the Temple in Jerusalem. . . . Lift up your hands, palms facing away from your body, and begin in your imagination to chant the word "Shalom". . . . Let your eyes be closed and enter into the mood of the chant, continuing to picture your friend's face in your mind's eye. . . .

Imagine that healing energy is being sent from your hands in the direction of your friend. . . . The combination of your hands and your voice send healing energy toward your friend in a very powerful way. . . . As you continue to chant, together with all other members of the group doing the same thing, more and more healing energy is being sent in the direction of your friend. . . .

As the word Shalom is chanted, let the second syllable of the word ("lom") be held for a longer period of time. . . . Continue repeating it in a slow, quiet chant filled with deep feelings of caring and warm wishes. . . .

[At this point the facilitator, or another designated person, can quietly chant the traditional Hebrew prayer for healing in the background (the *mee she-bayrakh*). Alternatively, the beautiful prayer of healing by songwriter Debbie Friedman can be chanted. It too begins with the traditional Hebrew words *Mee she-bayrakh*].

As you continue to open your hands in your imagination, in the direction of your friend, you may wish to form your fingers in the configuration that the ancient Kohanim used when blessing the people. They would form the Hebrew letter "shin" by forming the fingers into three prongs: the thumb, the next two fingers together, and the fourth finger and pinky together. If you find this too difficult to achieve, simply continue to face your palms toward your friend, and chant the word "Shalom" quietly in the person's direction. . . .

If you would like, you may also picture in your imagination an ancient biblical Kohen holding his hands up in the same direction, with the fingers formed into the Hebrew letter "shin." "Shin" stands for the Hebrew word Shaddai or "Almighty," one of God's seventy names according to tradition.

As you continue to send your own healing energy, feel the healing energy of the entire group moving in the direction of your friend. . . . As the ancient Kohen joins you, the healing energy of the universe and that of God is also directed towards this special person. . . . Imagine that healing is taking place more and more fully the longer you and your group continue to send healing energy towards this special person. (Pause).

When you are ready, begin to let your imagery fade away, open your eyes and stretch your limbs, until you are feeling very comfortable. . . . Continue to rest for a while, and think for a moment of how good it feels to send love and caring to another person. ○

Index Of Guided Imagery Scripts

Dov Peretz Elkins is well-known as a prominent Rabbi and innovative Jewish educator. Youthful, dynamic and passionate in his ideas and programs, he has earned the respect and admiration of colleagues and students throughout the world for his many previous books on self-esteem, experiential learning and spiritual renewal. He has lectured and conducted workshops throughout North America, Europe, Russia, Africa and Israel. His twenty previous books have earned him a reputation as one of the most prolific and trail-blazing spiritual leaders of the modern age.

Dr. Elkins' well-known writing, a unique blend of religion, education, psychology and spirituality, mixed with a deep commitment to social change and human betterment, have earned him the reputation of a leading change agent and religious spokesman of our day.

Rabbi Elkins lives with his wife, Maxine, in Princeton, New Jersey, where he is spiritual leader of The Jewish Center. Their six children live in Israel, Los Angeles, Philadelphia, and Princeton.

ACCOMPANYING CASSETTE TAPE AVAILABLE

Those interested in a cassette tape with scripts presented by a professional reader, please send $13., including postage & handling, pre-paid, payable to Growth Associates, and ask for *Jewish Guided Imagery Scripts* cassette tape.

Growth Associates
212 Stuart Road East
Princeton, NJ 08540-1946

MORE SCRIPTS FOR JEWISH GUIDED IMAGERY

Be a part of our next book! After practicing Guided Imagery we invite you to create your own scripts and submit them for a new volume titled *More Scripts For Jewish Guided Imagery*. We will be happy to give all authors full credit. Send your guided imagery scripts to:

Dr. Dov Peretz Elkins
Growth Associates Publishers
212 Stuart Road East
Princeton, NJ 08540-1946
609/497-7375
E-mail: elkins@tigger.jvnc.net

GROWTH ASSOCIATES
HUMAN RELATIONS CONSULTANTS AND PUBLISHERS
212 STUART ROAD EAST   PRINCETON, NJ 08540
(609) 497-7375

EASE PRINT OR TYPE   E-mail: elkins@tigger.jvnc.net   web site: www.DPElkins.com

AME_____ DATE_____

DDRESS_____

Y_____ STATE_____ ZIP_____

ail_____

EDUCATIONAL MATERIALS BY DR. DOV PERETZ ELKINS

ty.	Titles Available	Cost	Total
	A Shabbat Reader: Universe of Cosmic Joy ISBN 0-8074-0631-7	$14	
	Hasidic Wisdom: Sayings From the Jewish Sages by Simcha Raz ISBN 0-7657-9972-3	$35	
	Jewish Guided Imagery: A How-To Book for Rabbis, Educators and Group Leaders Optional accompanying audiocassette with sample imagery scripts ISBN 0-918834-16-3	$35 $10	
	Jewish Chicken Soup for the Soul: 101 Stories to Open the Heart and Rekindle the Spirit	available 2000	
	Forty Days of Transformation: Daily Reflections of Teshuvah for Spiritual Growth — From Rosh Hodesh Elul to Yom Kippur	$15	
	Meditations for the Days of Awe: Reflections, Guided Imagery and Other Creative Exercises to Enrich Your Spiritual Life	$20	
	Melodies From My Father's House: Hasidic Wisdom for the Heart and Soul ISBN 0-918834-15-5	$12	
	Moments of Transcendence: Inspirational Readings for Rosh Hashanah ISBN 0-87668-506-8	$40	
	Moments of Transcendence: Inspirational Readings for Yom Kippur ISBN 0-87668-504	$40	
	Moments of Transcendence: Annual Supplements Annuals — 1992-1997 $20 each Enlarged Editions — 1998 and 1999 $30 each	$20 $30	
	The Tallit: Some Modern Meanings	$3	
	Shepherd of Jerusalem: A Biography of Rabbi Abraham Isaac Kook ISBN 1-56821-597-5	$20	
	Prescription for a Long and Happy Life: Age-Old Wisdom for the New Age ISBN: 0-918834-14-7	$20	
	My Seventy-Two Friends: Encounters With Refuseniks In the USSR ISBN 0-918834-11-2	$10	
	God's Warriors: Dramatic Adventures of Rabbis In Uniform	$10	
	Humanizing Jewish Life: Judaism and the Human Potential Movement ISBN: 0-498-01912-8	$12	
	Rejoice With Jerusalem: Prayers, Readings and Songs for Israel Observances	$6	
	Organization Development for Jewish Institutions	$7.50	
	A Treasury of Israel and Zionism: A Source Book for Speakers, Writers and Teachers ISBN 0-918834-17-1 Optional computer disk — $25	$50 $25	

OVER

EDUCATIONAL MATERIALS BY DR. DOV PERETZ ELKINS (cont'd.)

Qty.	Titles Available	Cost	Total
	Four Questions On the Weekly Sidrah	$45	
	Sidrah Sparks and Questions for Discussion	$45	
	More Sidrah Sparks and Questions for Discussion	$45	
	Loving My Jewishness: Jewish Self-Pride and Self-Esteem ISBN 0-918834-04-X	$10	
	Experiential Programs for Jewish Groups: Thirty Full-Length Programs ISBN 0-918834-05-8	$10	
	Clarifying Jewish Values: Values Clarification Strategies for Jewish Groups ISBN 0-918834-02-3	$10	
	Jewish Consciousness Raising: A Handbook of 50 Experiential Exercises ISBN 0-918834-03-1	$10	
	The Ideal Jew: Values Clarification Program	$10	
	Why Did Susan Cohen Desert Judaism? A Values Clarification Program On Intermarriage and Assimilation	$10	
	Teaching People To Love Themselves: A Leader's Handbook of Theory and Technique for Self-Esteem Training ISBN 0-918834-06-6	$22	
	Self-Concept Sourcebook — Ideas and Activities for Building Self-Esteem ISBN 0-918834-09-0	$19	
	Glad To Be Me: Building Self-Esteem In Yourself and Others ISBN 0-918834-10-4	$12	
	Twelve Pathways To Feeling Better About Yourself ISBN 0-918834-08-2	$7.50	

SHIPPING & HANDLING:
   USA: 15% of order (10% of orders over $150)
 Canada: 20% of order
 Foreign: 30% of order

Subtotal:_____
Shipping & Handling:_____
TOTAL:_____

All orders must be prepaid by credit card or check.
Minimum on all orders: $3

❑ My check is enclosed.
   Please make checks payable to Dov Peretz Elkins (US Funds only).

❑ Charge my: ❑ VISA   ❑ MasterCard

Account Number: Expiration Date:_____

| | | | | | | | | | | | | | | | | | | |

Name on card: _____

Signature:_____

_____Check here if interested in inviting Dr. Elkins to give lectures, workshops, retreats, and/or other training events for group, board, staff or faculty, etc.

ORDER FORM

GROWTH ASSOCIATES
HUMAN RELATIONS CONSULTANTS AND PUBLISHERS
212 STUART ROAD EAST   PRINCETON, NJ 08540
(609) 497-7375

E-mail: elkins@tigger.jvnc.net   web site: www.DPElkins.com

#1 New York Times BESTSELLER

Chicken Soup for the Soul
for the Soul

101 Stories To
Open The Heart And
Rekindle The Spirit

WRITTEN & COMPILED BY
Jack Canfield
Mark Victor Hansen

PLEASE PRINT OR TYPE

NAME _____ DATE _____

ADDRESS _____

CITY _____ STATE _____ ZIP _____

E-mail _____

CHICKEN SOUP FOR THE SOUL

Qty.	Titles Available	Cost	Total
	Jewish Chicken Soup for the Soul: 101 Stories to Open the Heart and Rekindle the Spirit	available Sept. 2000	
	Chicken Soup for the Soul	$12.95	
	A 2nd Helping of Chicken Soup for the Soul	$12.95	
	A 3rd Serving of Chicken Soup for the Soul	$12.95	
	A 4th Course of Chicken Soup for the Soul	$12.95	
	A 5th Portion of Chicken Soup for the Soul	$12.95	
	A 6th Cup of Chicken Soup for the Soul	$12.95	
	Chicken Soup for the Couple's Soul	$12.95	
	A Cup of Chicken Soup for the Soul	$8.95	
	A Dog of My Own — Chicken Soup for Little Souls	$14.95	
	Chicken Soup for the Woman's Soul	$12.95	
	A Second Chicken Soup for the Woman's Soul	$12.95	
	Chicken Soup for the Christian Soul	$12.95	
	Chicken Soup for the Country Soul	$12.95	
	Chicken Soup for the Kid's Soul	$12.95	
	Chicken Soup for the Mother's Soul	$12.95	
	Chicken Soup for the Pet Lover's Soul	$12.95	
	Chicken Soup for the Soul at Work	$12.95	
	Chicken Soup for the Soul Cookbook	$12.95	
	Chicken Soup for the Surviving Soul	$12.95	

OVER

CHICKEN SOUP FOR THE SOUL

Qty.	Titles Available	Cost	Total
	Chicken Soup for the Teenage Soul	$12.95	
	Chicken Soup for the Teenage Soul II	$12.95	
	Chicken Soup for the Teenage Soul Journal	$12.95	
	Chicken Soup for the Golfer's Soul	$12.95	
	Condensed Chicken Soup for the Soul	$8.95	
	Chicken Soup for the Single's Soul	$12.95	
	Chicken Soup for the College Soul	$12.95	
	Chicken Soup for the Unsinkable Soul — Stories of Triumph & Overcoming Obstacles	$12.95	

No shipping/handling charges added.

TOTAL:_____

All orders must be prepaid by credit card or check.

❑ My check is enclosed.
   Please make checks payable to Dov Peretz Elkins (US Funds only).

❑ Charge my: ❑ VISA   ❑ MasterCard

Account Number: Expiration Date:_____

| | | | | | | | | | | | | | | | | | | |

Name on card: _____

Signature:_____

____Check here if interested in inviting Dr. Elkins to give lectures, workshops, retreats,
   and/or other training events for group, board, staff or faculty, etc.